When John Wesley felt his h[eart...] 1738, one of the great revival[s...] continues to resound powerfully into the present day. The story of John and Charles Wesley, their spiritual awakening and their careers as preachers, teachers and writers of extraordinary energy, is one that needs to be told anew for every generation. I am sure many will be inspired by Julian Wilson's lively and timely biography.

TIM COSTELLO, CEO World Vision Australia

There is much we could learn from John and Charles, and Julian Wilson's extensively researched and wonderfully told story of the Wesleys may be the clarion call to today's Church to once again reach the common man and change our nations with the Gospel.

ROBIN MARK, Internationally-acclaimed composer, singer, song writer and worship leader

The lives of John Wesley and Charles Wesley have often been studied separately. The great merit of this book is that it looks at these two outstanding figures together. If you have wanted to gain more understanding of the Wesley brothers' relationship and their individual and combined achievements, this is the book for which you've been waiting.

IAN M. RANDALL, Research Associate, Cambridge Centre for Christianity Worldwide.

In *The Wesleys—Two Men Who Changed the World*, Julian Wilson has produced a very inspiring book which will be useful for both the student and those who have never read about these remarkable men of the eighteenth century. With skill, Wilson weaves into his narrative an account of two lives, so intricately bound together and yet the impact of each is unique. I warmly commend the book as a reliable and well-documented account of two people who may have been among the greatest of a generation and whose influence has stretched far beyond their own day and still speaks meaningfully in the twenty-first century.

REV. KEITH V. GARNER AM, Superintendent/CEO Wesley Mission

THE
WESLEYS

== TWO MEN WHO CHANGED THE WORLD ==

JULIAN WILSON

Authentic

Published by Authentic Publishers
188 Front Street, Suite 116–44
Franklin, TN 37064
USA

28 West Parade
West Ryde NSW 2114
Australia

Authentic Publishers is a division of Authentic Media, Inc.

Library of Congress Cataloguing-in-Publication Data

Wilson, Julian
    The Wesleys: two men who changed the world / Julian Wilson

p. cm.

ISBN 978-1-78078-119-8
    978-1-78078-240-9 (e-book)

Printed in the United States of America
21 20 19 18 17 16 15   10 9 8 7 6 5 4 3 2 1

To John and Charles Wesley
Two of the greatest men of God who have ever lived.

CONTENTS

ACKNOWLEDGMENTS

As with all biographers, I owe a debt of gratitude to those who have gone before. Arguably the finest biographies of John and Charles Wesley are, in my opinion, the following: *The Young Mr. Wesley* and *John Wesley*, both by V. H. H. Green; *Assist Me to Proclaim: The Life and Hymns of Charles Wesley*, by John R. Tyson; and Gary Best's *Charles Wesley*.

Get these three Principles fixed in your hearts: that Things
eternal are much more considerable than Things temporal; that
Things not seen are as certain as the Things that are seen;
that upon your present choice depends your eternal lot.

—JOHN WESLEY

Peter Martin, former ostler of the London Inn in Redruth, Cornwall, used to reminisce fondly how that in 1786 he had driven John Wesley to St. Ives to fulfill a preaching engagement. While Wesley was engrossed as usual in reading and writing in his carriage, Martin drove the twelve miles to Hayle, but when they arrived, the sands along the shore, into which the road disappeared, were fast becoming submerged by the rising tide.

A frantic ship's captain approached the carriage and begged them to return at once. But Wesley was adamant that they must press on as he had to preach in St. Ives at a certain hour. Looking out of the window, he shouted to Martin, "Take the sea! Take the sea!" Soon the horses were up to their necks in the water, and Martin expected any moment to be swept away and drowned. But Wesley poked his head out of the window again, his long white hair dripping with salt water, and enquired, "What is your name, driver?"

"Peter," the ostler replied.

"Peter," he said, "fear not; thou shalt not sink."

At last, after battling through the rising tide, they arrived at St. Ives and Martin was convinced that it was a miracle. Wesley's first concern, according to Martin, was "to see me comfortably lodged at the tavern." Wesley ensured the ostler had warm clothing, a roaring fire, and refreshments, then, completely oblivious of himself and drenched to the skin by the sea, he proceeded to the chapel, where he preached as though nothing had happened. He was then in his eighty-third year.

✠ ✠ ✠

May 1743. Birmingham and Nottingham were relatively quiet, but in Sheffield, Charles Wesley found the Methodists "as sheep in the midst of wolves." The local clergy organized a mob to pull down the recently built Methodist meeting place. The house where he was staying also came under attack and was showered with stones. When Charles stepped outside to confront the mob, someone hurled a stone that struck him in the face. An army officer was also heard to utter, "You shall see, if I do but hold my sword to his breast he will faint away."

As soon as Charles began preaching to the mob outside, the officer drew his sword and charged at him shouting obscenities with the intention of thrusting the weapon through Wesley's heart. Charles recalled of the terrifying incident: "My breast was immediately steeled. I threw it open, and, fixing mine eye on his, smiled in his face, and calmly said, 'I fear God and honour the King.' His countenance fell in a moment, he fetched a deep sigh, put up his sword, and quietly left the place."

ENGLAND IN THE EIGHTEENTH CENTURY

Ungodliness is our universal,
our constant, our peculiar character.

—JOHN WESLEY

The England of the first half of the eighteenth century was one of political corruption, moral disorder, lawlessness, and ecclesiastical indifference. The population in the early eighteenth century was probably between five and six million. London was growing rapidly and was the largest city in England, with a population of more than 500,000, which would expand to more than 800,000 by the 1770s, followed by Bristol with approximately 40,000, and Norwich with around 30,000. By 1742, 7,000,000 gallons of gin were consumed annually, and by 1749 there were 17,000 gin houses in London alone, which often pitched for customers with the line, "Drunk for a penny, dead drunk for two pence." Women with young children drank as heavily as the men. The orgy of spirit drinking reduced resistance to disease, increased infant mortality, became a substitute for food, and ruined work discipline.

The country was infested with highwaymen and footpads (robbers on foot). Youths formed groups called mohocks that terrorized ordinary citizens, breaking their victims' noses and gouging out eyes. In 1718 it was said that there were so many thieves in the City of London that people were afraid to shop or visit coffeehouses after dark in the district "for fear that . . . they may be blinded, knock'd down, cut or stabbed."

Hogarth's graphic cartoons of life in London were a realistic depiction of life in the capital. Such was the filth that in 1708 a plague of flies was so dense in London that people's feet left impressions "as visible as in snow" on the dead insects on the streets. According to the historian J. H. Plumb, "In every class there is the same taut neurotic quality—the fantastic gambling and drinking, the riots, the brutality and violence and everywhere and always a constant fear of death."[1]

Drunkenness, gambling, and violence were rife, and according to one historian, "The mob was a persistent and violent element in the Georgian scene." When the anti-Catholic Gordon Riots erupted in London in 1780, Charles Wesley described the mob as a "vile, rebellious race [in a] proud metropolis . . . where Satan's darkest works abound." There was no police force in eighteenth-century England, so burning, looting, and destruction by the mob were commonplace.

To deal with rampant crime, laws became ever more draconian so that by the 1740s there were 225 offenses that were punishable by death. One author has commented, "If a man injured Westminster Bridge, he was hanged; if he cut down a young tree, if he shot a rabbit, if he stole property valued at four shillings, he was hanged," and even a child caught stealing a handkerchief worth a shilling could be hanged. Hangings became so frequent that the famous writer Dr. Samuel Johnson expressed his fear that the navy might run short of ropes. Criminals were publicly whipped, pilloried, and hanged, while traitors were drawn and quartered. The heads of Jacobites (those who supported the deposed King James II and his Stuart heirs) were impaled on spikes on Temple Bar until 1777, while until 1789, women were still burned alive at the stake for murdering their husbands, though a sympathetic hangman might strangle them before they were consumed by the flames.

London teemed with brothels and had an excess of ten thousand prostitutes plying their trade at theatres and on the streets. Wrote one observer, John Macy: "they are more numerous than at Paris and

---

[1] J. H. Plumb, *England in the Eighteenth Century* (London: Penguin Books, 1950), 95.

have more liberty and effrontery than at Rome itself. About nightfall they range themselves in a file in the footpaths of the great streets, in companies of five or six, most of them dressed very genteelly. . . . Whole rows of them accost passengers in the broad day-light, and above all, foreigners."

The new towns as well as London were characterized by filth and squalor. There was no sanitation with sewage, and rubbish was often thrown out onto the streets, while the houses of the poor were usually one- or two-room hovels with ten or more to a room. As historian Roy Porter has said: "Food hygiene was no better than personal hygiene. The omnipresence of animals meant streets were awash with dung. What we have lost above all from the world we have lost in stench. Small consolation that eyes may have been less offended than noses, for much was invisible in a world lit by candlelight, rushlight and moonlight."[2] In 1771 Tobias Smollet observed:

> If I would drink water, I must quaff the mawkish contents of an open aqueduct, exposed to all manner of defilement, or swallow that which comes from the River Thames, impregnated with all the filth of London and Westminster. Human excrement is the least offensive part of the concrete, which is composed of all the drugs, minerals, and poisons used in mechanics and manufacture, enriched with the putrefying carcasses of beasts and men, and mixed with the scourings of all the wash-tubs, kennels, and common sewers within the bills of mortality.

Medicine was crude and expensive, and there were no anesthetics, with alcohol considered the best painkiller. Diseases such as smallpox, typhus, typhoid, cholera, dysentery, and influenza raged through the packed tenements so that the average lifespan in eighteenth-century England was only thirty-seven years old; only one child in four survived infancy. The gentry were not immune to early death and disease either. Edward Gibbon, the eminent historian, had six brothers and sisters who died in infancy, and he barely survived himself. None of Queen Anne's

---

[2] Roy Porter, *English Society in the Eighteenth Century* (London: Penguin Books, 1982), 19.

children lived to adulthood. Industrial diseases such silicosis, cancer, and lead-poisoning were rife, as were rheumatism, rickets, scurvy, gout, and dropsy, while cosmetic poisoning scarred and killed the wealthy. Lady Coventry, for example, reputedly died from being poisoned by her lead-based makeup.

Poverty added yet another painful reality to life in England. According to Porter:

> Poverty spelt lives of deprivation and dependence: a taste-less, unsatisfying diet of bread; freezing in shacks and cellars, with farm animals occasionally living under the same roof; enduring the petty tyranny of poor-law overseers; engaging in back-breaking toil for pittances under often brutal masters, and the prospect ahead only of pinching old age or the poor-house.[3]

Thomas Davis, the steward of the Marquis of Bath, commented on the plight of the working poor:

> Humanity shudders at the idea of the industrious labourer, with a wife and five or six children, being obliged to live or rather exist, in a wretched, damp, gloomy room, of 10 or 12 ft square, and that room without a floor; but common decency must revolt at considering, that over this wretched apartment, there is only one chamber, to hold all the miserable beds of the miserable family.

Most children were beaten at home and school, and child labor was universal. In 1767, Jonas Hanway, protesting the forcing of boys as young as four to become chimney sweeps, wrote, "These poor black urchins . . . are treated worse than a humane person would treat a dog."

In the 1720s, the population actually plateaued and then declined in part because of epidemics of disease. Dr. Hilary at Ripon reported in 1727 that the poor were dying like flies: "Nor did any other method which art could afford relieve them; insomuch that many of the little country towns and villages were almost stripped of their poor people."

---

[3] Ibid., 15.

In 1721, one commentator observed what happened to those who died in poverty:

> They dig in the courtyards, or other annexed burial places, large holes or pits in which they put many of the bodies of those whose friends are not able to pay for better graves and then those pits or holes (called the Poor's Holes), once opened are not covered till filled with such dead bodies. . . . How noisome the stench is that arises from these holes so stowed with dead bodies, especially in sultry seasons and after rain, one may appeal to all who approach them.

Blood sports, such as cockfighting, were highly popular. Such was the cruelty to animals that celebrated poet Alexander Pope wrote a furious letter of complaint to the *Guardian*, stating, "I know nothing more shocking or horrid than the prospect of . . . kitchens covered with blood and filled with the cries of creatures expiring in tortures."

Most roads, until the establishment of a network of turnpike roads, were little more than rutted, potholed tracks that turned into swamps in winter. At St. Ives in Cornwall, wrote Celia Fiennes, "the road was so full of holes and quick sands I dare not venture," and on the way to Leicester she found "very good land but very deep bad roads . . . being full of sloughs, clay deep way, that I was near 11 hours going but 25 mile." Twice she was nearly drowned in a pothole, and John Wesley himself only just escaped possible death on the Great North Road. Wesley mentioned riding in torrential rain along flooded roads. Returning from Warwick to Banbury, the roads were so bad that he was forced to ride in the fields on either side. He also recorded that once his horse became so tired that by the time he reached the town of Newark in Nottinghamshire he had to walk. The following day his horse fell into a ditch, and it required six men to drag it out. Even in 1781, at the age of seventy-seven, John recorded in his *Journal*: "Having appointed to preach at Blackburn I was desired to take Kabb [sic] in my way. But such a road sure no carriage ever went before; I was glad to quit it and use my own feet." As late as 1765, a French visitor to the City of London complained of how the streets were "eternally covered with dirt and paved in such a manner that it is scarce possible to find a place to set one's foot and absolutely impossible to ride in a coach."

Parliament was corrupt, venal, and unrepresentative, its main purpose being to serve the interests of the ruling elite. England was riddled with rotten boroughs that had virtually no inhabitants, but still returned one or two members of Parliament, while the emerging industrial towns of the north had no representation. It is estimated that only 5 percent of the men in England had the right to vote during the eighteenth century, while Scotland with a population of 2,000,000 had only 3,000 voters. The first two Hanoverian monarchs, George I and George II, were flagrantly dissolute, while Sir Robert Walpole, the prime minister between 1721 and 1742, lived in undisguised adultery with his mistress.

The Church of England, that the Wesleys were to defend so loyally, was in a state of decline. As the clergy became ever more lax and indolent, spiritual duties were neglected, daily services were abandoned, Holy Communion became infrequent, and church buildings were allowed to fall into disrepair. John himself described the clergy as "dull, heavy, blockish ministers; men of no life, no spirit, no readiness of thought; who are consequently the jest of every pert fool." As one historian has commented: "Archbishops in the eighteenth century were potentates if not princes. A carriage with six horse and a private state barge on the Thames with livery-clad crew were the normal appurtenances of such dignity." The Bishop of Winchester was notorious for using foul language, but excused himself by claiming that he swore only in the company of baronets, not bishops.

The distinguished writer William Thackeray, reviewing the eighteenth century, railed against the corrupt life at the court of George II, while praising John Wesley and George Whitefield:

> No wonder that the clergy were corrupt and indifferent amidst this indifference and corruption: No wonder that sceptics multiplied and morals degenerated, so far as they depended on the influence of such a king. No wonder that Whitefield cried out in the wilderness, that Wesley quitted the insulted temple to pray on the hill-side. I look with reverence on these men at that time.

The poet and playwright Oliver Goldsmith commented on the sermons preached in Anglican churches: "Their discourses from the pulpit are generally dry, methodical and unaffecting, delivered with the most insipid calmness." And Judge Blackstone asserted that he "heard not a single sermon which had more of the gospel in it than the writings of Cicero." The practice of pluralism—whereby a clergyman could hold a number of parishes at the same time—was rife. The Bishop of Winchester, for example, only visited his diocese once in twenty-one years.

In 1728, the philosopher Montesquieu wrote that "In England there is no religion and the subject, if mentioned in society, evokes nothing but laughter." According to Bishop John Ryle: "From the year 1700 till about the era of the French Revolution, England seemed barren of all good. There was a gross, thick, religious and moral darkness; a darkness that might be felt." The Bishop of Lichfield observed in 1724: "The Lord's Day is now the devil's market day. More lewdness, drunkenness, more quarrels and murders, more sin is contrived and committed on this day than all the other days of the week together." In 1736, Joseph Butler, Bishop of Durham, commented that most people no longer looked on Christianity even as a subject of inquiry, "its fictitious nature being so obvious," while Bishop Watson suggested "that there never was an age since the death of Christ, never once since the commencement of this history of the world, in which atheism and infidelity have been more generally confessed." And Butler lamented in the same year: "The influence of religion is more and more wearing out of the minds of men. The number of those who call themselves unbelievers increases, and with their number, their zeal. The deplorable distinction of our age is an avowed scorn of religion in some and a growing disregard of it in generality." Even secular authors such as Dean Swift commented on this phenomenon in his *A Project for the Advancement of Religion* (1709): "I suppose it will be granted that hardly one in a hundred among our people of quality or gentry, appears to act by any principle of religion; that great numbers of them do entirely discard it, and are ready to own their disbelief of all revelation in ordinary discourse. Nor is the case much better among the vulgar, especially in great towns." And in

1722, the celebrated author Daniel Defoe stated that "no age, since the founding and forming of the Christian Church in the world, was ever like, (in open, avowed atheism, blasphemies and heresies), to the age we now live in." As one historian has commented on the Christianity of the Church of England: "It was not a religion which had much appeal to the men and women living brutal and squalid lives in the disease-ridden slums of the new towns and mining villages. They needed revelation and salvation."[4]

John Wesley himself was well aware of the godlessness of the age in which he lived: "Ungodliness is our universal, our constant, our peculiar character . . . a total ignorance of God is almost universal among us—High & low, cobblers, tinkers, hackney coachmen, men and maid servants, soldiers, tradesmen of all rank, lawyers, physicians, gentlemen, lords are as ignorant of the Creator of the World as Mohametans & Pagans."

The answer to secularism, Deism, the ritualistic religion offered by the Church of England, and the deadness of the non-conformist churches proved to be Methodism, although both John and particularly Charles regarded it as a renewal movement within the Established Church, not a separate denomination. At Methodist meeting houses freedom of expression and emotion was permitted, joyful hymns were sung, love feasts (the Eucharist) and watch night services were held, salvation and justification by faith were preached, and the Holy Spirit was allowed to move without prejudice and restraint. But it was more than just a religious movement, suggests Methodist theologian Ralph Waller: "Methodism was a source of life and purpose, a 'solution' both in physical and spiritual terms. It saved men and women from poverty, aimlessness and degradation, and gave them a glimpse of heaven. It taught them hope in the hereafter, but it also made them stable parents, good citizens and caring people."[5]

[4] Plumb, *England in the Eighteenth Century*, 90.

[5] Ralph Waller, *John Wesley: A Personal Portrait* (London: The Continuum International Publishing Group, Inc., 2003), 128.

According to Plumb, while Methodism certainly aided those in poverty, "Methodism was not a religion of the poor but for the poor."[6] It drew its membership from the working and lower middle classes, particularly in the new industrial towns where Anglican churches were few. Industrialization was driving many of the rural poor into the new towns in search of work, where they had no roots and where there were no institutions that could provide for their physical and spiritual needs. Methodism offered its members a social identity, a sense of purpose and belonging, and through it many rose to positions of prominence and responsibility in their communities.

It was also thought by many, including the renowned Anglican theologian Frederick Denison Maurice (1805–1872), that Methodism prevented Britain from following France into revolution during the 1790s. According to Maurice's son:

> As I referred to the name of Wesley . . . I will say that I have often heard my father speak of Wesley. It is always in the mode represented by the answer he once gave to the question—"How do you account for the fact that England at the end of the eighteenth century escaped a revolution like that of France?" "Ah," he said at once, "there is not the least doubt as to that. England escaped a political revolution because she had undergone a religious revolution." "You mean that brought about by Wesley and Whitefield?" "Of course."

So influential was Methodism that Plumb has asserted: "By 1760 Methodism was easily the most highly coordinated body of opinion in the country, the most fervent, the most dynamic. Had it been bent on revolution in Church or State nothing could have stopped it."[7]

John Wesley railed against Britain's corrupt and narrow parliamentary system, questioning: "By what right do you exclude a man from being one of the people because he has not forty shillings a year? Is he not a man, whether he be rich or poor? Has he not a soul and a

---

[6] Plumb, *England in the Eighteenth Century*, 95.

[7] Ibid, 94. This may be an exaggeration of Methodism's influence in Britain, considering there was a relatively small number of Methodists scattered throughout the country.

body?" He even supported female suffrage: "I ask, by what argument do you prove that women are not naturally as free as men? Are they not rational creatures?" John urged all Methodists who had the right to vote to participate in all elections, but to vote "without fee or reward for the person they judged most worthy." Paradoxically, he also wrote, "The greater the share the people have in government, the less liberty, civil or religious, does a nation enjoy." And he was convinced that the people of Britain "enjoy at this day throughout these kingdoms such liberty, civil and religious, as no other kingdom or commonwealth in Europe, or in the world, enjoys," and that they were "screaming out for liberty while they have it in their hands."

Initially, John sympathized with the American colonists, but when they opposed the British government and sought independence, he became an implacable critic. Far from being a revolutionary, John Wesley was autocratic, anti-democratic, an avowed monarchist, and an intransigent conservative who regarded the French Revolution as the direct work of Satan and loathed radical thinkers like Rousseau and Voltaire. For Wesley, the transformation of society could only occur through a change in the hearts of individuals through salvation and spiritual rebirth, not through revolution and political change.

1

THE EARLY YEARS

A brand plucked from the burning.

—JOHN WESLEY

I believe it was just at that time I waked, for I did not cry as they imagined, unless it was afterwards. I remember all the circumstances as distinctly as though it were but yesterday. Seeing the room was very light, I called to the maid to take me up. But none answering, I put my head out of the curtains, and saw streaks of fire on top of the room. I got up and ran to the door, but could get no farther, all the floor beyond it being in a blaze. I then climbed up on a chest, which stood near the window: one in the yard saw me and proposed running to fetch a ladder. Another answered: "There will not be time; but I have thought of another expedient. Here I will fix myself against the wall: lift a light man and set him on my shoulders." They did so, and he took me out of the window. Just then the whole roof fell in; but it fell inward or we had all been crushed at once.

This is how John Wesley described the famous rectory fire of 1709 in Epworth and himself as "a brand plucked from the burning." He would recall the incident forty years later in 1749, writing in his *Journal*: "At about eleven o'clock it came into my mind that this was the very day and hour in which forty years ago I was taken out of the flames. I stopped and gave a short account of that wonderful providence. The voice of praise and thanksgiving went up on high and great was our rejoicing before the Lord."

The blaze started in the middle of the night. The fire may have been an arson attack by some of John's father Samuel Wesley's disgruntled parishioners. Susanna, who was almost eight months pregnant, had no time to get dressed but ran naked from the burning rectory. Her face and neck were burnt when three times she ran back into the flames to try to ensure all her children were saved. Baby Charles owed his escape to a quick-thinking maid who carried him to safety, but five-year-old John, or Jacky as he was affectionately known, was trapped inside. Repeatedly, Samuel tried to get up the burning stairs, but beaten back by the intense flames, he knelt down and commended young Jacky's soul to God. But Jacky did not perish in the flames.

The family stood naked and shivering with cold, despite the heat of the fire, in the yard of the rectory as their home went up in flames. Recalled Susanna, "So by the infinite mercy of almighty God our lives were well preserved by little less than [a] miracle, for there passed but a few moments between the first discovery of the fire and the falling of the house." But even though they had lost everything, she said, "He has given me all eight children: let the house go, I am rich enough." Samuel echoed Susanna's thoughts: "When poor Jacky was saved I could not believe it till I had kissed him two or three times. . . . I hope my wife will recover and not miscarry, but God will give me my nineteenth child. She has burnt her legs, but they mend."

The fire of 1709 was not the first time the rectory had burned down. In 1702 fire destroyed three-quarters of the building. Samuel was again philosophical about the damage, writing to Archbishop Sharp: "My wife, children and books were saved. . . . I shall go on, by God's assistance, to take my tithe; and when that is in, to rebuild my house, having at last crowded my family into what's left, and not missing many of my goods."

The ever-impatient Samuel immediately started to rebuild the rectory after the second fire, but thirteen years later it was still incomplete, and the money he had borrowed to replace the furniture and clothes had still not been repaid. Samuel's presence in London—where he was determined to be involved in the debates occurring within the Church of England—and subsequent lack of revenue from his estates left his family in poverty, with one of his daughters commenting bitterly, "For seven winters my father was in London, and we at home in intolerable want and affliction . . . vast income but no comfort or credit from it." And John and Charles' sister, Emily, was to describe the family as being "in scandalous want of necessities."

While Samuel was in London, he engaged a curate to carry on the work of the parish, but the curate proved uninspiring and incompetent. Susanna then stepped in and invited parishioners to the rectory on Sunday evenings for prayer, Scripture reading, and discussion. These services became so popular that she soon had more followers than the curate. However, the meetings contravened Anglican Church law, and Samuel, envious of his wife's success and stung by the sneering comments of his fellow clergy, protested strongly, but Susanna stood her ground: "If you think fit to dissolve this assembly, do not tell me that you desire me to do it, for that will not satisfy my conscience; but send me your positive command, in such full and express terms as may absolve me from all guilt and punishment for neglecting this opportunity of doing good." John was to say of his mother that she "did not feel for others near so much as my father did; but she did ten times more than he did."

Susanna had hoped to obtain some financial support for the family from her wealthy brother, Samuel Annesley, who was returning to England after serving with the East India Company. She traveled to London with Charles to meet his ship. However, when the ship docked, Samuel failed to disembark and was never heard of again, presumed murdered. This was a cruel blow to Charles' remaining unmarried sisters, for now they had no hope of receiving dowries that could help them attract husbands.

✠ ✠ ✠

Samuel Wesley was raised as a Dissenter, and his grandfather, Bartholomew Westley (Samuel changed the family name to "Wesley"), was rector of Charmouth in Dorset before being ejected for non-conformity. Samuel's father, John Westley senior, had been a minister of the Church of England until he, like his father, was removed from office in 1662 for refusing to conform to the Act of Uniformity which attempted to establish a national, all-inclusive Church that required the acceptance of the new Book of Common Prayer. Samuel's father John died in 1678 at only forty-two after years of poverty and persecution.

The young Samuel attended a number of Dissenting schools before rejecting the faith of his ancestors and joining the Church of England to gain access to Oxford University. He entered Exeter College as a "pauper scholar" or servitor, the lowest rank of undergraduate, who was expected to serve the wealthier students.

On a winter's morning, with only eight farthings left in his pocket and with expulsion from Oxford looming, Samuel went out early for a walk in one of the city's parks. While walking he heard a child weeping and found an eight-year-old boy under a hedge whose clothes had frozen to the ground. Samuel rubbed the boy's hands and legs to get his circulation going again, and then discovered that his mother and father had died and that he and his sister were reduced to begging for food. Filled with compassion, Samuel gave the boy his last eight farthings and took him to Oxford to buy bread. On his return to the College, Samuel found that his mother had sent him a large cheese, a relative had given him half a crown, and his tutor would later pay his college expenses.

Born in 1669, Susanna also came from a Dissenting background. Her father, Dr. Samuel Annesley, was an ordained minister who was forced out of his parish in 1662 for refusing to adhere to the Act of Uniformity. However, his wealth enabled him to avoid the destitution experienced by other Dissenting clergy, and he was able to provide financial support for many ex-ministers in need. Admired for his piety and principles, Annesley was described by the famous writer Daniel Defoe, who was one of his pupils, as having "nothing in him that was little or mean."

Samuel met the beautiful and scholarly Susanna (also known by her nickname, Sukey) when she was only thirteen. They married six years later in 1688. Their wedding coincided with the Glorious Revolution of 1688–9, in which the Catholic James II was deposed in favor of his daughter, the Protestant Mary and her Dutch husband,

William of Orange. Susanna was brought up as a Dissenter but later embraced the Church of England, which may have been due to her husband's influence.

Samuel was ordained by the Bishop of London in February 1689. His first appointment was as curate of St. Boltolph's in Aldersgate, London, where he received an annual salary of £28. Unable to make ends meet, he accepted the post of chaplain aboard a Royal Navy warship in the Irish Sea on £70 per annum. So appalling were the conditions aboard ship that Samuel resigned after six months, complaining, "I was very ill used, and nearly starved and poisoned . . . nor had we fish or butter in our ship and our beef stunk intolerably." During his absence, Susanna gave birth to their first child, Samuel junior, in 1690. After a number of clerical appointments and attempting to supplement his meager income through freelance writing, Samuel secured a position as rector of St. Andrew's Church in Epworth, a small farming parish on the marshy Isle of Axholme in Lincolnshire, potentially worth between £150 and £200 a year.

Samuel and Susanna were very different in character and personality, and their relationship through forty-six years of marriage was often tense, punctuated by arguments and stand-offs, particularly about their differing political views and Samuel's endless debts. About this, John wrote sadly in later life: "Were I to write my own life, I should begin it before I was born, merely for the purpose of mentioning a disagreement between my father and my mother." Said Susanna about her relationship with her husband: " 'Tis an unhappiness almost peculiar to our family that your father and I seldom think alike." On the surface, Susanna continued to demonstrate her respect for her husband, calling him "Sir" and "My Master," but inwardly she resented his high-handed, domineering manner.

With the death of Queen Mary, her husband became William III, but Susanna had never accepted the removal of James II and would not accept that the new king had any right to the throne. The dispute came to a head in the beginning of 1702 when Susanna refused to say "Amen" after Samuel's prayers for William. When Samuel enquired why, she replied, "Because I do not believe the Prince of Orange to be

King." Enraged, Samuel declared, "You and I must part; for if we have two Kings, we must have two beds." Susanna recalled of the incident:

> I was a little surprised at the question and don't remember what I answered, but too well I remember what followed. He immediately kneeled down and imprecated the divine Vengeance upon himself and all his posterity if ever he touched me more or came into a bed with me before I had begged God's pardon and his, for not saying "Amen" to the prayer for the King.

The standoff between them continued even though William died in March 1702 and was succeeded by the Stuart Queen Anne. Samuel may have used the disagreement as an excuse to leave the family to attend Church of England meetings in London where debates raged about the Church's role and organization, but according to Susanna, Samuel "met a clergyman to whom he communicated his intentions . . . and he prevailed upon him to return." Coincidentally, in 1702, the Epworth rectory was set ablaze, maybe by a disaffected parishioner, but both Samuel and Susanna believed that it was the result of "the finger of God" due to their quarrel and Samuel's curse. Samuel rushed home from London. He and Susanna were reconciled, and on June 17, 1703, John Benjamin Wesley was born.

Samuel Wesley was a scholar and a prolific writer. In addition to many minor works, he wrote a *Life of Christ* and the *History of the Old and New Testaments*, as well as his mammoth Latin commentary *Dissertations on the Book of Job*. Alexander Pope, the great English writer, declared of Samuel, "I call him what he is, 'a learned man.'"

Samuel was brave, compassionate, and principled, but also obstinate, narrow-minded, and a terrible manager of money, remaining in debt throughout his life. When he opposed the Whig candidate at a contested election in Lincolnshire, the latter's friends demanded he repay a small loan of £30, and when unable to do so, Samuel was arrested and thrown into the debtor's prison in Lincoln Castle. Samuel endured the humiliation and appalling conditions with courage and stoicism. Susanna sent him her gold rings so he could sell them and get better treatment in prison, but he returned them immediately. He remained in prison for three months while friends and supporters raised the funds required for his release. While in prison he wrote to the Archbishop of York, Dr. John Sharp, in June 1705:

> I don't despair of doing some good here . . . and it may be, do more in this parish than in my old one; for I have leave to read prayers every morning and afternoon here in prison, and to preach once a Sunday, which I choose to do in the afternoon, when there is no sermon at the Minster. And I am getting acquainted with my brother jail-birds as fast as I can; and shall write to London next post, to the Society for Propagating Christian Knowledge, who, I hope will send me some books to distribute among them.

When he was released Samuel returned to Epworth and to his hostile, sullen parishioners. He stoically informed the Bishop of York in 1705 that "Most of my friends advise me to leave Epworth if l e'er I should get from hence. I confess I am not of that mind, because I may yet do good there, and 'tis like a coward to desert my post because the enemy fire thick upon me. They have only wounded me yet, and I believe CAN'T kill me."

Charles Wesley was born on December 18, 1707 and, according to Dr. John Whitehead, he "appeared dead rather than alive when he was born. He did not cry nor open his eyes and was kept wrapt [sic] up in soft wool until the time when he should have been born according to the usual course of nature, and then he opened his eyes and cried." It was only Susanna's constant care that ensured the infant Charles did not die. And it is possible that Charles' later health problems may have stemmed from his premature birth.

Both John and Charles Wesley grew up in a household where singing psalms, reciting prayers, and reading passages of Scripture were regular daily features and where religion was a way of life and not just a matter of certain outward observances. Susanna told one of her daughters, "'Tis not learning these things by rote, nor the saying a few prayers morning and evening, that will bring you to heaven; you must understand what you say, and practise what you know." One commentator has suggested that "In the household of the Epworth rectory can be traced the real origin of Methodism."

Susanna's world became her children. Even Samuel had to admit she was "the best of mothers." The children were taught to "cry softly" to avoid an "abundance of correction," presumably at the hand of Samuel who hated to be disturbed by "that most odious noise of crying"; to recite the Lord's Prayer as soon as they could speak; to do exactly as they were told; and to seek permission before doing anything. When the Wesley children addressed each other, it had to be with the prefix of "brother" or "sister." Shouting, bad manners, snacks between meals, mixing with other children, and borrowing without the permission of the owner were not permitted, while lying, stealing, or playing in church were severely punished. Six hours of intense studying per day were expected without excuse. Contended Susanna:

> Self-will is the root of all sin and misery, so whatever cherishes this in children insures . . . [their] wretchedness and irreligion; whatever checks and mortifies it promotes their future happiness and piety. . . . Religion is nothing else than doing the will of God in the renewing and saving a soul. The parent who indulges it does the devil's work; makes religion impracticable [and] salvation unattainable.

Jacky and Charles, like the rest of the Wesley children, were not taught to read until the age of five, so they developed a good memory by listening, particularly to Bible stories. The day after his fifth birthday, John was taught the letters of the alphabet and told to read the first verses of the Book of Genesis. Within two days he was able to read, while Charles apparently managed it in a day. Each evening during the week, Susanna taught one of the children individually: Charles' special time with his mother was on Saturdays and John's turn was on Thursdays. These one-on-one sessions were so important to John that while at Christ Church, Oxford, in a letter to his mother he wrote, "If you can spare me only that little part of Thursday evening which you formerly bestowed upon me in another manner, I doubt not it would be as useful now for correcting my heart as it was for forming my judgement."

One of the keys to Susanna's success was her astonishing patience. On one occasion, Samuel was astounded to hear his wife go over a subject twenty times with one of the children. When he questioned her, she replied: "If I had satisfied myself by mentioning it only nineteen times, I should have lost all my labour. It was the twentieth time that crowned it." And she was to comment, "There are few, if any, that would entirely devote twenty years of the prime of life in hope of saving the souls of children; for that was my principal intention, however unskillfully managed."

Her children did not just work hard. Susanna never withheld praise or encouragement where it was due, and there were moments of kindness and levity. Recalled the seventy-year-old John, "My mother had a dancing master to come to her house who taught all of us what was sufficient in her presence." Once when Samuel junior wrote her a letter and addressed her as "Madam," she replied: "Sammy—I do not love distance and ceremony. There is more love and tenderness in the name of mother than in all the complemental titles in the world."

In January 1714, at the age of ten, John left Epworth for Charterhouse School in London after being given a free place on the recommendation of Samuel's former patron, the Duke of Buckinghamshire. John's school uniform as a gownboy consisted of a black jerkin with a white collar, knee-length breeches, long black coat, and hat.

In the bitterly cold dormitories, pupils slept two to a bed, while below in the seventy-foot-long great hall, or Writing School as it was called with one of the finest paneled ceilings in Europe, classes sat together to recite the Greek and Latin classics. John's father had instructed him to run round the school's playing field called Green, which he did three times daily before breakfast. The boys rose at five, but breakfast was not until 8.00 a.m. and consisted of bread, cheese, and beer (beer was much cheaper than tea—a pound of the latter could buy 360 pots of beer). Supper was the same again, but lunch was more substantial, although the older boys stole the meat of the younger boys. John remarked later that the older boys pinched the younger pupils' meat so that he had to exist mainly on bread, which he claimed explained his small stature, even though all the Wesleys were short. However, in later life, he attributed his spartan diet at school as one of the reasons for his good health: "I can hardly believe that I am this day entered into my sixty-eighth year of my age. How marvellous are the ways of God. How has he kept me even from a child. From ten to thirteen or fourteen I had little but bread to eat, and not great plenty of that. I believe this was so far from hurting me, that it laid the foundation of lasting health."

Reminiscing on his childhood, John Wesley considered that by the age of ten he had not lost his innocence, "having been strictly educated and carefully taught that I could be saved 'by universal obedience, by keeping all the commandments of God,' in the meaning of which I was diligently instructed." John believed that his regular chapel going, combined with morning and evening prayers and Bible reading, would earn him eternal salvation. But he admitted that when he left home, he slackened without his mother's strict spiritual discipline: "Outward restraints being removed, I was much more negligent than before, even of outward duties, and almost continually guilty of outward sins, which I knew to be such, though they were not scandalous in the eyes of the world."

In 1716, his brother Samuel married Ursula "Nutty" Berry, and Charles entered Westminster School at Samuel's expense until he was elected a King's Scholar and his fees were paid by the school. Charles remarked that he had to be careful in dealing with his brother's wife as she could be severe towards him, although John told his mother that "She has always been particularly civil to me." Samuel acted as a surrogate father to Charles until he went to university. He undoubtedly moulded Charles' views on the Church of England, inspiring him with a deep love of its modes of worship.

At Westminster, Charles was required to rise at 5.15 a.m., recite morning prayers on his knees, and then wash in cold water before attending prayers in Latin at 6.00 a.m. This was followed by the study of Latin and Greek until breakfast at 8.00 a.m. Study then continued, with a break for dinner at noon, only to resume through to supper, with bed at 8.00 p.m.

Four years later, John was nominated for a scholarship to go to Oxford. On June 24, 1720, a week after his seventeenth birthday, he entered Christ Church College as a Commoner with an annual stipend of £20, paid in quarterly installments, with Samuel senior being delighted at his son's success. In 1726 his brother Charles joined him at Christ Church, Oxford.

2

OXFORD AND
THE HOLY CLUB

They imagine that they cannot be saved
if they do not spend every hour, indeed minute,
of their lives in the service of God.

—RICHARD MORGAN

John Wesley entered Christ Church College, Oxford, as a Commoner on June 24, 1720, a week after his seventeenth birthday, and in 1724, he graduated with a Bachelor of Arts degree. Soon after graduating, his parents put pressure on him to become an ordained minister, with his mother writing, "I heartily wish you were in orders," and his father suggested that he prepare for Holy Orders, commenting, "You don't admire a callow clergyman any more than I do."

When he finally agreed to seek ordination in December 1724, Samuel appeared to have second thoughts, informing John he opposed "your going hastily into Orders," suggesting instead that he spend a year assisting him to collate the Hebrew, Greek, Syrian, and Latin texts of the New Testament for the polyglot Bible he was working on, adding: "You ask me which is the best commentary on the Bible. I answer, the Bible." Susanna, however, was against any delay, advising John, "I think the sooner you are a deacon the better." Samuel had a change of heart and wrote to John in March 1725: "I've changed my mind since my last, and now incline to your going this summer into Orders." John began preparing for his ordination, but there was a remark in one of his mother's letters that made an impact on him. She had advised him to "enter now upon a serious examination of yourself, that you may know whether you have a reasonable hope of salvation by Jesus Christ, that is whether you are in a state of faith and repentance or not."

John discovered an old red notebook that belonged to his Puritan grandfather, John Westley, and began recording his daily self-examination. His more intimate notes were written in a code he developed that was so complex it was not deciphered accurately until 1972. For example, on March 26, 1725 he wrote: "Too much addicting to light behaviour at all times. . . . Listening to too much idle talk, and reading vain plays and books. . . . To avoid idleness, freedom with women, and high-seasoned meats." He also determined "to resist the very beginnings of lust, not by arguing with, but by thinking no more of it or by immediately going into company."

John wrote of his early years at Oxford: "I began to alter the whole form of my conversation, and to set in earnest upon a new life. I set apart an hour or two a day for religious retirement. I communicated every week. I watched against all sin, whether in word or deed. I began to aim at, and pray for inward holiness." However, on the night before his ordination in Christ Church Cathedral on September 19, 1725, John wrote in cipher in his diary: "Boasting, greedy, praise, intemperate sleep, detraction, lying—Lord have mercy—heat in arguing."

John established an unvarying routine at Oxford. He rose between four and five, said his prayers and read the Bible, breakfasted sometimes in the coffeehouses, instructed his pupils, dined in hall, conversed in the common room, walked, rode, read, and composed the sermons that he preached in the village churches around Oxford or in Oxford itself, all before he retired at nine or ten to bed.

In March 1726, John was elected a Fellow of Lincoln College by the twelve fellows of the College. His proud father exclaimed, "Wherever I am, my Jacky is a Fellow of Lincoln." John took his responsibilities to his students as a Fellow seriously, lecturing in Logic, Greek, and later Philosophy, commenting, "I should have thought myself little better than a highway man if I had not lectured them every day of the year but Sundays."

The annual stipend of £30 was critical, as a debt-ridden Samuel was struggling to fund his son at Oxford, writing to John in 1726:

> The last £12 pinched me so hard that I am forced to beg time of your brother Sam till after harvest, to pay him the £10 that you say he lent you. Nor shall I have so much as that (perhaps not £5) to keep my family till after harvest. I do not expect that I shall be able to do anything for Charles when he goes to the University. What will be my own fate before the summer be over God only knows.

Fortunately, in 1726, Charles was awarded a King's Scholarship to Christ Church College, Oxford, which was worth £100 per year, by coming top in his final exams. Charles arrived at Oxford in October, but, despite his scholarship, found himself in debt. On one cold January day, while sitting miserably by a fireless grate, he wrote to John regarding his pressing financial needs: "'Tis in the power of a few Epworth or Wroot guineas and clothes to give things the favourable turn, and make a gentleman of me. Come money, then, and quickly, to rescue me from my melancholy maxim, ex nihilo nihil fit—I can't possibly 'save nothing, where there is nothing to save.'"

It was a condition of John Wesley's Oxford fellowship that he should remain single, but he had a fondness for attractive young women and loved flirting with them. John also spent considerable time boating and swimming, drinking with friends, and playing chess, billiards, and backgammon, behavior that he later regretted when he lamented "the sensual pleasures, the desire of the sexes and [the] pernicious friendships" of his youth.

Charles felt he was equally entitled to a similar freedom before settling down to his studies, especially since for the first time he was not under the watchful eye of either his parents or oldest brother. He admitted freely later that he was "dead to God and asleep in the arms of Satan."

John continued to flirt with the opposite sex, and he introduced Charles to a circle of women who lived in a number of Cotswold villages with whom he corresponded, including Anne Granville, her sister Mary Pendarves, and the three sisters Sally, Betty, and Damaris Kirkham. John and these women adopted classical nicknames, with Anne becoming "Selima," Mary "Aspasia," and Sally "Varanese." John himself became "Cyrus," while Charles chose the nickname "Araspes." But just as Charles was enjoying his freedom, John began withdrawing from what he described as "trifling acquaintances," writing to his brother Samuel on December 5, 1726: "Leisure and I have taken leave of one another. I propose to be busy as long as I live." Throughout the winter of 1726, John worked on his Master of Arts, taking his degree in February 1727 by submitting three lectures in Latin on the subjects of Julius Caesar, the souls of animals, and the love of God.

John became concerned about Charles' lack of diligence and religious fervor. He was also annoyed at his brother's habit of entering his rooms and then reciting poetry and rifling through his papers. But when he challenged him, Charles replied, "What, would you have me a saint at once?" and would hear no more. A heated quarrel then transpired between the brothers, and Charles resolved never to quarrel again, writing to John later, "I shall never quarrel with you again till I do with my religion, and that I may never do that I am not ashamed to desire your prayers."

Charles claimed that he was "very desirous of knowledge but can't bear the drudgery of it. . . ." He was not as academic as his brothers and found himself "bewildered" in reading anything difficult: "My head will by no means keep pace with my heart and I'm afraid I shan't reconcile it in heart to the extraordinary business of thinking."

To supplement his income, Samuel senior had taken on the nearby parish of Wroot for an additional £50 per annum. John had assisted his father during the spring and summer of 1726, but in August 1727 he returned home to serve as his father's curate until November 1729, with Lincoln College renewing his leave of absence every six months. His mother's health was deteriorating. She almost died in June that year. His father commented to John, "Though she has now and then some very sick fits, yet I hope the sight of you will revive her."

In 1725, John and Charles' beautiful and highly educated sister, Hetty, had fallen in love with a handsome Oxford graduate called John Romley, who was then acting as Samuel's curate. Unfortunately, Samuel heard Romley singing a song that he considered vulgar, so he banished him from the parish. On the rebound, Hetty eloped with a local lawyer named Will Atkins. She returned home after one night, but her father refused to forgive her. When he discovered she was pregnant, he married her off to a rough, ill-educated glazier called William Wright from the nearby town of Louth, declaring harshly of Hetty: "Gangrene, farewell! She is lost to me [though] not so well as dead." John recorded that his father "never spoke of her in my hearing but with the utmost detestation." Susanna and Charles supported Samuel senior, but John was filled with compassion for his sister and preached a sermon on forgiveness at Wroot parish church. He showed the sermon to his mother who commented: "You wrote this sermon for Hetty. The rest was brought in for the sake of the last paragraph." Samuel realized it was directed at him and was enraged at John's audacity, complaining to Charles, "You hear how he contradicts me, and takes your sister's part before my face. Indeed, he disputes with me. . . ." When Charles informed John of Samuel's displeasure—"My father last night was telling me of your disrespect to him. He said you had him at open defiance"—John was stunned that he had offended his father. He burst into tears of contrition for contradicting him and not helping him with his writing, adding "but now I promise to do whatever you please." His father kissed him and wept, replying, "I always knew you were good at bottom and I will employ you next day." In penance, John spent hours composing sermons for his father and transcribing Latin quotations for his magnum opus on the Book of Job, before his return to Oxford.

During 1728, Charles became far more religious and studious. This may have been due to his narrow escape from the clutches of a London actress named Molly Buchanan, who was appearing in *The Virgin Queen* at the Theatre Royal in London. Charles had formed an attachment to her on his visits to the capital, and Molly's mother did all she could to ensure Charles would seduce her daughter in order to force his hand into marriage. Charles later confided to John: "To do the Old Lady justice, she did give us opportunities enough could I have had the Grace to have laid hold of them. . . . Hints were lost upon so dull stupid Fellow as I was; and as such no doubt I have been sufficiently laughed at." John helped his brother extricate himself from the situation. Charles also determined never to get himself into such a position again: "From henceforth . . . I shall be less addicted to gallantry . . . and liking woman simply for being woman. . . . But enough of her—I'll blot my brain and paper no longer with her." Charles promised to abandon all diversions, to start reading seriously, and to follow John's example in keeping a daily record of his spiritual progress. Frivolity was replaced with solemnity. He assured John, "It is through your means that, I firmly believe, God will establish what He has begun in me; and there is one person I would so willingly have to be the instrument of good to me as you."

When Charles stayed with Samuel and his family during his Christmas vacation in 1728, Charles confided in a letter to John how they noticed the changes in him: "They wonder here I'm so strangely dull (as indeed mirth and I shook hands and parted) and at the same time pay me the compliment of saying I grow extremely like you," although the "compliment" was not intended by Samuel. The latter wrote to John that Charles was "so entirely infected with your gravity that every motion and look made me almost suspect it was you; indeed, I begin now to think he will hardly ever lay aside the present solemnity of his person and behaviour."

Charles did not find Oxford conducive to learning or the development of his new-found faith. He described the university as a place "where learning keeps its loftiest seat, and hell its firmest throne. . . . Christ Church is certainly the worst place in the world to begin a reformation in. A man stands a very fair chance of being laughed out of his religion at his first setting out, in a place where 'tis scandalous to have any at all." By January 1729, without John's presence, Charles feared that he would return to his old ways, writing:

> One who has for thirteen years been utterly inattentive
> at public prayers can't expect to find there [at Oxford] that

warmth, he has never known, at his first seeking. . . . [But] I
look upon this coldness as a trial . . . [and] I won't give myself
to leisure to relapse for I'm afraid if I have no business of my
own, the Devil will soon find me some. . . . I am not ashamed
to desire your prayers. 'Tis owing in great measure to somebody's (my Mother's most likely) that I am come to think as
I do, for I can't tell myself How or When I first awoke out of
my Lethargy—only that twas not long after you went away.

Charles informed John that he needed to surround himself with
a supportive group of like-minded friends. He persuaded a couple of
fellow students to join him in weekly communion: Robert Kirkham,
brother of Sally, and William Morgan, who was the eldest son of a
Dublin lawyer. Charles described Morgan as "a modest, humble,
well-disposed youth" who, with his encouragement, "resolved to spare
no plans in working out his salvation."

John was recalled to Oxford in November 1729 by the Rector of
Lincoln College to provide supervision and instruction to the under-
graduates. By mutual consent John took over the leadership of the
group from Charles, while also acting as his brother's tutor in Classics.
In his diary John described the meetings in which they prayed and read
Scriptures and other books: "In November 1729, four young gentlemen
of Oxford, Mr. John Wesley, Fellow of Lincoln College; Mr. Charles
Wesley, Student of Christ Church; Mr. Morgan, Commoner of Christ
Church; and Mr. Kirkham of Merton College; began to spend some
evenings in a week together, in reading chiefly the Greek Testament."

In the summer of 1730, William Morgan began visiting a man in an
Oxford prison who was sentenced to death for murdering his wife. He
approached John and Charles about joining him, telling John that "it
would do much good if anyone would be at the pains of now and then
speaking with them." John was not sure whether it was appropriate for
dons and undergraduates to visit prisons. He wrote later to his father
and the Bishop of Oxford, John Potter, for their opinions. Both were
unequivocal in their support: Potter replying that he "was greatly
pleased with the undertaking," and Samuel revealing that he too in
his Oxford days had visited prisoners "and reflect on it with grave satisfaction to this day" and that "none but such as are out of their senses

would be prejudiced against your acting in such a manner." Samuel also commented: "I have the highest reason to bless God that he has given me two sons together in Oxford to whom he has given grace and courage to turn the war against the world and the devil. . . . I think I must adopt Mr. Morgan to [also] be my son."

On August 24, John and Charles accompanied Morgan to the prison which would become a regular experience. John preached once a month at the Castle and at Bocardo prison, where most of the debtors were incarcerated, with members of the Holy Club. They visited the prisons daily, and twice a week read prayers to the prisoners. On December 11, 1730, John wrote to his father that "On Sunday they had prayers and a sermon at the Castle; on Christmas Day we hope they will have dinner; and the Sunday after, a communion." Samuel senior was impressed by John's activities, remarking, "I hear my son John has the honour of being styled the 'Father of the Holy Club': if it be so, I am sure I must be the grandfather of it; and I need not say that I had rather any of my sons should be so dignified and distinguished than to have the title of 'His Holiness.'"

The work of the Holy Club also extended to the inmates of St. Thomas' workhouse, a fund to buy medicine, assistance to help debtors pay off their debts, and a school for poor children. One of the Club's members said: "The school was of Mr. Wesley's [so he thought] own setting up; however he [William Morgan] paid the mistress and clothes some, if not all of the children. When they went thither, they inquired how each child behaved, saw their work (for some knit and spin), heard them read, heard them their prayers of their catechism, and explained part of it."

When John and Charles returned from Epworth in the summer of 1731, John informed his father sadly that "our little company that used to meet us, is shrunk into almost none at all." But still the work continued, including the prison ministry where John recorded that the inmates of Castle prison "have still the Gospel preached to them, and some of their temporal wants supplied, our little fund rather increasing than diminishing. Nor have we yet been forced to discharge any of the children which Mr. Morgan left to our care."

Their prison visiting and charitable activities attracted more students, including Francis Gore and John Boyce, the son of a former mayor of Oxford. John Gambold of Christ Church College, who later became a Moravian bishop, and John Clayton, a tutor at Brasenose College, joined the group in 1732. Before leaving Oxford six months later to become a clergyman, Clayton urged them to keep the fasts of the primitive church and to fill every hour with prayer or action. Charles was instrumental in attracting two of the most important members of the group who were to play significant roles in the growth of Methodism: Benjamin Ingham and George Whitefield. Others who joined the group included Charles Kinchin, Thomas Boughton, and James Hervey.

In November 1730, some fellow students started to jokingly describe John and Charles' society as "the Holy Club" or the "Godly Club" and the members as "Bible Moths" and "Bible Bigots." They also called them the "Super-Rogation Men" because of their fanatical observance of Church of England ceremonies, particularly fasting. Others scathingly labeled them "the Sacramentarians" as they walked through the streets of Oxford every Sunday to celebrate the Lord's Supper at the university's St. Mary's Church. By September 1732, a new name had been coined for the members of the Holy Club—Methodists, maybe because they were attempting to be "methodical" in their worship and lifestyle. The term had first been used in the seventeenth century as a derogatory description of nonconformists who followed the teachings of Jacobus Arminius, a Bible professor and theologian who opposed Calvinism. By 1732, even Samuel senior felt the need to tell John to stop behaving like "a wild enthusiast or fanatic." Emily Wesley criticized the group's constant self-examination, commenting that it "seems to me like Church tyranny, and assuming to yourselves a dominion over your fellow creatures which was never designed by God."

John became obsessed with encouraging an ascetic lifestyle, including rising at 4.00 a.m. (rising early enabled him to overcome the insomnia that had been troubling him for years) and fasting on Wednesdays and Fridays. He adopted a system in which he listed his daily activities hour by hour and, after daily self-interrogation rather than meditation, rated his "temper of devotion" on a scale of one to nine. His obsession with the state of his faith made him resentful of his parents' increasing desire to see him return to Epworth. He prayed at intervals throughout the day, particularly on the hour, what he described as ejaculatory prayer, with one Holy Club member observing, "[He] thought prayer to be more his business than anything else and I have seen him come out of his closet with a serenity of countenancy that was next to shining."

John and Charles displayed a disciplined, frugal lifestyle. For example, John would often sit in his rooms without a fire to save money or as a penance. Moreover, the two Wesleys walked everywhere, including the one hundred and fifty miles to Epworth, which concerned their father so much that he wrote in 1731, "I should be pleased to see you here this spring, if it was not upon the hard conditions of your walking here, but that always terrifies me, and I am commonly so uneasy for fear you should kill yourselves with coming so far on foot that it destroys much of the pleasure I should otherwise have in conversing with you." And their mother expressed her feelings about their regular fasting: "I must tell you, Mr. John Wesley, Fellow of Lincoln, and Mr. Charles Wesley, Student of Christ Church, that you are two scrubby travellers, and sink your characters strangely by eating nothing on the road . . . to save charges. I wonder you are not ashamed of yourselves." But John was determined to adhere to his punishing regime, asserting, "Fasting is not a means of chastity only, but of deadness to pleasure and heavenly-mindedness and consequently necessary . . . to all persons in all times of life." An observer said of the Holy Club members, "they stint themselves to twopence meat and a farthing bread, and a draught of water when they eat at their own expense; and as for supper, they never eat any."

Not all members were able to follow John's example. Benjamin Ingham managed to sleep without a mattress or sheets, but when it came to rising early from bed each morning, the regime proved too much. He used an alarm clock and asked a friend to wake him up and even imposed penalties on himself for failing to get up on time. Still, rising from bed at such an early hour turned out to be a discipline he could not keep.

Charles and William Morgan, however, did follow John in rising early and fasting, which may have affected their health. Charles' mother described how he was unable to "eat a full meal, but must presently throw up again." One of Charles' doctors was to attribute his frequent bouts of ill health to excessive fasting while at Oxford. Morgan's father was also concerned about his son's involvement in the group, writing scathingly to William:

> You can't conceive what a noise that ridiculous Society which you are engaged in has made here. Besides the particulars of the great follies of it at Oxford . . . it gave me sensible trouble to hear that you were noted for your going into villages about Holt, entering into poor people's houses, calling their children together, teaching them their prayers and catechism and giving them a shilling at your departure.

In February 1732, John Wesley informed his mother, rather coldly, that he thought William Morgan was dying: "He can neither sleep, read, stand nor sit. . . . Surely now he is a burden to himself and almost useless in the world; his discharge cannot be far off." In June 1732, William Morgan did indeed become seriously ill and had to return to Ireland where he died insane on August 26. His father said of his son, "The Wesleys he raved of most of all in his illness."

Oxford was swept with rumors and accusations that Morgan had become ill and died because of excessive fasting imposed on him by John Wesley. John wrote to Richard Morgan, William's father, asserting that his son had stopped fasting a year and a half before his death and that John had only begun fasting six months before. However, in December 1732, an anonymous letter was sent to the London newspaper *Fogg's Weekly Journal*, which described "the Methodists" and their "enthusiastic madness": "The University at present is not a little pestered with these sons of sorrow whose number daily receives addition. . . . They avoid . . . any pleasant and grateful sensation. All social entertainments and diversions are disapproved of, and in endeavouring to avoid luxury, they not only exclude what is convenient, but what is absolutely necessary for the support of life." The letter went on to describe how the members of the Holy Club were making the university "nothing but a monastery," and complained of their "absurd and perpetual melancholy . . . gloomy and disconsolate way of life. . . . Weighed down by a habitual sorrow . . . superstitious scruples [and] . . . gloomy stupidity."

John responded to his critics by preaching a sermon on January 1, 1733 at St. Mary's Church in Oxford. His sermon centered on holiness and expounded his doctrine of Christian perfection for the first time, proclaiming the need to be so "renewed in the spirit of our mind" as to be "perfect as our father in heaven is perfect." An anonymous pamphlet entitled *The Oxford Methodists* (probably written by the mystic and theologian William Law) also helped stem what Wesley described as "the torrent rolling down from all sides upon me." But he still had to accept "the ill consequences of my singularity," being deserted by friends and pupils, and the loss of his reputation. He was even confronted by a hostile mob at the gates of Lincoln College.

Despite his criticism of John Wesley's lifestyle, William Morgan's father accepted John's rebuttal of his accusations, was grateful for the kindness the Wesleys had shown William, and was still willing to entrust his youngest son, Richard, to John's care as his tutor, even though Richard railed against John's strictness. On January 14, 1734, John entered Richard Morgan's room and was incensed at finding a letter to Morgan's father complaining bitterly about his tutor's regime:

> . . . a society of gentlemen . . . whom the world calls Methodists, of which my tutor is president. They imagine that they cannot be saved if they do not spend every hour, indeed minute, of their lives in the service of God. And to that end they read prayers every day in the common jail, preach every Sunday and administer the sacrament once every month. They almost starve themselves to be able to relieve the poor and buy books for their conversion. They endeavour to reform notorious whores and allay spirits in haunted houses. They fast two days in the week, which has emaciated them to that degree that they are a fearful sight. . . . They rise every day at five of the clock and till prayers, which begin at eight, they sing psalms and read some piece of divinity. They meet at

each other's rooms at six of the clock five nights in the week, and from seven to nine read a piece of some religious book. In addition, six to seven they read over the petitions of poor people and receive their wants, dispose of pious books and fix the duties of the ensuing day.

Richard went on to complain that:

> I am as much laughed at and despised by the whole town as any of them and always shall be so while I am his pupil. The whole College makes a jest of me and the Fellows themselves do not show me common civility, so great is their aversion to my tutor. . . . He has lectured me scarce in anything but books of devotion. He has given me a book of Mr. Nelson to abridge this Christmas. By becoming his pupil I am stigmatized with the name of a Methodist, the misfortune of which I cannot describe. . . . I think it incumbent upon me to inform you that it is my opinion that if I am to continue with Mr. Wesley I shall be ruined.

John wrote in his diary that "there was little prospect of Morgan because no sincerity in him." Ironically, however, Richard Morgan became one of John's most dedicated disciples and was among those who saw the Wesleys off at Gravesend when they sailed for Georgia in October 1735.

The Oxford Methodists not only survived the crisis over William Morgan's death but increased in number, largely due to the efforts of John Clayton and Charles. Benjamin Ingham proved to be one of Charles' most dedicated disciples, declaring, "I trust that by God's mercy and grace I shall be enabled to inure myself to hardship and to fight manfully against the world, the flesh and the devil." He renounced all "the pomp and vanities of the world . . . all proud and vain thoughts of my own worth [and] all the sinful ways of the flesh." He and a fellow student, James Hervey, began visiting a workhouse and working with the poor at a hospital and in the slums of Oxford. The members of the society also attempted to live on the same amount of money each year. As their incomes increased, they gave the remainder to charity.

Back in Epworth, Samuel was desperate for John to take on the responsibility of running his parish, particularly as his health was deteriorating after a serious accident in 1731 in which he fell from a wagon and hit his head. By 1734, Samuel, knowing that Susanna would be evicted from the Epworth rectory when he died, demanded that one of his sons return and take over from him. Samuel junior was headmaster of Blundell's School in Devon and Charles was not ordained, so that left John. But John refused to acquiesce, informing his father callously that he had no wish to repeat the latter's failures and no desire to work among "lukewarm Christians" when his personal salvation required that he should stay in Oxford.

In November 1734, his father wrote to John again, urging him to accept the position and carry on the work he had been pursuing for forty years and on "account of the love and longing the poor people have for you." John replied in December in a long, rambling letter. This epistle contained around five thousand words and was methodically numbered in sections from one to twenty-six. In it John defended his decision not to return: "In Epworth, on the other hand, I should be no use at all. I could not do any good to these boorish people, and I should probably fall back in to habits of irregularity and indulgence. Moreover, there should be no difficulty in finding someone else far better suited than I am to take the living. My present vocation is here, in Oxford, and not elsewhere." He concluded that "I may not likely to do that good anywhere, not even at Epworth, which I may do at Oxford."

John also stopped writing regularly to his mother. This, along with his perceived callous attitude towards their father, incensed his brother Samuel who wrote scathingly to John: " I judge every proposition flatly false . . . I see your love to yourself but love to your neighbour I do not see." The letter suggests a selfishness in John and an unwillingness to reveal the truth—namely, that he preferred the life of an Oxford don to that of a rector in some obscure rural parish. As V. H. H. Green has concluded:

> If Wesley wanted the life of self-denial and contempt, the
> bearing of the cross, all things which he stressed so much,
> then the parish of Epworth provided them as richly as did

Oxford. He had in fact to justify his refusal of the living to himself rather than his father. The letter revealed, lucid and carefully argued as it was, a mind in a considerable state of confusion. Yet within two years of writing this letter, Wesley, though still a fellow of Lincoln, was working as a missionary in Georgia.[8]

By the time a remorseful John relented and applied for the position of rector, it was too late. The Bishop of London, Edmund Gibson, decided John was unfit for the position. He considered John too much of a fanatic, and ironically the parish was given to John Romley, the man Hetty wanted to marry. Romley was to prove a bitter critic of the Wesleys until his death in 1751.

Charles had already written to his brother Samuel in July 1734: "My father declines so fast, that before next year he will, in all probability, be at his journey's end; so that I must see him now, or never more with my bodily eyes. My mother seems more cast down at the apprehension of his death than I thought she could have been; and what is still worse, he seems so too." John said of his father:

> What he experienced before, I know not; but I know that during his last illness, which continued eight months, he enjoyed a clear sense of his acceptance with God. I heard him express it more than once, although at that time I understood him not. "The inward witness, son, the inward witness," said he to me, "that is the proof, the strongest proof, of Christianity." And when I asked him (the time of his change drawing nigh), "Sir, are you in much pain?" he answered aloud, with a smile, "God does chasten me with pain—yes, all my bones with strong pain; but I thank Him for all, I bless Him for all, I love Him for all!"

When his father died on April 25, 1735, Charles wrote again to Samuel junior, "The fear of death he had entirely conquered, and at last gave up his latest human desires of finishing Job, paying his debts, and seeing you." And in another letter to his brother, Charles wrote, "His passage was so smooth and insensible that, notwithstanding the

[8] V. H. H. Green, *The Young Mr. Wesley* (London: Wyvern Books, 1963), 235.

stopping of his pulse, and the ceasing of all signs of life and motion, in doubt whether the soul was departed or no. . . ."

John and Charles were present at their father's death, and both were stricken with grief. Even though the latter's relationship had been highly formal—Charles still addressed Samuel senior as "Honoured Sir"—he had great affection for his father and held him in awe, writing again to his brother Samuel, who was unable to return home in time: "You have reason to envy us, who could attend him in the last stage of his illness. The few words he could utter I saved, and hope never to forget. . . . He appeared full of faith and peace . . . [and] often laid his hand upon my head, and said, 'Be steady. The Christian faith will surely revive in this Kingdom. You shall see it, though I shall not.'"

3

AMERICA

My chief motive, to which all the rest are subordinate,
is the hope of saving my own soul.

—JOHN WESLEY

O n August 28, 1735, John Wesley was walking down Ludgate Street near St. Paul's Cathedral in London when he bumped into Dr. John Burton, a theologian, fellow of Corpus Christi College, Oxford, and trustee of the newly founded colony of Georgia in America. John was in London to oversee the printing of his father's six-hundred-page Latin commentary *Dissertations on the Book of Job*, which was to be presented to Queen Caroline. The Georgian colony had been established in 1732 by General James Oglethorpe, a former soldier and Member of Parliament. He had named the colony after King George II.

Burton arranged for John to meet Oglethorpe, who encouraged John to return to Georgia with him to minister to the colonists and the native Indians. Burton also introduced John to the Society for the Propagation of the Gospel (SPG), calling John a man "inured to contempt of the ornaments and conveniences of life." The SPG offered him the chaplaincy in Savannah, the capital of the colony, on a salary of £50 per annum. John accepted the position after consulting with mystic and former Anglican clergyman William Law, John Clayton and his brother, Samuel. Fortunately, John could retain his Lincoln College Fellowship, although he was never to return to the university as a tutor.

Both John and Charles' grandfathers had intended to be missionaries in America. Their father Samuel had also expressed a desire to go to the New World. In a letter written to Oglethorpe and dated November 7, 1734, Samuel said: "I had always so dear a love for your colony, that if it had but been ten years ago, I would gladly have devoted the remainder of my life and labours to that place." Their elder brother Samuel was also excited by the prospects for mission work and donated a communion set for use in the colony. He even published a celebratory poem called "Georgia" in honor of John and Charles' venture.

In 1730, John and his sister Kezzy went to Lincoln to see the Indian kings, possibly Cherokee chiefs, who had been brought from America to England by Sir Alexander Coming. In 1732, John had become a member of the Society for the Propagation of Christian Knowledge (SPCK). He and his family held James Oglethorpe in high esteem for his humanitarianism and religious ideals, with Samuel senior describing him as "a guardian angel" for initiating an investigation into the condition of prisoners. In fact, Oglethorpe had established the colony partly as a haven for poor debtors, displaced Scottish highlanders, and persecuted Protestant minorities, including the Moravians and Salzburghers.

Disillusionment of life at Oxford (despite rigorously defending his decision to stay rather than succeed his father), a determination to do penance for refusing Epworth, and a string of failed romances may also have played a part in John's unexpected departure to the New World. It seems that more than anything else, though, he left out of a deep desire to save his own soul. As he expressed to Dr. Burton: "My chief motive, to which all the rest are subordinate, is the hope of saving my own soul. I hope to learn the true sense of the Gospel of Christ by preaching to the heathen." Historian V. H. H. Green has commented: "John Wesley was introspective by nature. He did not feel that the work that he was doing gave him the inward peace and spiritual serenity which should be the mark of the true Christian."[9] Green also suggests that John's correspondence with Burton had an emphasis on "escape

---

[9] V. H. H. Green, *John Wesley* (Lanham, MD: University Press of America, 1987), 34.

rather than of fulfilment. In another age and another church Wesley must surely have been a monk at least for a time."[10] John believed that the forthcoming hardships would guarantee an ascetic lifestyle. He was also extraordinarily naive about the native Indians, remarking that they would be like "little children, humble, willing to learn and eager to do the will of God." He also wrongly hoped that living in a place where there would be few women, except for Indians who were "a different species from me," would solve the problem of sexual temptation.

John wrote to Dr. Burton in October 1735: ". . . you will perhaps ask: Cannot you save your own soul in England as well as in Georgia? I answer, No; neither can I hope to attain the same degree of holiness here which I may there; neither if I stay here, knowing this, can I reasonably hope to attain any degree of holiness at all." According to Green, "The mission to Georgia thus offered an escape and a challenge. He sailed for America in a state of considerable emotional and spiritual perturbation."[11] The voyage was also going to be a challenge for John. He had never been on a ship before and hated the sea, remarking a few years earlier of his "fear of the sea, which I had both dreaded and abhorred from my youth."

Charles had no desire to leave Oxford. He and his brother Samuel knew that he lacked the physical and emotional strength to survive in such a harsh environment. Charles later commented: "I took my Master's Degree, and only thought of spending all my days at Oxford. But my brother, who always had the ascendant over me, persuaded me to accompany him and Mr. Oglethorpe to Georgia. I exceedingly dreaded entering into holy orders; but he overruled me here also." Charles was given the position of Secretary for Indian Affairs and minister to the colonists, but was in reality Oglethorpe's personal assistant at his beck and call. George Whitefield questioned Charles' decision to go to Georgia as Oglethorpe's secretary:

> My friend will not take it amiss if I enquire why he chooses
> to be secretary to Mr. Oglethorpe, and not go where labourers

---

[10] Green, *The Young Mr. Wesley*, 240.

[11] Ibid., 265.

> are wanted, in the character of a missionary. Did the Bishop
> ordain us, my dear friend, to write bonds, receipts, and etc.
> or to preach the Gospel? Or dare we not trust God to provide
> for our relations without endangering or at least retarding,
> our spiritual improvement? But I go too far. Habe me escu-
> satum [Please excuse me]. You know I was always heady and
> self-willed.

Much to his brother Samuel's annoyance, Charles felt he could
not deny John's request, so he agreed to go with him. The only person
who could have persuaded Charles to ignore John was their widowed
mother, but she gave the venture her blessing, saying, "Had I twenty
sons, I should rejoice that they were thus employed."

It appears that John was more concerned about going to Georgia
than about the best interests of his brother. He not only ignored
Charles' reluctance to go and the protests of his brother Samuel, but
insisted that Charles should be ordained a minister even though he
felt no calling to be one and "exceedingly dreaded" the prospect.
The experience of trying to live a holy life among like-minded fellow
students had made it difficult for Charles. An emphasis on showing one
was saved by performing good works had only succeeded in making
him feel that his faith was inadequate and his lifestyle unworthy of
a true Christian. Nevertheless, Charles was ordained as a deacon by
John Potter, Bishop of Oxford, on September 21, 1735, and in rapid
succession as a minister by Edmund Gibson, Bishop of London, on
September 29. Following his ordination, he commented rather sadly
that "Jack knew his strength and used it. . . . I freely own it was the will
of Jack, but am not convinced it was the will of God."

John was able to persuade two other Oxford Methodists to join
him—Benjamin Ingham and twenty-one-year-old Charles Delamotte.
John expressed his delight at the ascetic life that lay ahead: "The
pomp and show of the world have no place in the wilds of America.
. . . I cannot hope to attain the same degree of holiness here, which I
may there. . . . [I will be] cut off from all occasions of gratifying those
desires which, unless speedily rooted out, will drown . . . [the] soul in
everlasting perdition."

On October 14, 1735, the four Oxford missionaries set sail for Georgia from Gravesend, Kent on the *Simmonds* with 257 passengers and crew. Before they left they had agreed that they would support each other, believing that it would be "impossible to promote the work of God among the heathen without an entire union among ourselves." They further agreed to consult each other about everything and accept the majority decision. If they were divided equally on an issue, they would draw lots to settle the matter.

They were given a cabin partitioned off in the forecastle of the ship, which gave them privacy to pursue a rigorous daily schedule they had agreed upon once at sea. For the two-month voyage to America, they agreed to abstain from meat and wine, and to consume only rice and biscuits. John left a detailed account of how they lived on board during the voyage:

> Our common way of living was this: from four in the morning till five each of us used private prayer. From five to seven we read the Bible together, carefully comparing it (that we might not lean to our own understandings) with the writings of the earliest ages. At seven we breakfasted. At eight were the public prayers. From nine to twelve I usually learned German, and Mr. Delamotte, Greek. My brother writ sermons, and Mr. Ingham instructed the children. At twelve we met to give an account to one another what we had done since our last meeting, and what we designed to do before our next. About one we dined. The time from dinner to four we spent in reading to those of whom each of us had taken charge, or in speaking to them severally, as need required. At four were the evening prayers, when either the Second Lesson was explained (as it always was in the morning), or the children were catachized and instructed before the congregation. From five to six we again used private prayer. From six to seven I read in our cabin to two or three of the passengers (of whom there were about eighty English on board), and each of my brethren to a few more of theirs. At seven, I joined the Germans in their public service, while Mr. Ingham was reading between the decks to as many as desired to hear. At eight we met again, to exhort and instruct one another. Between nine and ten we went to bed, where neither the roaring of the

> sea nor the motion of the ship could take away the refreshing
> sleep which God gave us.

The newly ordained Charles preached a number of times while on board the ship, including a sermon concerning the reluctance of people to give up their all for the gospel: "The world with her pomps and vanities, pleasures and delights, entertainments and diversions, has monopolized a large share of our affections. . . . We have offered part of our service to other masters . . . [yet] the gospel informs us that to be disciples of Christ we must forsake . . . [everything] which the world counts dear."

Behind the bravado, Charles agonized over whether he should have embarked with his brother. The seas were very rough. He suffered miserably from seasickness, which plunged him into a severe depression: "I find no words to express myself. There is no writing down my sensations. I feel the weight and misery of my nature, and long to be freed from this body of corruptions." Charles wrote to Sally Kirkham: "In vain have I fled myself to America; I still groan under the intolerable weight of inherent misery! . . . Go where I will, I carry my Hell about with me; nor have I the least ease in anything."

John spent considerable time ministering to Beata Hawkins, the wife of the ship's surgeon, and her pregnant friend Anne Welch. They flirted with John, but he was convinced that the two women's motives were genuine, commenting:

> Mrs. Hawkins expressed a desire of receiving the Holy
> Communion. Several being informed of it, warned me of her
> insincerity, and laid many crimes to her charge, of which I
> informed her. In the evening she replied clearly and calmly
> to every article of the charge, and with such an appearance
> of innocence . . . that I could no longer doubt of her desire to
> be not only almost but altogether a Christian.

Charles, however, saw through the pretense of both women and argued with John, believing he was making a fool of himself. In response, John wrote "Charles perverse" several times in his *Journal*.

In January, the ship encountered a series of severe storms. John recorded: "I was vaulted over with water in a moment, and so stirred I scarce expected to lift my head till the sea should give up her dead. . . . The winds roared about us. . . . The ship not only rocked to and fro with the utmost violence, but shook and jarred with so unequal, grating a motion, that one could but with great difficulty keep one's hold of anything, nor stand a moment without it." Then on the evening of January 17, John and Charles were with Oglethorpe in his cabin when the ship was hit by a massive wave. John described what happened:

> The sea broke over us from stem to stern; burst through the windows of Mr. Oglethorpe's cabin, where three or four of us were sitting with a sick woman, and covered her all over. . . . About eleven I lay down . . . and in a short time fell asleep, though uncertain whether I should awake alive. . . . O how pure in heart must he be who would rejoice to appear before God at a moment's warning.

At midnight he added a further note to his diary: "Stormy still and afraid."

There was another group of passengers on board who, unlike the Wesleys, were unafraid of death: the twenty-six German members of the Church of the United Brethren, or the Moravian Church[12] as they were more usually known, led by their bishop, David Nitschmann. These individuals were admired for their serenity and willingness to undertake tasks that the English immigrants felt were beneath them. Despite being insulted, vilified, and even physically assaulted, they refused to retaliate.

Another storm struck the ship a few days later. One of its huge waves knocked John off his feet. Though unscathed, he was unsettled by his all-consuming fear: "I could but to say to myself, 'How is it that

---

[12] Also known as the United Brethren (or Unitas Fratum in Latin, meaning "Unity of the Brethren"), the Moravian Church evolved from the Hussite movement led by John Hus (1369–1415) who objected to some practices in the Roman Catholic Church. Hus was burned at the stake for heresy by the Catholic Church in 1415. The first Protestant church, the United Brethren became known as the Moravian Church due to those who fled to Saxony in 1722 from the province of Moravia, now in the Czech Republic, to escape persecution. The Moravian Church placed great emphasis on Christian unity, personal piety, missions, and music.

you have no faith?' being unwilling to die." The storm continued and on Sunday evening, John joined the Moravians as they held a service, singing their hymns in his limited German. Regarding that event he wrote:

> In the midst of the psalm wherewith their service began, the sea broke over, split the mainsail in pieces, covered the ship, and poured in between the decks, as if the great deep had already swallowed us up. A terrible screaming began the English. The Germans looked up and without intermission calmly sang on. I asked one of them afterwards, "Was you not afraid?" He answered. "I thank God, no." I asked, "But were not your women and children afraid?" he replied mildly, "No; our women and children are not afraid to die." This was the most glorious day which I have hitherto seen.

John recorded two years later: "[They] endeavoured to show me 'a more excellent way.' But I understood it not at first. I was too learned and too wise. So that it seemed foolishness to me. And I continued preaching, and following after, and trusting in that righteousness whereby no flesh can be justified." Benjamin Ingham wrote of the Moravians:

> They are more like the primitive Christians than any church now existing. . . . They live together in perfect love and peace, having for the present all things in common. They are more ready to serve their neighbours than themselves. In business they are diligent, in all their dealings strictly just; and in everything they behave themselves with meekness, sweetness and humility.

On February 5, 1736, the ship arrived off the coast of Georgia. As the *Simmonds* was moored off Tybee Island, Charles commented despondently: "God has brought an unhappy, unthankful wretch here, through a thousand dangers, to renew his complaints, and loathe the Life which has been preserved by a series of Miracles. . . . I still groan under the intolerable weight of inherent misery!"

Oglethorpe went ashore and returned, bringing with him August Spangenberg, the leader of the Moravian Herrnhut settlement in

Georgia. Samuel Quincy, the clergyman John was going to replace, had not yet vacated the parsonage in Savannah. Quincy had tried to seduce one of his parishioners, which led to the trustees terminating his contract. John and Charles Delamotte would stay for the time being at the Moravian settlement.

John engaged Spangenberg in conversation and was surprised by his response:

> I asked Mr. Spangenberg's advice with regard to myself— to my own conduct. He told me he could say nothing till he had asked me two or three questions: "Do you know yourself? Have you the witness within yourself? Does the Spirit of God bear witness with your spirit that you are a child of God?" I was surprised and knew not what to answer. He observed it and asked, "Do you know Jesus Christ?" I paused and said, "I know he is the Saviour of the world." "True," replied he, "but do you know He has saved you?" I answered, "I hope He has died to save me." He only added, "Do you know yourself?" I said, "I do." But I fear they were vain words.

However, Spangenberg was not as hard on John as Wesley was on himself, writing in his diary, "I observe that grace really dwells and reigns in him."

Oglethorpe also brought on board Chief Tomo-chachi, who was dressed in English clothes. On another occasion Oglethorpe had presented the chief to King George II in London. Tomo-chachi was the chief of the Savannah nation. He was wrapped in a large blanket, his hair bedecked with beads, and a red feather tucked behind one ear. Chief Tomo-chachi made a solemn speech that was interpreted by an Indian woman married to an English trader. This gave John hope that he could reach the Indians with the gospel. However, in time it proved a false hope, and he considered his lack of success in converting the native Indians as one of the foremost failures of his time in Georgia.

The Moravian John Töltschig revealed to John that, in his opinion, the American Indians were worse than animals and drank so heavily that they rolled around on the ground. A disappointed Wesley described the Indians as liars, thieves, hooligans, murderers, adulterers, idlers, and sensualists, and he had never "as yet found or heard of any Indians on the continent of America who had the least desire of being instructed in the Christian religion."

Savannah consisted of about five hundred colonists, a hundred dwellings, and four public buildings, with the courthouse doubling as a church. When he eventually moved there, John was initially impressed by the colonists' "deep attention with which they received the word." Some of them told him they were thankful to God for "all the goodness . . . [and] great many benefits" of his ministry. However, John soon became unpopular with the colonists for trying to impose a regime that was too severe: enforced Sunday observance; a service divided into two parts with a meeting at five in the morning; an insistence on trine immersion for baptism rather than just sprinkling the head of the baby with water; and his refusal to conduct a burial service for a dissenter. He also alienated many by supporting the colony's anti-slavery policy, strict trading laws, and a ban on drinking rum.

John offended the colonists by questioning their morality. When he reproved one of them for his slack religious life, the man replied scathingly: "I like nothing you do. All your sermons are satires upon particular persons, therefore, I will never hear you more; and all the people are of my mind for we won't hear ourselves abused. Besides they say that they are Protestants. But as for you they cannot tell what religion you are of. They never heard of such religion before. They do not know what to make of it."

Meanwhile, Charles and Benjamin Ingham accompanied Oglethorpe to establish a new settlement called Fort Frederica on St. Simon's Island, one hundred miles south of Savannah. The settlement consisted of a few tents and huts. A depressed Charles wrote home, unsure of whether he would survive such a hostile environment: "I wandered to the north end of the island and stood upon the narrow point which . . . [projects] into the ocean. The vastness of the watery waste, as compared with my standing place, called to mind the briefness of life and the immensity of its consequences."

Oglethorpe gave Charles permission to act as chaplain to the colonists. Charles wrote in his journal that his spirits revived because

"God gave me, like Saul, another heart." However, he hated his administrative duties, reporting "I was wholly spent in writing letters for Mr. Oglethorpe. I would spend six days more in the same manner for all Georgia." According to Green, Charles was out of his depth in both roles: "Charles proved incompetent as a secretary and disastrous as the pastor at Frederica."[13]

In the absence of a church building, Charles held four services a day in the open air, with a drum roll summoning the colonists. They came to resent his sermons, most of which had been written by John about sin and God's vengeance. Like John, Charles refused to baptize babies by sprinkling water and insisted on trine immersion. On his second day in Frederica, Charles wrote in his journal: "I began talking to M. Germain, about baptizing her child by immersion. She was much averse to it, though she owned a strong healthy child. I then spoke to her husband, who was soon satisfied, and brought his wife to be so too. However, four days later, the Germain's had a change of heart and retracted their consent."

When Oglethorpe banned shooting on Sunday, Charles got the blame, and when Hawkins, the former ship's surgeon turned settlement doctor, was arrested for firing his gun, his wife publicly denounced Charles "with the utmost bitterness and scurrility," no doubt recalling his suspicions of her and her friend on board ship: "[She said] she would blow me up, and my brother . . . [and that] she would be revenged, and expose my damned hypocrisy, my prayers four times a day by beat of drum, and abundance more, which I cannot write, and thought no woman . . . could have spoken."

Charles' reputation among the colonists was damaged further when a Mrs. Lawley lost her baby and the doctor Hawkins was still in prison unable to assist her. Her husband, a sailor, blamed Charles for the child's death and claimed to Oglethorpe that he was a traitor and "stirrer-up of sedition." Charles then had an encounter with Mrs. Hawkins' maid that led to a tense stand-off with Hawkins herself:

---

[13] Green, *John Wesley,* 44.

After prayers, I met Mrs. Hawkins's maid, in a great
passion of tears, at being struck by her mistress. She seemed
resolved to make away with herself, to escape her Egyptian
bondage. With much difficulty I prevailed upon her to return,
and carried her back to her mistress. Upon my asking Mrs.
Hawkins to forgive her, she refused me with the utmost rough-
ness, rage, and almost reviling.

That evening, Charles was on the receiving end of barbed comments from Oglethorpe, reporting that he "heard the first harsh word
from Mr. Oglethorpe, when I asked for something for the poor woman.
The next day I was surprised by a rougher answer, in a matter that
deserved still greater encouragement. I know not how to account for his
increasing coldness." A week later Charles declared, "I was enabled to
pray earnestly for my enemies, particularly for Mr. Oglethorpe, whom
I now looked upon as the chief of them."

But Oglethorpe's coldness was not Charles' only problem. The
"meek and teachable" Mrs. Welch he suddenly "found all storm and
tempest" and "so wilful, so untractable, so fierce" that he "could not
bear to stay with her." Soon after, while Oglethorpe was away hunting
for two days, Beata Hawkins and Anne Welch confided to Charles
that Oglethorpe had seduced them on board the *Simmonds*. Charles
naively believed them and distanced himself from Oglethorpe. The
two women then informed Oglethorpe that Charles was spreading
rumors that he had committed adultery. The women also claimed that
Charles had attempted to rape Welch. A furious Oglethorpe cut off all
communication with Charles and ordered everyone else to ostracize
him. Remarked Charles ruefully:

Knowing that I was to live with Mr. Oglethorpe I had
brought nothing with me from England except my clothes
and books, but this morning, asking a servant for something
I wanted (I think a tea-kettle), I was told Mr. Oglethorpe
had given orders that no one should use any of his things. I
answered that order I supposed did not extend to me. "Yes,
sir", says she, "you was excepted by name."

Even Charles' few remaining friends seemed to be avoiding him. He wrote despondently: "[I was] abused and slighted . . . [and] trampled upon. . . . The people have found out I am in disgrace. . . . My few well-wishers are afraid to speak to me. Some have turned out of the way to avoid me. Others desired I would not take it ill, if they seemed not to know me when we should meet." Even the "servant that used to wash my linen sent it back unwashed." Oglethorpe vindictively provided nowhere for Charles to sleep, except on the floor of a Mr. Read's hut. Charles reported dejectedly, "I was forced to exchange my usual bed, the ground, for a chest, being almost speechless through a violent cold."

Matters went from bad to worse. Charles discovered that there were some surplus wooden boards and tried to obtain a few to make a makeshift bed, but even this request was refused. Then when a man died in Frederica and Charles was given his bed, he was only able to sleep on it for one night before it was removed. Wrote Charles, "Mr. Oglethorpe gave away my bedstead from under me and refused to spare one of the carpenters to mend me up another."

The strain of the situation was wearing Charles down. He confided to his brother Samuel his doubts about whether he had ever been a genuine Christian. Samuel tried to allay his fears: "That you had lived eighteen years without God I either do not understand, or absolutely deny." His strained relations with Oglethorpe and the colonists also contributed to a breakdown in his health. On April 1, 1736, he was stricken by fever and what he described as "bloody flux." He would have died if it were not for the care of a colonist called Davison and his wife. When John discovered from Ingham Charles' plight, he went straight to Frederica. When he arrived he found his brother desperately ill with fever and dysentery lying on the earthen floor of his tent. Charles' physical condition was worsened by his determination not to ask for food from the colonists.

Eventually Oglethorpe confronted Charles about the alleged rumors, and Charles vigorously defended himself: "I told him: 'I absolutely deny the whole charge. I have neither raised nor spread this report, but whenever I heard it, checked it immediately.'" Oglethorpe accepted Charles' explanation concerning the incident and realized they had both been deceived by Hawkins and Welch. Recorded Charles: "When I had finished this relation he seemed entirely changed, full of his old love and confidence in me. He condemned himself for his anger, (God forgive those who made me the object of it!) which he imputed to his want of time for consideration. He ordered me whatever he could think I wanted; [and] promised to have me an house built immediately."

On April 24, 1736, Oglethorpe revealed to Charles melodramatically before embarking on an expedition into Spanish territory: "I am now going to my death. You will see me no more." He then gave Charles a diamond ring to present to the colony's trustees in the event of his death. However, five days later he returned unscathed and Charles returned the ring, commenting, "I need not Sir, and indeed cannot, tell you how joyfully and thankfully I return this." Soon after, Charles informed John, "The trial is at last over, but has left me as a man in whom is no strength."

Meanwhile, Mrs. Hawkins was convinced that Charles had earlier slandered her in a letter he had written in Greek to John that she and Mrs. Welch had somehow had the chance to read. When she confronted John, he did not deny the charge, admitting that it referred to "only two persons, you and Mrs. Welch." Seeking revenge, Hawkins enticed John to her home where she threatened to shoot him with a pistol: "Sir, you have wronged me, and I will shoot you through the head this moment with a brace of balls." Recalled John: "I caught hold of her hand with which she presented the pistol, and at the same time of her hand in which she had a pair of scissors. On which she threw herself upon me and forced me down upon the bed, crying out all the while, 'Villain, dog, let go of my hands', swearing bitterly with many imprecations both of herself and me, that she'd either have my hair or my heart's blood." She then bit his arm and with the scissors hacked off one side of his long hair before being dragged away by her husband.

When a chastened John returned to Savannah, a young colonist, Philip Thicknesse, recorded that "such was his humility, that he appeared the Sunday following at Church, in his partial and ear-crop'd head of hair. Thicknesse was highly amused to observe John preach "with his hair so long on one side, so short on the other [those] fine long Adonis locks of auburn hair—hair which he took infinite pains to have in the most exact order which, with his benign and humble countenance, gave him a very pleasing aspect." Töeltschig wrote in his diary about the incident: "Mr. Wesley told us that a grand lady had wanted to shoot him, but that he had anticipated her by grasping hold of the pistol, and while he held her hands she had bitten large pieces of flesh in her rage. He showed us the places. The reason had been that he told her the truth too plainly."

Charles had not recovered when John departed, and his continued ill health forced him to request that Oglethorpe permit him to return to England. John agreed to return to Frederica with Charles Delamotte and take on Charles' role of secretary to Oglethorpe, which appealed to the governor, for as Stanley Ayling has commented: "What Oglethorpe obviously did recognize in [John] Wesley—and found lacking in his brother Charles—was business efficiency."[14] John left Benjamin Ingham to conduct church services in Savannah and described in his *Journal* the long journey by boat: ". . . near Skidoway Island, where the water, at flood, was twelve or fourteen feet deep. I wrapped myself up from head to foot in a large cloak, to keep off the sand-flies, and lay down on the quarter-deck. Between one and two I waked under water, being so fast asleep that I did not find where I was till my mouth was full of it."

A relieved Charles left Frederica for good in July 1736. "I was over-joyed by my deliverance out of this furnace, and not a little ashamed for being so." He informed Samuel of his homecoming plans. While waiting in Savannah for news of a ship leaving for England, Charles assisted Ingham, including caring for a terminally ill girl:

> I visited a girl of fifteen, who lay a-dying of an incurable illness. She had been in that condition for many months. . . . I started at the sight of a breathing corpse. Never was a real corpse half so ghastly. Her groans and screams alone distinguished her from one. They had no intermission: yet she was perfectly sensible, as appeared by her feebly lifting up her eyes when I bade her trust in God, and read [her] prayers. . . . We were all in tears. She made signs for me to come again.

[14] Stanley Ayling, *John Wesley* (Glasgow, Scotland: William Collins, 1979), 67.

Charles' physical deterioration continued, and he confided in a letter to John:

> All my friends urge me to see a physician, but 'I cannot afford so expensive a funeral.' . . . Though I am apt to think that I shall at length arrive in England to deliver what I am entrusted [documents given to him by Oglethorpe], yet I do not expect, or wish for, a long life. How strong must the principle of self-preservation be, which can make such a wretch as I am willing to live at all! Or rather unwilling to die; for I know greater pleasure in life, than in considering that it cannot last for ever.

Despite his poor health, nothing was going to stop Charles from leaving for England: "I am just no much worse than ever; but nothing less than death shall hinder me from embarking." In the three days that he had to wait for weather good enough to embark, he recorded, "I vomited, purged, bled, sweated, and took laudanum, which entirely drained me of the little strength I had left."

On October 25, 1736, Charles was so weak that friends had to carry him on board the *Hannah*, which was bound for England. The voyage was rough, with Charles reporting that often "the sea streamed in at the sides so plentifully, that it was as much as four men could do by continual pumping, to keep her above water." Riven by fear, he prayed fervently, "I prayed for power to pray, for faith in Jesus Christ, continually repeating his name, till I felt the virtue of it at last, and knew that I abode under the shadow of the Almighty."

Worse was to follow when they left Boston and were hit by a storm that lasted for ten days, forcing the captain to cut down the ship's mizzen mast to stop the ship from sinking. Wrote Charles:

> In this dreadful moment, I bless God, I found the comfort of hope; and such joy in finding I could hope, as the world can neither give nor take away. I had that conviction of the power of God, present with me, overruling my strongest passion, fear, and raising me above what I am by nature, as surpassed all rational evidence, and gave me a taste of the divine goodness. . . . Toward morning the sea heard, and obeyed, the divine voice, "Peace, be still."

Throughout the rest of the voyage, Charles suffered from bouts of dysentery, recording, "I often threw myself upon the bed, seeking rest, but finding none." Finally reaching England on December 2, 1736 and disembarking at Deal the following day, Charles wrote of his joy and relief at making it home: "I knelt down and blessed the Hand that had conducted me through such inextricable mazes; and desired I might give up my country again to God; when He would require it."

Back in Georgia, John made the fatal error of falling in love with one of his parishioners, seventeen-year-old Sophy Hopkey, the attractive and innocent niece of the wife of the chief magistrate of the colony, Thomas Causton. John had informed Burton that one of the benefits of life in Georgia would be the absence of eligible young women, but he soon realized that he was mistaken, writing to Charles only six weeks after he arrived: "I stand in jeopardy every hour. Two or three women are here, young, pretty, God-fearing. Pray for me that I know none of them after the flesh."

Typically, John vacillated about taking the final step of matrimony, even though he had given the strongest hint that he would propose, telling her, "Miss Sophy, I should think myself happy if I was to spend the rest of my life with you." Sophy had been engaged to a rogue called Thomas Mellichamp, but had second thoughts and assured John she was free to marry. Her uncle, Thomas Causton, also made it clear to John that he had free rein, telling him: "I give her to you. Do what you will with her. Take her into your own hands. Promise her what you will. I will make it good." Instead, John informed Sophy that if he were to marry he would not "do it till I have been among the Indians." Twelve days later he called on the Caustons and found Sophy alone. He wrote of her, "Her words, her eyes, her air, her every motion and gesture, were full of such softness and sweetness!" He took her hand and almost proposed, then the following day he recorded that "my resolution failed" and he almost proposed again. Yet still undecided, Wesley resorted to drawing lots with Charles Delamotte, with the latter drawing the card that read "Think of it no more".

Ultimately, Sophy grew weary of waiting and married another colonist, William Williamson. When John discovered that Sophy had

been seeing Williamson for at least two weeks before their sudden
engagement, shocked and angry he contested the marriage on the
grounds that the minister who married them in Purrysburg had not
published the marriage banns. He also prohibited Sophy from Holy
Communion, claiming she had not been honest with him. On July 5,
1737, John wrote a letter to Sophy explaining his case:

> 1) You told me over and over you had entirely conquered
> your inclination for Mr. Mellichamp. Yet at the very time you
> had not conquered it. 2) You told me frequently, you had
> no design to marry Mr. Williamson. Yet at the very time you
> spoke you had the design. 3) In order to conceal both these
> things from me, you went through [a] course of deliberate
> dissimulation. Oh how fallen! How changed! Surely there was
> a time when in Miss Sophy's life there was no guile. Own these
> facts, and own your fault, and you will be in my thoughts as
> if they had never been.

An enraged and humiliated Sophy, who had just miscarried, which
was blamed on Wesley by her aunt, persuaded Williamson to instigate
a lawsuit against John for defamation of character, claiming damages
of £1,000, an immense sum in 1737. A rigged Grand Jury of forty-four
colonists, hand-picked by the chief magistrate Causton, decided that
Wesley was answerable to ten charges, most of which were ecclesiastical
in nature, for which they had no jurisdiction. Denied the chance of a
trial on numerous occasions and fearing he was going to be framed,
John decided to leave Georgia and made his intentions clear by pinning
a notice to the courthouse door that he would depart on December 2.
Williamson countered with a notice of his own concerning his £1,000
claim. When the magistrates issued an order that Wesley should be
prevented from leaving the colony, John decided to make his escape
before it was too late. John wrote of fleeing Georgia in his *Journal*:
"Being now only a prisoner at large . . . I saw clearly that the hour was
come for me to fly for my life, leaving this place; and as soon as evening
prayers were over, about eight o'clock, the tide then serving, I shook
off the dust of my feet, and left Georgia, after having preached the

Gospel there . . . not as I ought, but as I was able, one year and nearly nine months."

With three equally desperate traveling companions, John made his way through forests and swamps, losing his way and almost running out of water before eventually arriving in Charleston ten days later. It is likely that no attempt was made to detain him, with the authorities in Savannah probably relieved to see him go. He boarded the *Samuel* bound for England on December 22, 1737, and never returned to America. A member of the Salzburgher community in Georgia, Grönau wrote in his diary on December 15, 1737, "received news that Mr. Wesley had gone secretly at night to Charlestown by way of Purrysburg, to go from there in all haste to London. I do not know at all what moved him to so quick a resolution, so hurtful both to his office and to God's honour."

It appeared that John's American adventure had been a complete disaster, but Green suggests that the Georgia experience was not entirely wasted: "It may not have taught John Wesley very much about human nature but it made him realize that the life of the Holy Club, austere and self-sacrificing as it undoubtedly was, yet lacked a certain dynamic quality when it came to dealing with a group of hard-bitten worldly men and women."[15] Green has also suggested that "His own [John's] and his brother's lack of experience and their limited knowledge of human nature were a disservice and they were at once made the stalking-horse of intriguers who sought to vilify Oglethorpe."[16] Reflecting on his experiences in Georgia, John remarked that they had taught him "to beware of men."

Both John and Charles failed as missionaries in Georgia, but it could be argued that the foundations of the future Methodist movement were established in the colony. In the spring of 1736, John founded an American version of the Holy Club that met once or twice a week. And both John and Charles experimented with extempore prayer and preaching, small core groups or classes, hymns in worship, and the use of lay preachers.

---

[15] Green, *The Young Mr. Wesley*, 266.

[16] Ibid., 265.

George Whitefield was effusive and probably too generous in his appraisal of John's achievements in Georgia: "What the good Mr. Wesley has done in America is inexpressible. His name is very precious among the people, and he has laid a foundation that I hope neither men nor devils will ever be able to shake." Ironically, John had written to Whitefield in late 1736, imploring him to join him in Georgia: "Only Mr. Delamotte is with me, till God shall stir the hearts of some of His servants, who putting their lives in His hands, shall come over and help us, where the harvest is so great, and the labourers so few. What if Thou art the man, Mr. Whitefield?"

4

STRANGELY WARMED

I went to America to convert the Indians;
but oh! who shall convert me?

—JOHN WESLEY

harles arrived off the coast of England on December 2, 1736, disembarking at Deal the following day and making straight for London. That month he received a letter from George Whitefield informing him that he had applied to become a missionary in Georgia and offered to accompany Charles to the colony. Charles described Whitefield in his journal as "a minister of fervent spirit—if I may say so, a second Timothy. God has wonderfully aroused by his means the twice-dead populace. The churches will not contain his hearers." Whitefield's letter, along with Charles' improved physical and mental health, reignited his dream of returning to America, this time as a bona fide missionary rather than as General Oglethorpe's secretary, a position from which, in any case, he would soon resign. His conviction to return to America was confirmed when he survived an attack by a highwayman while traveling to Westminster and was convinced that this was a sign of God's favor. In late January 1737, however, he visited Mary Pendarves just as she was reading a letter reporting his death. Charles commented despondently: "Happy for me, had the news been true! What a world of misery would it save me."

Charles also visited former Anglican clergyman William Law in Putney on the outskirts of London, whom he described effusively as "our John the Baptist." However, Law was becoming increasingly irrational, depriving himself of sleep as he viewed it as a wasteful sin. Law's only advice to Charles was "Renounce yourself and do not be impatient." But Charles was impatient and, not satisfied with this advice, returned to see Law but was coldly rebuffed, with Law replying to Charles' questions, "Sir, I have told you my opinion." Later, when he came to believe that holiness was only obtainable to someone who had first experienced justification by faith alone, Charles informed Law: "I told him he was my school master to bring me to Christ; but the reason I did not come sooner to Him, was my seeking to be sanctified before I was justified."

Charles, however, was not destined to return to America. Struck down by dysentery and possibly malaria, he was physically incapacitated and had instead to be content with farewelling Whitefield off to Georgia on New Year's Eve 1737. "One consequence of my sickness you will not be sorry for," he wrote to his brother Samuel, "it's stopping my sudden return to Georgia. For the doctor tells me to undertake a voyage now would be certain death."

Meanwhile, on board the *Samuel* on his return to England, John wrestled with doubt, unbelief, and a sense of abject failure, "Continually doubting whether I was right or wrong and never out of perplexities and entanglements." Doubts about his faith and even the truth of the gospel plagued him throughout the voyage: "I went to America to convert the Indians; but oh, who will convert me? Who, what is it that will deliver me from this evil heart of unbelief? I have a fair summer religion. I can talk well; indeed and believe myself, while no danger is near. But let death look me in the face, and my spirit is troubled." Yet even in the midst of his spiritual crisis, he was able to report: "In this dreadful moment, I bless God, I found the comfort of hope; and such joy in finding I could hope, as the world can neither give nor take away. I had that conviction of the power of God present with me, overruling my strongest passion, fear and raising me above what I am by nature, as surpassed all rational evidence and gave a taste of the divine goodness."

On February 1, 1738, John landed at Deal on the south coast of England while it was still dark and in a state of depression and despondency. He discovered that George Whitefield was aboard the *Whitaker* bound for Georgia to join him. Unable to decide whether to wait in Deal to see if Whitefield's ship would be delayed so he could see him or to head to London, he decided to draw lots. In the inn where he was staying he wrote the alternatives on pieces of paper. He drew a lot and it read "Let him return to London." He enclosed it in a note that he left at the inn in case Whitefield returned and then hurried on to the capital. Whitefield, his ship becalmed, did indeed discover to his grief that John had left for London. This incident would have an impact on their relationship in the years to come.

Two days after John arrived back in Britain, Charles heard to his astonishment that his brother had returned. That night he appeared at the Huttons' home where Charles was lodging.

In February 1738, John wrote in his *Journal*, "The faith I want is, 'A sure trust and confidence in God, that, through the merits of Christ, my sins are forgiven and I reconciled to the favour of God.'" The answer came in an unexpected form. On Tuesday, February 7, 1738, John and Charles Wesley met a young German, Peter Böhler, who was on his way to be a missionary to the African slaves in South Carolina, at the home of a Dutch merchant called Weinantz. Born in Frankfurt, the twenty-six-year-old Böhler studied theology at the University of Jena and was a member of the Moravian Brethren, having been ordained by its founder Count Nikolaus von Zinzendorf. In later life, Böhler became a Moravian bishop and spent his final years at the Moravian settlement in Fulneck, Yorkshire, where he died in 1775. John and Charles struck up a warm friendship with Böhler. They conversed in Latin, for Böhler at the time could not speak English. When the Wesleys visited Oxford with Böhler, the undergraduates laughed at his shabby clothes. Unperturbed, Böhler said of the episode to John, "Brother, it does not even stick to our clothes."

Böhler contended that a true faith in Christ resulted in two fruits: "Dominion over sin and constant peace from a sense of forgiveness." John was "quite amazed and looked upon it as a new gospel. If this was so, it was clear I had not faith." John, however, disputed with Böhler "with all my might," arguing that forgiveness and peace must be earned by continual effort. "My brother, my brother, that philosophy of yours must be purged away," retorted Böhler. Not to be deterred, Böhler continued to press John: "Believe and you will be saved. Believe in the Lord Jesus with all your heart and nothing shall be impossible to you! This faith, like the salvation it brings, is the free gift of God. Seek and you will find. . . . Strip yourself naked of your own good works, and your righteousness and go naked to him! For everyone that comes to him he will in no wise cast out."

Böhler wrote to Zinzendorf describing his encounter with the Wesleys: "The elder John is a good-natured man. He knew he did not believe on the Saviour and was willing to be taught. His brother is at present very much distressed in his mind, but does not know how he shall begin to be acquainted with the Saviour."

In late February 1738, Charles became ill with a severe case of pleurisy. He wrote of the episode in his journal:

> At eleven I waken in extreme pain, which I thought would quickly separate my soul and body. Soon after Peter Böhler came to my bedside. I asked him to pray for me. He seemed unwilling at first, but, beginning very faintly, he raised his voice by degrees, and prayed for my recovery with strange confidence. Then he took me by the hand, and calmly said, "You will not die now." I thought within myself, "I cannot hold out in this pain until morning. If it abates before, I believe I may recover." He asked me, "Do you hope to be saved?" "Yes." "For what reason do you hope it?" "Because I have used my best endeavours to serve God." He shook his head, and said no more. I thought him very uncharitable, saying in my heart, "What, are not my endeavours a sufficient ground of hope? Would he rob me of my endeavours? I have nothing else to trust to."

On Sunday, March 5, John suddenly realised that Böhler was right. The plain meaning leaped out of the Greek Testament that they were studying together: "I was clearly convinced of unbelief, of the want of that faith whereby alone we are saved." John also recalled the poverty-stricken porter in his days at Oxford who was continually giving thanks to God, despite having "nothing to wear, nothing to eat and no bed to lie upon." Remarked the porter, "I thank Him that He has given me life and being; and a heart to love Him and a desire to serve Him." Continued John:

> Immediately it struck into my mind, "Leave off preaching. How can you preach to others, who have not faith yourself?" I asked Böhler, whether he thought I should leave it off or not. He answered, "By no means." I asked, "But what can I preach?" He said, "Preach faith till you have it; and then, because you have it, you will preach faith." Accordingly, Monday, 6, I began preaching this new doctrine, though my soul started back from the work.

Thus on March 6, John Wesley visited Oxford prison and preached "salvation by faith alone" to a prisoner called Clifford who had been sentenced to hang. Recalled Wesley: "Peter Böhler had many times desired me to speak to him before. But I could not prevail on myself to do so, being still (as I had been many years) a zealous asserter of the impossibility of a death-bed repentance." John visited Clifford again, accompanied by his friend, Charles Kinchin, the day he was to be hanged. They prayed on their knees with Clifford. When he rose from his knees, Clifford declared, "I am now ready to die. I know Christ has taken away my sins and there is no more condemnation for me." He remained calm and composed as he was taken to the gallows to be hanged. Wesley and Kinchin went with him in the cart to the place of execution. John commented later that "in his last moments he was enjoying a perfect peace, in confidence that he was 'accepted in the Beloved.'"

Böhler went a step further and claimed that faith could come instantaneously, that the worst sinner could receive immediate salvation if they repented of their sins and trusted in Christ alone. John was stunned by this revelation and knew that he had not experienced the instantaneous conversion experience that Böhler spoke of. John remarked, "I could not understand how this faith should be given in a moment: how a man could at once be turned from darkness to light, from sin and misery to righteousness and joy in the Holy Ghost."

When John examined the Book of Acts, he found to "my utter astonishment" that almost all conversions were instantaneous and "scarce any so slow as that of St. Paul who was three days in the pangs of the new birth." When Böhler brought three men who had been instantaneously saved with him the next evening to see John, he vowed to bring eight more if necessary. Wesley had to confess that he could raise no other objection. "I can only cry out, 'Lord, help Thou my unbelief.'" John, with tears in his eyes, asked Böhler again whether he should stop preaching, but Böhler replied: "No. Do not hide in the earth the talent God has given you." Böhler wrote about the incident, "He is a poor sinner, who has a broken heart and who hungers after a better righteousness than that which he has had till now, namely after the righteousness which is in the blood of Jesus Christ."

Two days later, John was with his brother and Charles Delamotte and to them dropped the bombshell about his new belief. Charles recorded: "We sang and fell into a dispute whether conversion was gradual or instantaneous. My brother was very positive for the latter and very shocking; mentioned some late instances of gross sinners believing in a moment. I was much offended at his worse than unedifying discourse. Mrs. Delamotte left us abruptly. I stayed and insisted a man need not know when first he had faith." But John vehemently disagreed. "His obstinacy in favouring the contrary opinion drove me at last out of the room," recalled Charles. John also said of the encounter, "My brother was very angry and told me I did not know what mischief I had done by talking thus."

On May 11, 1738, the English Moravian John Bray visited Charles as he was about to move to the home of John Hutton. Bray persuaded Charles to reside at his own house instead. Charles was still too ill with pleurisy to walk, so he had to be carried to Bray's in a sedan chair. Charles noted in his journal:

> I was going to remove to old Mr. Hutton's when God sent
> Mr. Bray to me, a poor ignorant mechanic who knows nothing
> but Christ; yet knowing him, knows and discerns all things. . . .

Mr. Bray is now to supply Böhler's place. We prayed together
for faith. I was quite overpowered and melted into tears, and
hereby induced to think it was God's will that I should go to his
house, and not Mr. Hutton's. He was of the same judgement.

Charles' pleurisy worsened and for the next nine days he battled
both the disease and spiritual highs and lows. He also received a final
visit from Peter Böhler who was leaving for America: "He stood by my
bedside and prayed over me, that now at least I might see the divine
intention, in this and my late illness. I immediately thought it might be
that I should again consider Böhler's doctrine of faith."

On May 12 he wrote in his journal: "I waked in the same blessed
temper, hungry and thirsty after God. I began Isaiah, and seemed to
see that to me were the promises made, and would be fulfilled, for
that Christ loved me. I found myself more desirous, more assured I
should believe." He spent the entire day praying, reading the Bible, and
talking about his faith, but the following day was struggling again. That
evening, John called on Charles, who found he had to encourage his
brother: "At night my brother came, exceedingly heavy. I forced him (as
he had often forced me) to sing a hymn to Christ, and almost thought
He could come while we were singing: assured He would come quickly."
The next day, he was initially down again when he awoke, feeling "very
heavy, weary and unable to pray; but the desire soon returned, and I
found much comfort both in prayer and in the word, my eyes being
opened more and more to discern and lay hold on the promises. I
longed for Christ, that I might show him to all mankind; that I might
praise and, that I might love him."

The following day a friend gave Charles a copy of Martin Luther's
Commentary of Galatians. Reading Luther's insights into justification by
faith seemed to transform Charles' own faith. "From this time," wrote
Charles, "I endeavoured to ground as many of our friends as come [to
visit] in this fundamental truth, salvation by faith alone, not an idle,
dead faith, but a faith which works by love, and is necessarily productive
of all good works and all holiness." He realized without any doubt that
Christ loved him and died for him. "I laboured, waited and prayed to
feel 'who loved me.' When nature was near exhausted, forced me to

bed, I opened the book upon 'For he will finish the work, and cut it short in righteousness, because a short work will the Lord make upon the earth.' After this comfortable assurance that [Christ] would come, and would not tarry, I slept in peace."

However, Charles' physical condition worsened still further and it affected his spiritual well-being. He wrote on May 19, "I received the sacrament, but not Christ." The next day he was in the same depressed state: "I waked much disappointed, and continued all day in great dejection, which the sacrament did not in the least abate." May 21 was Pentecost Sunday (Whitsunday), and Charles recorded in his journal:

> I was composing myself to sleep, in quietness and peace when I heard one come in (Mrs. Musgrave, I thought by the voice) and say, "In the name of Jesus of Nazareth, arise and believe, and you shall be healed of all your infirmities." I wondered how it should enter into her head to speak in that manner. The words struck me to the heart. I sighed, and said within myself, "Oh that Christ would but speak thus to me!" I lay musing and trembling, then thought, "But what if it should be Him? I will send at least to see." . . . She [Mrs. Turner] went down, and, returning, said, "Mrs. Musgrave has not been here." My heart sunk within me at the word and I hoped it might be Christ indeed. However, I sent her down to inquire and felt in the meantime a strange palpitation of heart. I said, yet feared to say, "I believe, I believe!" She [Mrs. Musgrave] came up again and said, "It was I, a weak, sinful creature, spoke; but the words were Christ's. He commanded me to say them, and so constrained me that I could not forbear."

Despite the encouragement and prayers of John Bray, Charles felt himself embroiled in a spiritual conflict:

> I sent for Mr. Bray, and asked him whether I believed. He answered. I ought not to doubt of it. It was Christ that spoke to me. He knew it and willed us to pray together. . . . Still I felt violent opposition and reluctance to believe; yet still the Spirit of God strove with my own, and the evil spirit, till by degrees he chased away the darkness of my unbelief. I found myself convinced, I know not how nor when; and immediately fell to intercession. . . . I now found myself at peace with God and

rejoiced in hope of loving Christ. My temper, for the rest of the day, was mistrust of my own great, but before unknown, weakness . . . yet confident of Christ's protection.

On Monday he awoke and declared, "Today, I saw him in his power; but saw little of the love of Christ crucified, or of my sins past: though more, I humbly hope, of my own weakness and his strength." Late that day, John visited him, with Charles writing in his journal: "My brother coming, we joined in intercession for him. In the midst of prayer, I almost believed the Holy Ghost was coming upon him. In the evening we sang and prayed again. I found myself very weak in body, but thought I ought to pray for my friends, being the only priest among them. I kneeled down and was immediately strengthened, both mind and body." Charles described his new-found faith as making him feel as though he was "in a new heaven and a new earth." He revealed that he now felt "under the protection of Christ" because he had given himself "soul and body to Him." Yet when he took communion with some of his friends on May 24, he was deeply disturbed how his old "accustomed deadness" of heart had returned; he received the bread and the wine "without any sensible devotion, much as I use to be."

That same evening, John grudgingly agreed to accompany James Hutton to a Moravian meeting in the City of London. Hutton and Wesley reached Aldersgate Street, a few feet from Charterhouse, and turned into Nettleton Court. As John listened to a reading of Martin Luther's view on justification by faith, there followed one of the most famous conversion experiences in history:

> In the evening I went very unwillingly to a society in Aldersgate Street, where one was reading Luther's preface to the Epistle to the Romans. About a quarter before nine, while he was describing the change which God works in the heart through faith in Christ, I felt my heart strangely warmed. I felt I did trust in Christ, Christ alone for salvation; and an assurance was given to me that he had taken away my sins, even mine, and saved me from the law of sin and death.

The historian William Lecky commented of the incident that "It is scarcely an exaggeration to say that the scene which took place at the humble meeting in Aldersgate Street forms an epoch in English history." Charles recorded in his journal what happened that night:

> At eight I prayed by myself for love; with some feeling, and assurance of feeling more. Towards ten, my brother was brought in triumph by a troop of our friends and declared, "I believe." We sang the hymn with great joy and parted with prayer. At midnight I gave myself up to Christ, assured I was safe, sleeping or waking. Had continual experience of His power to overrule all temptation; and confessed, with joy and surprise, that He was able to exceeding abundantly for me, above what I can ask or think.

For John, though, the battle was just beginning:

> After my return home, I was much buffeted with temptations; but cried out and they fled away. They returned again and again. I as often lifted up my eyes, and he, "sent me help from his holy place." And herein I found the difference between this and my former state chiefly consisted. I was striving, yes, fighting with all my might under the law as well as under grace. But then I was sometimes, if often conquered; now, I was always the conqueror.

The following day, John recorded in his *Journal*, "The moment I awaked, 'Jesus, Master,' was in my heart and in my mouth, and I found all my strength lay in keeping my eye fixed upon him."

Not everyone was impressed by John's and Charles' conversion experiences. They faced opposition from those who questioned the events of that Pentecost Sunday and the influence they had on others. On June 6, 1738, the mother of John Hutton wrote to Samuel Wesley, "Your brother John seems to have turned a wild enthusiast, or fanatic, and, to our great affliction, is drawing our two children into those wild notions, by their great opinion of Mr. John's sanctity and judgement."

Once their initial elation had worn off, both John and Charles struggled with fears and doubts about their new-found faith. In his journal, Charles refers to three days in June 1738 as being "utterly dead" spiritually and "exceedingly heavy and adverse to prayer." He wrote, "I could not help asking myself, 'Where is the difference between what I am now and what I was before believing.'"

On New Year's Eve 1738, John recorded how he and Charles celebrated the Eucharist with around sixty Moravians: "About three in the morning, as we were continuing instant in prayer, the power of God came mightily upon us, insomuch that many cried out for exceeding joy, and many fell to the ground. As soon as we had recovered a little from that awe and amazement at the presence of his majesty, we broke out with one voice, 'We praise you, O God, we acknowledge you to be Lord!'"

Their brother Samuel was vehemently opposed to their new-found faith, informing them that he disliked "canting fellows . . . who talk of indwellings, experiences, getting into Christ, etc, etc," and that preaching extempore was "a natural inlet to all false doctrine, heresy and schism." He attributed John's behavior to "perpetual intenseness of thought [and] lack of sleep," concluding that "I heartily pray God to stop this lunacy."

John also expressed his disappointment over how little his life appeared to have changed. He was frustrated by the fact that, like Charles, he still had "no settled, lasting joy." In January 1739, John wrote to his brother Samuel, asserting: "My friends affirm that I am mad because I said I was not a Christian a year ago. I affirm I am not a Christian now. . . . I have . . . [not got] a peace which passeth understanding. . . . I have not the fruits of the Spirit of Christ."

Yet both John and Charles knew they would never be the same after their personal Pentecost, regardless of being plagued with doubts and, in Charles' case, ill health. They now believed that they could not earn their salvation. This released them from the fear of condemnation that paralyzed their former Christian ministry. From then on they began to preach full salvation more spontaneously, and Charles produced a flood of biblically based hymns.

Charles commented on the "continual experience" of God's power "to overrule all temptation," in particular the desire for alcohol. "[I was] amazed to find my old enemy, intemperance, so suddenly subdued, that I almost forgot I was ever in bondage to him." However, he also had to acknowledge that "I never knew the energy of sin till now that I experience the superior strength of Christ."

Despite his struggles with sin, Charles' new-found faith was accompanied by "a tidal wave of spiritual energy and action." This resulted in constant Bible reading and speaking to everyone he could about God's saving grace, including to Henry Piers, Vicar of Bexley, his wife and their maid, and Charles Delamotte and his family. Even Delamotte's gardener informed Charles, "Was I to die just now, I know I should be accepted through Jesus Christ," when he overheard Charles reading aloud one of John's sermons on faith. Charles even spoke of his faith while traveling by coach to a speaking engagement:

> I preached faith in Christ. A lady [in the coach] was deeply offended; avowed her own merits in plain terms; asked if I was not a Methodist; threatened to beat me. I declared I deserved nothing but hell; so did she; and must confess it, before she could have a title to heaven. This was most intolerable to her. The others [in the coach] were less offended; began to listen; asked where I preached; a maid servant devoured every word.

One consequence of the Wesleys' new-found faith was that they began to draw away from the practices of mystics like William Law. Writing in the preface of *Hymns and Sacred Poems*, which they published jointly in 1739, they made it clear that they now believed in justification by faith alone. "The sole cause of our acceptance with God . . . is the righteousness and death of Christ, who fulfilled God's law and died in our stead." John accused Law, whose writings had once made such a deep impression on him, of failing to direct him towards "a living faith in the blood of Christ." An exasperated Law replied: "Who made me your teacher or can make me answerable for any defects in your knowledge? You sought my acquaintance. You came to me as you pleased, and on what occasion you pleased, and to say to me what you pleased. . . . Pray, sir, be at peace with me."

Remarkably, despite the exponential growth of the Methodist movement and decades of successful ministry, John wrote to Charles nearly thirty years after his conversion in a state of despondency and doubt:

> In one of my last [letters] I was saying I do not feel the wrath of God abiding on me; nor can I believe it does. And yet (this is the mystery) I do not love God. I never did. Therefore I never believed in the Christian sense of the word. Therefore I am only an honest heathen, a proselyte of the Temple. . . . I have no direct witness, I do not say that I am a child of God but of anything invisible or eternal. And yet I dare not preach otherwise that I do, either concerning faith, or love, or justification, or perfection.

Even as late as the 1770s, John wrote to Charles, consumed, it appears, by depression and doubt in which he again questioned the whole worth of his ministry: "I often cry out, 'Give me back my former life!' Let me again be an Oxford Methodist! I am often in doubt whether it would not be best for me to resume all my Oxford rules, great and small. I did then walk closely with God and redeem the time. But what have I been doing these thirty years?"

Yet, despite his moments of doubt and depression, John Wesley never stopped preaching the gospel. He built a religious movement that would influence the very fabric of British society.

5

ALL THE WORLD
IS MY PARISH

A horrid thing, a very horrid thing!

—BISHOP JOSEPH BUTLER

n the early years of the Wesleys' ministry, the most vociferous opposition came from the Church of England clergy who perceived
the Methodists as disruptive enthusiasts (an eighteenth-century
euphemism for fanatics) who unsettled their parishioners. These
clergy also viewed Methodist meetings as conventicles[17] that were
illegal. Some critics claimed that John and Charles were antinomians,[18]

---

[17] The Conventicle Acts of 1662, 1664, and 1670 prohibited the reading of prayers
at "conventicles"—assemblies of worship in places other than Anglican churches
—and punished those who did with imprisonment and fines. The laws aimed
to force people to attend Church of England services and impose "uniformity"
in religion. The Toleration Act of 1689 allowed for non-Anglican worship by
Protestants (Roman Catholics were excluded) who had registered with the government as Dissenters. Dissenters also had to make certain oaths of allegiance
and were still excluded from political office and universities.

[18] Antinomianism (from the Greek meaning "lawless or "against the law") was a
term that emerged during the Protestant Reformation and refers to those who
believe that there is no fixed meaning and application of moral law and that
salvation is attained solely through faith and divine grace.

while others were convinced that Methodism was a veil for Jacobitism[19] or Roman Catholicism or represented the division and turmoil of a Puritan revival. According to Green, the parochial clergy "had the experience, never an enviable one, of seeing a fellow-minister invade their parish, attract large congregations and establish a religious society outside their control."[20] As one historian has commented, "Vicars, deans, curates, rectors, chaplains, and bishops issued forth with sermons, pastorals, and tractates abusing the Methodists and warning the people against them."

George Whitefield also angered the clergy by criticizing two well-known and revered devotional works: *The Whole Duty of Man*, which was published anonymously in 1658, and *Sermons*, by John Tillotson (1630–94), a former Archbishop of Canterbury, which Whitefield attacked as emphasizing the moral aspects of Christianity above faith. He infuriated the clerical establishment further by possibly commenting that Tillotson "knew no more of Christ than did Mahomet."

The verbal denunciations began as early as 1738 when the literary critic and churchman William Warburton (1698–1779), who would become the Bishop of Gloucester in 1759, wrote to a friend, sneering, "What do you think of our new set of fanatics, called the Methodists?" When he became Bishop of Gloucester, Warburton attacked the Methodists, maintaining that the work and outpouring of the Holy

---

[19] Jacobitism (from the Latin for James, Jacobus) was a political movement in Britain and Ireland that aimed to restore the Roman Catholic Stuart King James II after he was deposed during the Glorious Revolution of 1688–9 and replaced by his Protestant daughter Mary II and her husband William of Orange, who became William III. James II (James VII in Scotland) died in 1701 and was succeeded by his son, James Francis Edward Stuart, who would have become James III (James VIII in Scotland) but was universally known as the Old Pretender. James led a rebellion in Scotland in 1715 against the Hanoverian government of King George I, but it failed. In 1745, his son Charles Edward Stuart, the Young Pretender, popularly known as Bonnie Prince Charlie, led another Jacobite uprising in Scotland, defeating the Hanoverians at the Battle of Prestopans and then invading England. Charles and his army got as far as Derbyshire, but decided to return to Scotland when little support was forthcoming from English Jacobites. Charles won another victory against government forces at the Battle of Falkirk before being decisively defeated at the Battle of Culloden on April 16, 1745, which effectively ended the rebellion.

[20] Green, *John Wesley*, 84.

Spirit were limited to the time of Jesus and the apostles and had ceased at the end of the apostolic age. He also singled out John Wesley, attacking him for his "abuses of fanaticism." In 1762, Warburton published his *Doctrine of Grace,* in which he denounced Methodism. Curiously, Warburton allowed Wesley to read the manuscript before it was printed to correct any possible errors. Regarding the manuscript, John commented sardonically: "After correcting the false readings, improper glosses and other errors, I returned it. I was a little surprised to find Bishop Warburton so entirely unacquainted with the New Testament."

When Charles preached in the open air for the first time on November 7, 1738 to those watching executions at Tyburn in London, he shocked the Anglican clergy. They could not accept the fact that he was preaching outside of a church. Charles later remarked, "I was melted down under the word I spake." One of those who was stunned was Henry Piers, Vicar of Bexley in Kent, who refused to continue attending the Fetter Lane Society "through fear of the world's threatenings" and informed Charles that he could no longer preach at his church. An indignant Charles retorted: "Mr. Piers refused me his pulpit through fear of man; pretending tenderness to his flock. I plainly told him, if he rejected my testimony, I would come to see him no more. I walked back to town in the strength of the Lord."

The *Scots Magazine* vehemently denounced the Wesleys and Whitefield in an editorial published in 1739:

> Whitefield and the two Wesleys offend against the rules of the Christian church by preaching in opposition to the opinions and instructions of the bishops. The Wesleys are more guilty than Whitefield because they are men of more learning and judgement and cooler heads. Let them go over to their proper companies, their favourites, the Dissenters, and utter their extemporary effusions in a conventicle; but not be suffered in our churches hypocritically to use our forms, which they despise.

In February of that year, the editor of *The Weekly Miscellany* condemned Methodism as a new brand of Puritanism:

> At first we only looked upon the Methodists as well-meaning, zealous people . . . [who] would be righteous overmuch; and there were hopes that, when this devotional effervescence had boiled over, they would return to the proper medium where true piety and Christian prudence fix the centre. But instead . . . [they encourage] extempore effusions both in their prayers and expoundings . . . [and] pretend to a sort of sinless perfection and boast of inward joys above other Christians.

One London preacher published a vitriolic sermon claiming that the Methodists were guilty of having "spiritual pride, enthusiasm, false doctrine, heresy, uncharitableness . . . crude, indigested notions of dismal consequences." John Wesley replied, "O Sir, how could you possibly be induced to pass such a sentence, even in your heart, till you had done us the common heathen justice of hearing us answer ourselves?" The Reverend Ralph Skerret, chaplain to the Earl of Grantham, described the Methodists as "restless deceivers of the people, who make it their daily business to fill the heads of the ignorant and unwary with wild, perplexive [sic] notions." While the Reverend John Wilder branded the Methodists as "deceivers, babblers, insolent pretenders, men of capricious humours, spiritual sleight and canting craftiness," and "novices in divinity casting indecent, false and unchristian reflections on the clergy." Another cleric, a Dr. Trapp, claimed that "To pray, preach, and sing psalms in the streets and fields is worse, if possible, than intruding into pulpits by downright violence and breach of peace," and suggested that people should "shun them [the Methodists] like the plague."

"Who are these 'lay lubbers'?" enquired a leading Anglican official rhetorically. "They are Wesley's ragged legion of preaching tinkers, scavengers, draymen and chimney sweepers. No man would do this unless he were as unprincipled as a rock." To this charge John Wesley replied, "O sir, what an idle thing it is for you to dispute about lay preachers. Is not a lay preacher preferable to a drunken preacher; to a cursing, drunken preacher?"

In 1739, John Wesley wrote of the persecution that the Methodists faced for preaching the gospel:

Being convinced of that important truth, which is the foundation of all real religion, that, "by grace we are saved through faith," we immediately began declaring it to others. Indeed, we could hardly speak of anything else, either in public or private. It shone upon our minds with so strong a light, that it was our constant theme. It was our daily subject, both in verse and prose; and we vehemently defended it against all mankind. But, in doing this, we were assaulted and abused on every side. We were everywhere represented as mad dogs, and treated accordingly. We were stoned in the streets and several times narrowly escaped with our lives. In sermons, newspapers and pamphlets of all kinds, we were painted as unheard of monsters. But this moved us not; we went on testifying salvation by faith both to small and great and not counting our lives dear unto ourselves, so we might finish our course with joy.

Dr. Henry Stebbing, a royal chaplain and renowned writer, published a pamphlet in 1739 entitled *A Caution Against Religious Delusion: A Sermon on the New Birth Occasioned By the Pretensions of the Methodists*, in which he attacked the Methodists for disturbing the peace of the Church and "stealing sheep" from Anglican parishes. In reply, Wesley wrote to Stebbing defending his methods:

I do, indeed, go out into the highways and hedges to call poor sinners to Christ. But not "in a tumultuous manner," not "to the disturbance of the public peace" or the "prejudice of families." Neither herein do I break any law which I know, much less "set at naught all rule and authority." Nor can I be said to "intrude into the labours" of those who do not labour at all, but suffer thousands of those for whom Christ died to "perish for lack of knowledge."

He then uttered one of the most famous phrases in history, and one which was to be later inscribed on his memorial in Westminster Abbey: "I look upon all the world as my parish." And then he proceeded to explain what he meant by the remark: "I judge it meet, right and my bounded duty to declare, unto all that are willing to hear, the glad tidings of salvation. This is the work which I know God has called me [and he has withdrawn me] from all things else that I might singly attend on this very thing, 'and go about doing good.'"

George Whitefield also made the same statement while on his second voyage to America in 1739, declaring: "The whole world is now my parish. Wheresoever my Master calls me I am ready to go and preach the everlasting Gospel." He urged the Wesleys not to be discouraged and to regard such persecution as "the buffetings of a ridiculing world." He wrote:

> Let them examine their own lives before they condemn others for enthusiasts. It is manifest that . . . [some ministers] make no scruple of frequenting taverns and public houses. They make no conscience of playing several hours of billiards, bowls, and other . . . games, which they esteem as innocent diversions. . . . They don't catechise. They don't visit from house to house. They don't watch over their flocks by examining their lives. They keep up no constant religious conversation in families under their care.

John and Charles' brother Samuel, who died in 1739, opposed their conversion and ministry and railed against anyone preaching extempore, believing it to be "a natural inlet to all false doctrine, heresy and schism." He was convinced Charles was being misled by John, whose behavior he attributed to "perpetual intenseness of thought [and] lack of sleep," concluding, "I heartily pray God to stop this lunacy." Brother Samuel was also appalled at John and Charles' field ministry, and in 1739, shortly before he died, he appealed to their mother to intervene:

> They design separation [from the Church of England]. . . . They are already forbid all the pulpits in London, and to preach in that diocese is actual schism. . . . As I told Jack, I am not afraid the church should excommunicate him—discipline is at too low an ebb—but that he should excommunicate the church. It is pretty near it. . . . Love feasts are introduced and extemporary prayers and exhortations of Scripture, which last are enough to bring all into confusion.

But John vigorously defended their field preaching:

How is it that you can't praise God for saving so many souls from death, and covering such a multitude of sins, unless he will begin this work within "consecrated walls"? Why should he not fill heaven and earth? You cannot, indeed you cannot, confine the Most High within temples made with hands. I do not despise them, any more than you. But I rejoice to find that God is everywhere.

I love the rites and ceremonies of the Church. But I see, well-pleased that our great Lord can work without them. And howsoever and whatsoever a sinner is converted from the error of his way, indeed, and by whomever, I therein rejoice, yes and will you rejoice!

On August 16, 1739, John Wesley was summoned to give an account of his ministry by the Bishop of Bristol, Joseph Butler, who was celebrated for his recent book *The Analogy of Religion*. They immediately began arguing over the doctrine of justification by faith, with Butler claiming Wesley made God seem like a tyrant, for if some were justified without previous good works, then why were not all?

"Because, my lord," replied Wesley, "they resist his Spirit, because they 'will not come to him that they may have life;' because they suffer him not 'to work in them both to will and to do.' They cannot be saved because they will not believe."

"Sir, what do you mean by faith?" enquired Butler.

"My lord, by justifying faith I mean conviction wrought in a man by the Holy Ghost that Christ has loved him, and given himself for him and that through Christ his sins are forgiven."

Unconvinced, the bishop remarked that "some good men have this, but not all," and queried how John could prove this to be "the justifying faith taught by the Church." After continued debate of the matter, Butler uttered the statement for which he would become known: "Mr. Wesley, I will deal plainly with you. I once thought Mr. Whitefield and you well-meaning young men. But I can't think so now. For I have heard more of you—matters of fact, sir. And Mr. Whitefield says in his *Journal*, 'There promises still to be fulfilled in me.' Sir, the pretending to extraordinary revelations and gifts of the Holy Ghost is a horrid thing, a very horrid thing."

Retorted Wesley, "I pretend to no extraordinary revelations and gifts of the Holy Ghost—none but what every Christian may receive and ought to expect and pray for."

When John asked to know what "the matters of fact" were, Butler accused him of administering the sacrament in the societies, which Wesley denied. But Butler continued, "I hear, too, many people fall into fits in your societies and that you pray over them."

"I do so, my lord. When any show by strong cries and tears that their soul is in deep anguish, I frequently pray to God to deliver them from it. And our prayer is often answered in that hour."

"Very extraordinary indeed! Well, sir, since you ask my advice, I will give it to you freely. You have no business here. You are not commissioned to preach in this diocese. Therefore I advise you to go hence," said Butler.

"My lord, my business on earth is to do what good I can. Wherever therefore I think I can do most good, there must I stay as long as I think so. At present I can do most good here. Therefore here I stay." John reminded Butler that as an ordained Fellow of Lincoln College, Oxford, he was permitted to preach "to any part of the Church of England." The bishop did not dispute this fact and ended the interview with Wesley.

A second meeting followed in which the bishop did not prohibit Wesley from preaching, but John's preaching did not change Butler's theological position.

Edmund Gibson, Bishop of London, had ordained Charles as a priest in 1735, and initially he was well disposed towards both brothers when they had their first meeting in October 1738. Their relationship remained cordial for the next few years. In 1740, John even claimed that Gibson encouraged him to write and publish his sermon "Plain Account of Christian Perfection."

> I think it was in the latter end of the year 1740, that I had a conversation with Dr. Gibson, then Bishop of London, at Whitehall. He asked me what I meant by perfection. I told him without any disguise or reserve. When I ceased speaking, he said, "Mr. Wesley, if this be all you mean, publish it to all the world. If any one then can confute what you say, lie may

have free leave." I answered, "My Lord, I will;" and accordingly wrote and published the sermon on Christian perfection.

However, the storm clouds were gathering as early as the summer of 1739 when George Whitefield wrote to John, saying, "I hear we shall be excommunicated soon." Bishop Gibson said of Whitefield that he was "a pious, well meaning youth but was tainted with enthusiasm."

Charles then antagonized Bishop Gibson by baptizing adults of the religious societies without seeking official approval from the Church of England. Gibson, whom the Prime Minister, Sir Robert Walpole, described as a "pope" because of the ecclesiastical power that he wielded, was dismayed when he discovered what Charles had done, as he believed baptism was the responsibility of the parish minister. He bluntly told Charles that he was not a licensed curate and that "no man can exercise parochial duty in London without my leave." Gibson claimed that the Methodists and Moravians gave "shameful disturbance to the parochial clergy and use very unwarrantable methods to prejudice people against them and to seduce their flocks from them." Gibson added that they were guilty of "annoying the established ministry and drawing over to themselves the lowest and most ignorant of the people, by pretences to greater sanctity and more orthodox preaching." When Wesley was informed by the Church that ecclesiastical law forbade field preaching, he aptly retorted that the laws of the church also forbade the card playing which was so commonly practiced by the Anglican clergy.

In 1743, John published his *Earnest Appeal to Men of Reason and Religion*, in which he argued that the Methodists were supporting the Church of England rather than seeking to undermine it. He contended that the Methodists preached the true word of God and took the sacrament at their meeting houses. Wesley followed a year later with *A Further Appeal to Reason and Religion* in which he claimed that Methodism was not heretical and that they had not provoked the clergy: "We have not willingly provoked them at any time; neither any single clergyman."

The criticisms, however, were unabated. The same year, in 1744, *Observations upon the Conduct and Behaviour of a Certain Sect* was published anonymously. It was suspected that the author was Bishop Gibson. In this publication, it was claimed that Methodist societies were illegal

since they were neither registered as Dissenters nor were truly part of
the Church of England. By 1747, the Wesleys and Whitefield no longer
had access to Gibson. He now saw them as a threat to the existence
of the Church—a threat that had to be resisted at all cost. In his last
letter to the clergy in London, Gibson declared, "Reverend Brothers, I
charge you all to lift up your voice like a trumpet! And warn and arm
and fortify all mankind against the people called Methodists."

In a letter dated June 11, 1747, John, without any vitriol, defended
Methodism and appealed to Gibson on the grounds that both shared
a mission to preach the gospel of Jesus Christ:

> Could your Lordship discern no other enemies of the
> gospel of Christ? Are there no other heretics or schismatics on
> earth? . . . Have the Methodists (so called) already monopo-
> lized all the sins, as well as errors in the nation? Is Methodism
> the only sin? . . .
>
> By the fruits shall you know those of whom I speak . . . the
> habitual drunkard that was, is now temperate in all things;
> the whoremonger now flees fornication; he that stole, steals
> no more, but works with his hands; he that cursed or swore,
> perhaps at every sentence, has now learned to serve the Lord
> with fear and rejoice unto him with reverence; those formerly
> enslaved to various habits of sin are now brought to uniform
> habits of holiness. These are demonstrable facts; I can name
> the men with their places of abode.
>
> My Lord, the time is short. I am past the noon of my life
> and my remaining years flee away as a shadow. Your Lordship
> is old and full of days, having past the usual age of man. It
> cannot, therefore, be long before we shall drop this house
> of earth and stand naked before God: No, nor before we see
> the great white throne coming down from heaven and Him
> that sits thereon.

This defense and plea may have had an affect on Gibson. He stopped
his diatribes against the Methodists. The following year, he died.

The new Bishop of Exeter, George Lavington, was not initially
opposed to the Wesleys' ministry in Devon and Cornwall, but then in
1748 a forgery of the bishop's handwriting was circulated and printed,
suggesting that he was not only actively sympathetic to their cause

but preaching Methodist doctrine. Enraged, Lavington accused John Wesley and Whitefield of being behind the forgery, although he produced no evidence. Lavington continued his diatribe against Wesley, publishing two anonymous pamphlets on *The Enthusiasm of Methodists and Papists Compared* in which he denounced John's teachings and practices. In another attack on Wesley, Lavington publicized a report from the chancellor of his diocese and the archdeacon of Barnstable alleging John made indecent advances to the maid of a Mrs. Morgan in Cornwall, an allegation he easily refuted. Lavington also sneeringly commented, "The Methodist must set out on Foot, with a sanctified Countenance and high Pretences to Piety, which is to consist of unscriptural Perculiarities, whimsical Strictnesses and bitter Zeal against innocent and indifferent Things."

John hit back at Lavington's accusations in his Second Letter (1751), in which he concluded: "You regard neither mercy, justice, nor truth. To vilify, to blacken, is your one point. I pray God it may not be laid to your charge. May he show mercy, though you show none!" Yet as an example of John's magnanimity, eleven years later, only a couple of weeks before Lavington's death, he wrote: "I was well pleased to partake of the Lord's Supper [in Exeter Cathedral] with my old opponent, Bishop Lavington. O may we sit down together in the Kingdom of our Father!"

The attacks on the Wesleys and Methodism continued well into the 1760s, with the *London Magazine* condemning John as "an enemy to religion and a deceiver of the people; an enthusiast, a very great enthusiast with no more knowledge of and esteem for the Holy Scriptures than a Mahommedan. . . . Methodism was a spurious mixture of enthusiasm and blasphemy, popery and quakerism." Another writer scathingly described the Methodists as "a race of men, which seemed to bear a near resemblance to the new species of rats."

As late as June 1790, John was still trying to convince the Church of England establishment that the Methodists were not seeking separation, writing to the Bishop of Lincoln pleading with him not to force Methodists out of the Church:

Methodists in general, my Lord, are members of the Church of England. They hold her doctrines, attend her services, and partake of her sacraments. . . . O my Lord, for God's sake, for Christ's sake, for pity's sake suffer the poor people to enjoy their religious as well as civil liberty. I am on the brink of eternity! Perhaps so is your Lordship too! How soon may you also be called to give an account of your stewardship to the Great Shepherd and Bishop of our souls! May He enable both you and me to do it with joy!

The Church of England clergy were by no means the only opponents of the Wesleys. When John Wesley arrived at Bath at one thirty on the afternoon of June 5, 1739, many begged him not to preach "because no one knew what would happen." He arrived at the meadow to find that "I had gained a larger audience than usual, including many of the rich and great" sitting in their chariots or on comfortable chairs.

Richard "Beau" Nash was determined to confront Wesley and stop him from preaching in the city of Bath. Then nearly sixty-five, Nash was an adventurer and philanderer who lived primarily by gaming. For thirty-four years he had been the unofficial Master of Ceremonies at Bath, wielding considerable influence and making the spa town famous for entertainment, as well as a favorite of royalty and the aristocracy. He was, however, a notorious scoffer at religion. Nash always drove in a chariot drawn by six grey horses with footmen on the box who announced his arrival by blowing on French horns. His arrival at the back of the crowd was thus an interruption, and the people made way when he walked ponderously, in his lace-covered coat and enormous cream-colored beaver hat, toward John Wesley as he preached in his cassock, gown, and bands. Wesley paused. Nash demanded by what authority he was doing these things.

"By the authority," replied Wesley, "of Jesus Christ, conveyed to me by the Archbishop of Canterbury when he laid hands upon me, and said. 'Take your authority to preach the gospel.'"

"This is contrary to Act of Parliament," retorted Nash. "This is a conventicle."

"Sir," contended Wesley, "the conventicles mentioned in that Act are seditious meetings; but here is no shadow of sedition; therefore it is not contrary to that Act."

"I say it is; and beside, your preaching frightens people out of their wits!" replied Nash.

"Sir, did you ever hear me preach?" retorted Wesley.

"No."

"How, then, can you judge of what you never heard?"

"Sir, by common report."

"Common report is not enough. Give me leave, sir, to ask, is your name Nash?"

"My name is Nash."

"Sir," replied Wesley with wit, "I dare not judge you by common report: I think it not enough to judge by."

There was silence, and then Nash replied, "I desire to know what this people comes here for."

Before Wesley could reply, an old woman in the crowd spoke up: "Sir, leave him to me: let an old woman answer him. You, Mr. Nash, take care of your body; we take care of our souls; and for the food of our souls we come here."

Nash turned and walked away without uttering another word.

After Nash's departure, Wesley told what happened: "We immediately began praying for him, and then for all the despisers. As we returned, they hollowed and hissed us along the streets; but when any of them asked, 'Which is he' and I answered, 'I am he,' they were immediately silent."

6

WHITEFIELD AND
THE WESLEYS

*[He] had a heart susceptible to the most generous
and the most tender friendship.*

—JOHN WESLEY
SPEAKING OF GEORGE WHITEFIELD

n September 1733, Charles Wesley befriended Oxford undergraduate George Whitefield, who was to become one of the Holy Club's most prominent members. Whitefield was one of seven children born to the proprietor of The Bell Inn in Gloucester. Whitefield's father died when he was two, leaving his mother to run the family business until she remarried. Whitefield later admitted to stealing money from his mother and gambling and that his childhood was consumed by "lying, filthy talking, and foolish jesting. . . . Some of the things I did at the grammar school had a natural tendency to debauch the mind, to raise ill passions and to stuff the memory with things contrary to the Gospel of Jesus Christ as light to darkness, Heaven to Hell."

Whitefield's stepfather ruined the inn and then deserted the family, curtailing Whitefield's hopes of a university education, until he discovered that he could have his fees paid if he was willing to serve wealthier students. Thus in November 1732, just before his eighteenth birthday, Whitefield was granted a place at Pembroke College, Oxford. As a servitor, he was not permitted to associate with the other students, but he became a secret admirer of the Oxford Methodists: "For about twelve months my soul longed to be acquainted with some of them, and I was strongly pressed to follow their good example, when I saw them go through a ridiculing crowd to receive the Holy Eucharist at St. Mary's." He finally plucked up the courage to contact Charles Wesley, and this was the start of a remarkable and enduring friendship:

> He sent an invitation to me . . . to come to breakfast with him the next morning. I thankfully embraced the opportunity; and blessed be God! It was one of the most profitable visits I ever made in my life. My soul at that time, was athirst for some spiritual friends to lift up my hands when they hung down, and to strengthen my feeble knees. He soon discovered it, and, like a wise winner of souls, made all his discourses tend that way.

Charles said of Whitefield when they first met, "I saw, I loved and clasped him to my heart." Charles lent him books, including Henry Scougal's *The Life of God in the Soul of Man*, introduced him to John and his circle of friends, and became Whitefield's spiritual mentor. Commented Whitefield:

> [He] instructed me as I was able to bear it. By degrees he introduced me to the rest of his Christian brethren. They built me up daily in the knowledge and fear of God, and taught me to endure hardness as a good soldier of Jesus Christ. I now began, like them, to live by rule. . . . Never did persons strive more earnestly to enter in at the strait [sic] gate. . . . They were dead to the world, and willing to be accounted as the dung and offscouring of all things, so that they might win Christ. Their hearts glowed with the love of God.

Whitefield was also deeply affected by Scougal's book, recalling:

> . . . though I had fasted, watched and prayed, and received the sacrament so long, yet I never knew what true religion was, till God sent me that excellent treatise by the hands of my never-to-be-forgotten friend. . . . God showed me that I must be born again, or be damned! I learned that a man may go to church, say prayers, receive the sacrament, and yet not be a Christian. . . . Shall I burn this book? Shall I throw it down?

or shall I search it? I did search it, and holding the book in my hand I thus addressed the God of heaven and earth: "Lord, if I am not a Christian, or if not a real one, for Jesus Christ's sake show me what Christianity is, that I may not be damned at last!" God showed me, for in reading a few lines further, that "true Christianity is a union of the soul with God, and Christ formed within us," a ray of divine light was instantaneously darted into my soul, and from that moment, and not till then, did I know I must become a new creature.

Whitefield compared himself to Nicodemus, who through fear of ridicule, came to see Jesus at night. In time, though, Whitefield became more confident and courageous: "I confessed the Methodists more and more publicly every day. I walked openly with them, and chose rather to bear contempt with those people of God than to enjoy the applause of almost-Christians for a season." However, he paid a heavy price for his association with the Methodists, with many fellow students turning against him:

> I daily underwent some contempt at college. Some have thrown dirt at me; others by degree took away their pay from me; and two friends that were dear to me . . . forsook me. . . . My honourable friend, Mr. Charles Wesley . . . came to my room, soon found out my case, apprised me of my danger, if I would not take advice; and recommended me to his brother John, as more experienced in the spiritual life. . . . John advised me to resume all my external [activities] . . . and I was delivered from those wiles of Satan.
>
> Mr. Charles Wesley, whom I must always mention with the greatest deference and respect, walked with me in order to confirm me, from the church even to the College. I confess, to my shame, I would gladly have excused him; and the next day, going to his room, one of our Fellows passing by, I was ashamed to be seen to knock at his door.

George Whitefield was ordained on June 20, 1736 at Gloucester Cathedral by the Bishop of Gloucester. Whitefield was twenty-one at the time. He became known as the "boy parson" or "the Seraph" (the angel), while cynical caricaturists dubbed him "Dr. Squintum" due to his squint and florid rhetorical style. Whitefield always described himself as a Methodist.

His rhetorical abilities stood out, as Green has commented: "Whitefield's power lay in his eloquence which was without equal in his time. . . . He possessed a voice of unusual richness and power of penetration. His spell was such that even the more critical suspended disbelief."[21] Another stated that Whitefield "had probably the most musical and carrying voice that ever issued from a human throat. Its sweetness hung in the charmed ears of the crowd; its cadences resembled the rise and fall of the notes of some great singer." One of his friends, future American statesman Benjamin Franklin, reported in 1739 after hearing Whitefield preach in Philadelphia: "He had a loud and clear voice, and articulated his words and sentences so perfectly, that he might be heard and understood at a great distance, especially as his audiences, however numerous, observed the most exact silence. . . . I computed that he might well be heard by more than thirty thousand."

Whitefield turned out to be a phenomenally popular preacher in London and Bristol, preaching nine times a week in churches that would allow him to preach and twice as often to the Methodist societies. As Whitefield recorded in his journal:

> On Sunday mornings, long before the day, you see streets filled with people going to church, with their lanthorns [lanterns] in their hands, and hear them conversing about the things of God. Other Churches near at hand would be filled with persons who could not come where I was preaching; and those who did come were like persons struck with pointed arrows or mourning for a firstborn child. . . .In a short time I could no longer walk on foot as usual, but was constrained to go in a coach, from place to place, to avoid the hosannas of the multitude.

One observer recalled:

> It was wonderful to see how the people hung upon the rails of the organ loft, climbed upon the leads of the church,

---

[21] Green, *John Wesley*, 71.

and made the church itself so hot with their breath that the steam would fall from the pillars like drops of rain. Sometimes almost as many would go away from lack of room as came in. . . . Every accent, every emphasis, every modulation of voice, was so perfectly tuned and well placed, that . . . [it gave the listener] a pleasure of much the same kind with that received from an excellent piece of music.

In the summer of 1737, Whitefield preached about a hundred sermons in London. Of this Charles wrote: "The churches will not contain the multitudes that throng to hear him. Even members of the aristocracy came to hear him, among them the Duchess of Marlborough." While waiting in Deal to sail to America at the end of 1737, Whitefield divided the congregation of the church in which he was preaching into two sittings so that they could hear him. Even then the floor of the hall had to be strengthened to bear their weight.

Whitefield left for Georgia at the same time that John was returning to England in January 1738, and his ministry in the colony proved to be as triumphant as John's and Charles' had been disastrous. In Georgia, his gospel proved far more favorable than the Wesleys had been. When he left Georgia, he hoped to return before long, saying, "The longer I continued there, the larger the congregations grew. And I scarce knew a night, though we had Divine service twice a day, when the Church House has not been nearly full."

When he returned from his first American mission in November 1738, he was no longer a younger and somewhat subordinate colleague; his popularity and status among the Anglican evangelicals had eclipsed that of the Wesleys. Whitefield spent his first months preaching in London, praying for his opponents, moving the societies to tears with his words, and taking a collection for an orphanage in Georgia. In February 1739 he moved to Bristol. There his mission took off more spectacularly than ever. Turned away from most churches, he preached at the Methodist societies to so many people that the stairs and courts below were crammed with latecomers straining to hear.

Then one Sunday he visited the mining community of Kingswood outside of Bristol, an underclass with the worst living conditions in Britain where the miners worked underground stark naked. Shunned by the churches, Whitefield decided to take a momentous step: he preached outdoors. Charles Spurgeon remarked of this event: "It was a brave day for England when Whitefield began field preaching." Recalled Whitefield: "I went upon a mount and spoke to as many people as came unto me. They were upwards of two hundred people. Blessed be God, I have now broken the ice." The miners were so moved by his preaching that Whitefield described "the white gutters made by their tears, which fell plentifully down their black cheeks as they came out of their coal pits. Hundreds and hundreds of them were soon brought into deep convictions, which as the event proved, happily ended in a sound and thorough conversion." One of the miners, Thomas Maxfield, who would become one of John's "sons of the gospel," begged Whitefield to return, and he agreed, preaching four more times to the miners with the last meeting attracting 10,000 people.

Emboldened by his success among the Kingswood miners, Whitefield began preaching in the Bristol area to crowds of 20,000 or more, with people traveling miles to hear him. One who heard him preach reported:

> His deep-toned yet clear and melodious voice . . . is perfect music. It is wonderful to see what a spell he casts over an audience by proclaiming the simplest truths of the Bible. I have seen upwards of a thousand people hang on his words with breathless silence, broken only by an occasional half-suppressed sob. He impresses the ignorant, and, not less, the educated and refined . . . and few return [from hearing him] unaffected. . . . He speaks from a heart all aglow with love, and pours out a torrent of eloquence which is almost irresistible.

Charles was astounded by the impact that Whitefield made when he preached to an estimated 20,000 people at Moorfields in London. Reported Charles: "The cries of the wounded were heard on every side. What has Satan gained by turning him out of the churches?" One observer of Whitefield's meetings at Moorfields commented:

> . . . he found an incredible number of people assembled. Many had told him he would never come out of that place alive. He went in between two friends who by pressure of the

crowd were soon entirely parted from him and were obliged
to leave him to the mercy of the rabble. But these, instead of
hurting him, formed a lane for him and carried him along to
the Fields (where a table had been placed which was broken
to pieces by the crowd) and afterwards back again to the wall
that parted the upper and lower Moorfields; from whence
he preached without molestation to an exceedingly great
multitude.

Essayist and minister John Foster remarked about Whitefield:
"With all the advantage of such power of voice as perhaps no other man
possessed, there must still often have been the necessity of forcing it
to the last possibility of exertion, in order to enable his being heard by
congregations amounting to thousands." One author has suggested that
the congregations that Whitefield preached to were the largest ever in
history to be addressed without the use of some form of amplification.

John Wesley arrived in Bristol on Saturday, March 31, 1739 and was
shocked the following day to witness Whitefield preaching on a bowling
green, "having been all my life (till very lately) so tenacious of every
point relating to decency and order, that I should have thought the
saving of souls almost a sin, if it had not been done in church." The next
day, Whitefield left with John praying for "some portion of his spirit."
But rather than follow his example into the fields, Wesley preached at
one of the local societies to a packed and overflowing hall. The next
day, however, he went to one of Whitefield's pulpits, a mound in a
brickyard, and took the plunge: "At four in the afternoon, I submitted
to be more vile and proclaimed in the highways the glad tidings of
salvation, speaking from a little eminence in a ground adjoining the
city, to about three thousand people." It was not long before he was
drawing crowds of up to 5,000 people, although he did not have the
rhetorical flamboyance of Whitefield.

Throughout 1738, Whitefield had entrusted his work in London to
the Wesleys while he was in America. The closeness of their relationship
can be observed through their early comments and correspondence.
In November of that year, John wrote, "Hearing Mr. Whitefield was
arrived from Georgia I hastened to London. . . . God gave us once

more to take sweet counsel together." And Whitefield wrote to John in gushing prose in February 1739:

> Honourable sir, how shall I express my gratitude to you for past favours? I pray for you without ceasing. But that is not enough; I want to give you more substantial proofs. Believe me, I am ready to follow you to prison and to death. Today I was thinking, suppose my honoured friend was laid in a dungeon for preaching Christ. Oh how would I visit him! . . . I know you pray for, honoured sir, your affectionate son in the faith, George Whitefield.

Cracks, however, began to appear in the relationship between John and Charles and Whitefield. Green states that "John Wesley's relations with Whitefield were an uneasy combination of friendship and distrust. . . . He greatly respected Whitefield's qualities and success as an evangelist, and was perhaps a little envious of them; but he detested his predestinarianism."[22] In George Whitefield's opinion, John Wesley preached two heresies: universal redemption and Christian perfection. Whitefield believed that "Mr. Wesley and I preach two different gospels." He also commented scathingly, "That monstrous doctrine of sinless perfection, for a while, turns some of its deluded votaries into temporary monsters." As far back as the early 1740s, Whitefield had been an opponent of Christian perfectionism. He wrote to John criticizing him for believing that sinless perfection was possible in this life, declaring: "I cannot agree that the inbeing of sin is to be destroyed in this life. . . . What a fond conceit is it to cry up perfection and yet cry down the doctrine of final perseverance." So strong was his opposition to Wesleyan doctrine that he felt constrained "publicly to separate from my dear, dear old friends Messrs John and Charles Wesley, whom I still love as my own soul."

In June 1740, John decided "to strike at the root of the grand delusion" of predestination by preaching a sermon on "Free Grace"—a sermon he had already preached at Newgate prison in Bristol the year before—to expose Calvinism "in all its naked, hideous deformity."

---

[22] Ibid., 72.

Charles described Calvinism as "the hellish, blasphemous, explosive lie . . . the foulest tale . . . that has ever hatched in Hell." When Whitefield heard about the sermon, he wrote to John: "I hear, Honoured Sir, that you are about to print a sermon against predestination. It shocks me to think of it! What will be the consequences but controversy? Silence on both sides will be best." The Wesleys went further and published John's sermon as a pamphlet. It was a fierce denunciation of predestination, and Charles supported the publication by writing hymns that described predestination as the "horrible decree."

A distressed Whitefield wrote a number of letters to John while he was in America, urging him not to make predestination a prominent issue. On June 25, 1740, he wrote: "For Christ's sake, let us not be divided amongst ourselves. Nothing so much will prevent a division as our being silent on this hand." Whitefield also wrote, "The doctrine of election . . . of those that are truly in Christ, I am ten thousand times more convinced of, if possible, than when I saw you last." John, attempting to avoid conflict with Whitefield, replied in August 1740 in a conciliatory tone, claiming: "There are bigots both for predestination and against it. . . . Therefore for a time you are suffered to be of one opinion and I of another, but when his time is come, God will do what man cannot, namely, make us both of one mind."

Another major difference between John and Whitefield was their differing abilities and personalities. John Wesley's was "a patient, persistent evangelism in a myriad of dingy villages and seedy backstreets." G. R. Cragg has said: "Wherever Whitefield went, he left an overwhelming impression of impassioned eloquence. Wherever Wesley went, he left a company of men and women closely knit together in a common life," a fact that Whitefield himself realized: "My brother Wesley acted wisely, the souls that were awakened under his ministry, joining in class, he preserved the fruit of his labour. This I neglected and my people are a rope of sand." According to the historian William Lecky: "Whitefield was chiefly a creature of impulse and emotion. He had very little logical skill, no depth or range of knowledge, nothing of the commanding and organizing talent . . . so conspicuous in his colleague [John Wesley]."

When Whitefield returned in March 1741 from his second trip to America, it was clear that his relations with John Wesley had cooled. John arrived in London in April and heard about "Mr Whitefield's unkind behaviour since his return from Georgia." When they met three days later, John was in no mood to compromise. He attacked Whitefield's rebuttal of his sermon on free grace, declaring, "If you were constrained to bear your testimony, as you term it, against the error I am in, you might have done it by publishing a treatise, without calling my name in question." He also criticized Whitefield for making public the fact that he cast a lot in Deal in 1738 to decide whether to wait for him or to go on to London. This was sufficient, according to John, "to make an open breach between you and me." Despite their differences, Whitefield was willing to abase himself for the sake of reconciliation with Wesley. On October 10, 1741, he wrote to John:

> Reverend and Dear Brother, I have for a long time
> expected that you would have sent me an answer to my last;
> but I suppose you are afraid to correspond with me because I
> revealed your secret about the lot. Though much may be said
> for my doing it, yet I am sorry now that any such thing dropped
> from my pen and I humbly ask pardon. I find I love you as
> much as ever and pray God, if it be his blessed will, that we may
> be all united together. . . . May God remove all obstacles that
> now prevent our union! Though I hold Particular Election
> yet I offer Jesus freely to every individual soul. You may carry
> Sanctification to what degrees you will, only I cannot agree
> that the inbeing of sin is to be destroyed in this life. . . . In
> about three weeks I hope to be at Bristol. May all disputing
> cease and each of us talk of nothing but Jesus and him cruci-
> fied. This is my resolution.

Whitefield and John met again in 1742, with the former hoping they could reconcile their differences, but again John was not prepared to make any compromises, recording somewhat imperiously in his *Journal* that he spent "an agreeable hour with Mr. Whitefield. I believe he is sincere in all he says concerning his earnest desire of joining hand in hand with all that love the Lord Jesus Christ. But if (as some would persuade me) he is not, the loss is all on his side. I am just as I was: I go on my way, whether he goes with me or stays behind."

During the 1740s, the Wesleyans and Whitefieldites established separate organizations, with the latter establishing tabernacles in London and Bristol. An argument also erupted between the Wesleys and Whitefield when, short of funds for his Orphan House in America, Whitefield dared to question whether the Methodist societies in Bristol owed him some money because he had helped to purchase the land for the meeting house in Kingswood. A furious John rejected Whitefield's claim, asserting that the success of the work in Bristol was due to his and Charles' efforts alone.

The Wesleys and Whitefield would never be fully reconciled, but they remained friends and would preach for each other on occasion. In September 1747, when someone wrote to Whitefield with unsavory gossip about Charles, Whitefield corresponded with his friend, assuring him of his love and support: "Some have wrote me things to your disadvantage. I would not believe them. Love thinks no evil of a friend. Such you are to me. I love you most dearly." In March 1749, Charles consulted Whitefield about his intention to marry in accordance with a promise he had made during their membership of the Holy Club. And in October of that year, Charles remarked to his wife that "G[eorge] Whitefield, and my brother and I are one, a three fold cord which shall no more be broken."

When John lost the love of his life, Grace Murray, in 1749 when she married Methodist lay preacher John Bennet, it was Whitefield who rushed to his side to comfort him, with John recording, "Mr. Whitefield wept and prayed over me . . . he said all that was in his power to comfort me, but it was in vain." He was also instrumental in reconciling John and Charles, even though the latter's intervention had been decisive in wrecking John's chances of marriage.

Still, mutual doubts plagued their relationship, with Whitefield writing to Charles in December 1752, "I cannot help thinking he [John] is still jealous of me and my proceedings, but thank God, I am quite easy about it." However, when Charles was considering deserting John when their relationship was at a low ebb and becoming Lady Huntingdon's private chaplain or advisor in 1752, Whitefield selflessly urged him to remain with his brother:

> My dear friend. . . . The connection between you and your brother, has been so close and continued, and your attachment to him so necessary to keep up his interest, that I would not willingly for the world do or say anything that may separate such friends. . . . [God] knows how much I love and honour you, and your brother, and how often I have preferred your interest to my own. This, by the grace of God, I shall continue to do.

A year later, when it was believed that John was dying, it was Whitefield who rushed immediately to London "to pay my last respects to my dying friend. It may be that shortly Mr. John Wesley will be no more: the physician thinks his disease is a galloping consumption. I pity the church, I pity myself, but not him. We must stay behind in this cold climate while he takes his flight to a radiant Throne." When Charles left his wife, who had a severe case of small pox, to attend his brother's supposed death bed, Whitefield wrote generously: "The Lord help and support you. May a double spirit of the ascending Elijah descend and rest upon the surviving Elisha! . . . Now is the time to 'prove the strength of Jesus yours.'"

Yet, when in 1749 John suggested to Whitefield that they meet in London to discuss a union between their respective disciples, Whitefield replied: "I am afraid an external one is impracticable. I find by your sermons that we differ in principles more than I thought, and I believe we are on a different plan. My attachment to America will not permit me to abide very long in England; consequently I should but weave a Penelop's web—a never ending work always to be begun again, from the story in Homer—if I formed societies. And if I should form them I have not proper assistants to take care of them. You, I suppose, are for settling societies everywhere." John proposed an evangelistic campaign in Scotland, but was informed bluntly by Whitefield, "You have no business in Scotland; for your principles are so well known that if you spoke like an angel, none would hear you; and if they did, you would have nothing to do but to dispute with one and another from morning to night."

In 1763, John commented about Whitefield that "Humanly speaking, he is worn out." Then in 1765, John remarked that he "seemed to be an old, old man, being fairly worn out in his master's service, though he has hardly seen fifty years." A year before Whitefield's death, Wesley observed: "His soul appeared to be vigorous still, but his body was sinking apace; and unless God interposes with his mighty hand, he must soon finish his bodily labours." John's observations were accurate, for shortly before his death, probably from heart failure, Whitefield revealed to a supporter: "My breath is short and I have little hope, since my last relapse, of much further public usefulness. A few last exertions, like the last struggles of a dying man, or glimmering flashes of a taper just burning out, is all that can be expected from me. But blessed be God the taper will be lighted up again in heaven." In his last sermon, Whitefield proclaimed prophetically: "I go to a rest prepared; my sun has arisen, and by aid from Heaven has given light to many. It is now about to set. . . . I shall soon be in a world where time, age, pain and sorrow are unknown. My body fails, [but] my spirit expands. How willingly would I live to preach Christ! But I die to be with him!"

George Whitefield died on September 30, 1770 in Newbury Port, Massachusetts. It was Charles rather than John who genuinely felt his loss, weeping openly and declaring the debt all owed to "his abundant labour of love." After Whitefield's death, Charles wrote: "I wish I could say any thing to add to the best impressions of my late dear friend, Mr. Whitefield. One part of his character ever the most to be admired by me, was the most artless mind—'an Israelite indeed in whom there was no guile.'" Although not as close to Whitefield as Charles, John was still moved by his sudden death and remarked sadly about his erstwhile friend that he:

> . . . had a heart susceptible to the most generous and
> the most tender friendship. I have frequently thought this,
> of all others, was the distinguishing part of his character.
> How few have we known of so kind a temper, of such large
> and flowing affections. Was it not principally by this that the

hearts of others were drawn and knit to him? Can anything but love beget love? This shone in his very countenance, and continually breathed in his words whether in public or private. Was it not this which, quick as lightening, flew from heart to heart, which gave that lift to his sermons, his conversations, his letters?

John Wesley was asked to speak at Whitefield's three London chapels in November, making no mention of Whitefield's doctrine of election beyond saying, "There are many doctrines of a less essential nature, with regard to which even the sincere children of God . . . are and have been divided for many ages. In these we may think and let think; we may 'agree to disagree.'" The predestinarians were incensed at the omission, with a seething Augustus Toplady commenting on free will theology that it "ascends, on the ladder of blasphemy, to the mountain top of atheism," and of John Wesley, "I believe him to be the most rancorous hater of the gospel system that ever appeared in England."

Dr. Martyn Lloyd-Jones has described George Whitefield as "the greatest preacher that England has ever produced." In old age, John Newton, the ex-slave trader and writer of *Amazing Grace*, revealed to the young William Wilberforce that George Whitefield was without doubt the greatest preacher he had ever heard. According to Newton, Whitefield had:

> . . . a manner of preaching which was peculiarly his own. He copied from none, and I never met any one who could imitate him with success; they who attempted generally made themselves disagreeable. His familiar address, the power of his action, his marvellous talent in fixing the attention of the most careless, I need not describe to those who have heard him, and to those who have not the attempt would be vain. Other ministers could, perhaps, preach the Gospel as clearly, and in general say the same things. But I believe, no man living could say them in his way. Here I always thought him unequalled, and I hardly expect to see his equal while I live.

7

THE TWO WESLEYS

. . . was a man made for friendship.

—JOHN GAMBOLD
SPEAKING OF CHARLES WESLEY

He was only a little man, but when he spoke the houses shook..

—AN OBSERVER
SPEAKING OF JOHN WESLEY

There was a considerable difference in temperament between John and Charles Wesley.

In character, Charles was more like his father—passionate, volatile, impetuous, short-tempered, and, as one person observed, his preaching "all thunder and lighting." He was also prone to depression and melancholic lows, particularly when he ended his itinerant ministry in 1757 and stayed in one place. Charles almost had an obsession with death, and his hymns often spoke of it. "What would I give to be on that death-bed," wrote Charles of a woman he had just left, "ready for the Bridegroom;" and "I visited our sister Webb dying in child-bed. We sang that hymn over her corpse, 'Ah lovely appearance of death,' and shed a few tears of joy and envy." On Midsummer's Day, 1719, poet, playwright, and essayist Joseph Addison was buried in Henry VII's Chapel at Westminster Abbey. The King's Scholars, including Charles, stood around the open grave holding lighted tapers. This experience may have contributed to Charles' apparent fascination with death.

Their brother Samuel became a substitute father figure for Charles, and he was largely brought up by his brother and his wife. This upbringing undoubtedly molded his views on the Church of England, including his love of its ceremonies and rituals.

Charles, according to one biographer, "had the gift of inspiring love at first sight. He had the good looks, a little mitigated perhaps by extreme short stature." He was a man of warmth, capable of deep and lasting relationships, as witnessed by his emotional response—in contrast to John's cool reserve—to the death of George Whitefield. Charles also had an enduring friendship with Lady Selina Huntingdon, unlike John who could not bear her determination to have her own way in all matters. As one historian has commented, "He [John] had many friends among his fellow workers but like a sovereign he was very much alone."

Unlike John, Charles had a happy marriage and children and was a devoted family man. John could never bring himself to take the final step to matrimony and seemed to fear physical contact, until his disastrous marriage to Mary Vazeille. When contemplating marriage to Grace Murray in 1749, John perceived it as a practical, rational decision: "She observes my rules, when I am absent as well as when I am present, and takes care that others observe them." According to John, if they had children they would be packed off to Kingswood school to be brought up. As M. Léger has said, "God was, after all, the only lasting passion of John Wesley," and Green has commented that "the real intimacy of love, whether of man for man or of man to woman, passed him by."[23]

Charles, like John, was brave, tenacious, and a man of character, becoming captain of the school and a King's Scholar at Westminster, standing up to bullies at school, despite his small size, confronting mobs while preaching who attacked and stoned him, and courageously speaking in public against the persecution of Catholics during the violent anti-Catholic Gordon Riots in 1780. He also turned down the

---

[23] Green, *The Young Mr. Wesley*, 203.

chance to become the heir of a wealthy, distant relative, Garret Wesley, as it would take him away from Epworth and Westminster.

It also appears that Charles was a gifted conversationalist and had a beautiful speaking voice, for his friends loved to hear him speak aloud during evenings at their homes. But with Charles' personal warmth there occasionally came flashes of anger. When Charles was "all off the hooks," as John Wesley once wrote, one might as well "blow against the wind as try to reason with him."

John Pollock, in his biography of John Wesley, describes John as a young man as having an "open face, with full lips, a nose which was a little too long and . . . framed by luxuriant silky hair which fell to his shoulders in defiance of current fashion; it had an unusual colour, brown which looked auburn in certain lights."[24] John Wesley was around 5' 3" tall, weighed approximately 126 pounds, and had large, dark blue eyes. One observer said that John was "thin and pale, with steely eyes and an expression that was often supercilious; but he exuded a mysterious and pervasive charm. Disdaining the periwig he let his hair grow long and fall in curls upon his shoulders. When speaking he would often raise his slender hands to heaven." Green described John as having a "pleasing appearance, was always carefully and neatly but sombrely dressed [and] was exceptionally clean (in an age unpleasantly devoid of the virtue of personal cleanliness)."[25] And John's friend and later fellow member of the Holy Club, Robert Kirkham, wrote to Wesley in 1726 reminiscing amusingly about his "most deserving, queer character—your worthy personal accomplishments—your noble endowments of mind—your little and handsome person—and your obliging and desirable conversation." In later life John had an appearance that displayed "a pattern of neatness and simplicity. A narrow, plaited stock; a coat with small upright collar; no buckles at his knees; no silk or velvet in any part of his apparel, and a head as white as snow, gave an idea of something primitive and apostolic; while an air of neatness and cleanliness was diffused over his whole person."

---

[24] John Pollock, *Wesley the Preacher* (Eastbourne, England: Kingsway Publications, 2000), 42.

[25] Green, *John Wesley*, 70.

Horace Walpole, man of letters and Whig politician, who heard John Wesley preach at Lady Huntingdon's chapel in Bath on October 5, 1766, commented: "I have been at one opera, Mr. Wesley's. . . . Wesley is a lean, elderly man, fresh coloured, his hair smoothly combed . . . wondrous clean, but as evidently an actor as [David] Garrick [the famous actor and playwright]."

Johan Liden, a Swedish professor, recorded in his private journal his impressions of John Wesley, whom he met in 1769:

> He is a small, thin old man, with his own long and strait [sic] hair and looks as the worst country curate in Sweden, but has learning as a Bishop and zeal for the glory of God which is quite extraordinary. His talk is very agreeable, and his mild face and pious manner secure him the love of all rightminded men. He is the personification of piety and he seems to me as a living representation of the loving Apostle John. The old man Wesley is already sixty-six years, but very lively and exceedingly industrious. I also spoke with his younger brother, Mr. Charles Wesley, also a Methodist minister and a pious man, but neither in learning or activity can be compared with the older brother.

John inherited his mother's iron will, rational reserve, and persistence, and he had a more stable and even character than Charles. He was also remarkably cerebral, even as a child, with a tendency to analyze and deliberate over even trivial matters. Observed his father Samuel: "As for Jack, he will have a reason for everything he has to do. I suppose he will not even break wind, unless he had a reason for it." And it was his habit to respond to a question by saying: "I thank you; I will think of it." His father tried to disillusion his son: "Child, you think to carry everything by dint of argument, but you will find how little is ever done in the world by close reasoning." Stephen Tompkins has suggested that John's propensity to provide a logical answer for everything he did may have been his most obvious failing: "Throughout his life, the assumption that if he could give a logical argument for his actions he was justified in them, no matter what hurt he caused, was to be possibly Wesley's greatest weakness."[26]

His sisters, on occasion, found him cold and insensitive, with Emily challenging him bluntly: "I impute all your unkindness to one principle you hold, that natural affection is a great weakness, if not a sin." John denied the accusation and attacked her savagely: "You are of all creatures the most unthankful to God and man. I stand amazed at you. How little have you profited under such means of improvement." He could be astonishingly insensitive. He left Emily desperately in debt and reduced to selling her clothes for food when he suddenly left for a three-month trip to Germany in June 1738, and then had the audacity to write to her telling her of the wonderful time he was having. Her reply was uncompromising: "For God's sake, tell me how a distressed woman, who expects daily to have the very bed taken from under her rent, can consider the state of the churches in Germany. . . . I loved you tenderly. You married me to a man, and as soon as sorrow took hold of me you left me to it. . . . You, who could go to Germany, could you not reach Gainsborough?" When his sister Martha lost a child, he reminded her that in the past she had complained about the time she had to devote to the upbringing of her children: "Now that time is restored to you, and you have nothing to do but to serve our Lord." John rebuked the preacher Adam Clarke for "inordinate affection" because he grieved over the death of his infant daughter and informed John Ogilvie that it "should be a matter of great thankfulness" that he and his wife had "been enabled to give to God" their "lovely child."

Green has commented that John's *Journal*, which records sixty-six years of his daily activities, is "one of the most impersonal documents ever written . . . of deep affection, of intimacies which carry passions and excitements, Wesley seems to have been singularly void . . . [and] did not bare the depths of his personality."[27] Another has commented: "His journals are like the note-books of a physician—a curious, monotonous, wonderful narrative."

---

[26] Stephen Tompkins, *John Wesley: A Biography* (Grand Rapids, MI: William B. Eerdmans Publishing Co., 2003), 16.

[27] Green, *John Wesley*, 92.

Comparing the two Wesleys, Green said:

> John Wesley was a stronger and more forceful personality
> than Charles. His industry and his power of concentration
> revealed by the hour-to-hour diary of his daily activities were
> really amazing. Even on the occasions when he felt unwell
> (and he suffered much from bilious catarrh [congested air-
> ways]) he rarely permitted sickness to interfere with his daily
> routine. . . . There is little doubt that he had imposed a regime
> upon himself which demanded self-discipline and strong will
> power; if he rose, as he often did, between four and five, there
> is nothing to indicate that he went to bed at an abnormally
> early hour. There were times for prayer and times for work,
> times for pupils and times for visiting the Castle and Bocardo;
> and life went on with clockwork regularity.[28]

John, said Green, "had incredible powers of endurance, proof of
his excellent constitution and mental stamina. . . . His charm and grace
cloaked an iron will; he was granite in aspic."[29]

The Wesleys' doctor, John Whitehead, said of John Wesley, "For a
small person he possessed great muscular strength." And the historian
Stead commented: "Wesley could never have left so deep and broad
an impression on the world without that marvelous body, with muscles
of whipcord, and bones of steel, with lungs of leather, and a heart of
a lion."

He was completely fearless, as he proved when confronting hostile
mobs intent on injuring or killing him.

Charles had the ability to draw people to the Holy Club, but he
deferred to John's leadership and organizational skills when it came to
its development. John Gambold, a fellow Oxford student and member
of the Holy Club, was to write about John that he was "always the
same. . . . To this I may add that he had, I think, something of authority
in his countenance; though . . . he could soften his manner and point
it as occasion required."

[28] Green, *The Young Mr. Wesley*, 139.

[29] Green, *John Wesley*, 127.

John Wesley undoubtedly had prodigious energy and zeal, preaching 15 to 18 sermons week after week, traveling by horse and then chaise 4,000 to 5,000 miles in an average year (speed reading as he went), while yet still finding time to write thousands of books, pamphlets, hymns, handbooks, school primers, abridgements, anthologies, a daily journal, and regular correspondence with a multitude of people. In 1743, for example, John's itinerary included 14 weeks in London, 10 weeks in Bristol, 13 weeks in Newcastle, and 15 weeks in Cornwall. He usually traveled by horse, reading as he rode with a slack rein, allowing his horse to judge the best route. He slept and ate where he could, commenting that he was not disturbed by "a dinner ill dressed, or a hard bed, a poor room, a shower of rain, or a dusty road." He was given a chaise and two horses by a wealthy sympathizer in 1763, and from the 1770s onward, always traveled in his own carriage fitted with a bookcase and a board that could be let down to serve as a desk.

For John, every minute, both day and night, had its appointed work. "Joshua, when I go to bed, I go to bed to sleep, and not to talk" was his rebuke to a young preacher who once shared his room and wished to steal some of Wesley's precious moments of repose for conversation on some difficult problems. To one who asked him how it was that he got through so much work in so short a time, he answered, "Brother, I do only one thing at a time, and I do it with all my might."

From his youth, his mother Susanna had taught John, or Jacky as he was called when he was young, to believe that he had been selected by God for a special purpose, "a brand plucked from the burning." John commented on the power he wielded in the Methodist movement, but he claimed he had not sought it:

> What is that power? It is a power of admitting into, and excluding from, the societies under my care; of choosing and removing stewards; of receiving helpers; of appointing them when, where, and how to help me; and of desiring any of them to meet me, when I see good. And as it was merely in obedience to the providence of God, and for the good of the people, that I at first accepted this power, so it is on the same considerations, not profit, honour, or pleasure, that I use it at this day.

Wesley addressed the issue of his power in the Methodist movement again in 1766:

> But several gentlemen are much offended at my having so much power. My answer to them is this: I did not seek any part of this power. It came upon me unawares. But when it was come, not daring to bury that talent, I used it to the best of my judgement. Yet, I never was fond of it. I always did, and do now, bear it as my burden; the burden which God lays upon me; but if you can tell me any one, or nay five men, to whom I may transfer this burden, who can and will do just what I do now, I will heartily thank both them and you.

In 1790, when a Methodist preacher dared suggest the possibility of people selecting their own steward or minister, John Wesley gave him short shrift: "As long as I live, the people shall have no share in choosing either stewards or leaders among the Methodists." Another preacher, John Pawson, sarcastically said of Wesley when he was in his eighties, "What an astonishing degree of power does our aged father and friend exercise." John had no patience with those in the movement who wanted to choose their own leaders, declaring emphatically: "We have not, and never had, any such customs. We are no republicans, and never intend to be. It would be better for those that are so minded to go quietly away. I have been uniform both in doctrine and discipline for above these fifty years; and it is a little too late for me to turn into a new path now I am grey-headed."

When John was accused of attempting to assume the Apostolate of England or acting like a pope, he replied:

> . . . in plain terms, wherever I see one or a thousand men running into hell, be it in England, Ireland or France, yes, in Europe, Asia, Africa or America, I will stop them if I can: as a minister of Christ, I will beseech them in His name to turn back and be reconciled to God. Were I to do otherwise, were I to let any soul drop into the pit whom I might have saved from everlasting burnings, I am satisfied God would not accept my plea, "Lord he was not of my parish."

When it came to those who differed with him, John had a remarkable approach: "I have no more right to object to a man for holding a different opinion from mine than I have to differ with a man because he wears a wig and I wear my own hair; but if he takes his wig off and shakes the powder in my eyes, I shall consider it my duty to get quit of him as soon as possible." John once remarked to the Scottish minister Ralph Erskine, "Difference of opinion is indeed with me a very small thing." On the other hand, John usually insisted that he was right and that his opinion was "plain demonstrable fact," which often resulted in fiery debate with those who thought otherwise. Curiously, according to his first biographer John Hampson, he could accept fierce opposition from those outside the movement with equanimity, but was enraged by Methodist preachers who dared challenge his authority.

Many people were drawn to John. Green notes that John had a

> . . . radiant quality about his personality which made men and women (if rather more women than men) admire and revere him. . . . His personality imposed itself on his contemporaries in a way that none of his associates, including the redoubtable Whitefield, did. Before his death statuettes and mementoes in china and other ware were being produced in considerable quantities to satisfy his public.[30]

John's young assistant, Samuel Bradburn, who traveled with him thousands of miles and afterward became a prominent Methodist preacher, claimed that he never saw him "low-spirited in my life" and was "greatly struck with his cheerfulness and affability." Bradburn went on to say:

> From seeing him only in the pulpit, and considering his exalted station in the Church of Christ, I supposed he was very reserved and austere; but how agreeably was I disappointed when, with a pleasant smile, he took me by the hand and said, "Beware of the fear of man and be sure you speak flat and plain in preaching." It is not easy to express the good effect this advice had on my mind at that time.

---

[30] Ibid., 70.

John could also be incredibly gracious. A Dr. Bready remarked:

> [John] Wesley, the evangelist, was a man possessed of amazing grace. Never did he lose his temper; and always was he prepared to endure a blow, if the dealing of it would relieve the hysteria of the assailant. Repeatedly, when struck by a stone or cudgel, he quietly wiped away the blood and went on preaching without so much as a frown on his face. He loved his enemies; and do what they would, they could not make him discourteous or angry.

Alexander Knox, the Irish theological writer who, at the age of thirty-two, accompanied Wesley in Ireland, wrote of him rather sycophantically:

> So fine an old man I never saw! The happiness of his mind beamed forth in his countenance: Every look showed how fully he enjoyed "the gay remembrance of a life well spent."
>
> Wherever he went he diffused a portion of his own felicity. Easy and affable in his demeanour, he accommodated himself to every sort of company; and showed how happily the most finished courtesy may be blended with the most perfect piety. In his conversation we might be at a loss whether to admire most his fine classical taste, his extensive knowledge of men and things, or his overflowing goodness of heart. While the grave and serious were charmed with his wisdom, his sportive sallies of innocent mirth delighted even the young and thoughtless; and both saw in his uninterrupted cheerfulness, the excellency of true religion. . . . In him even old age appeared delightful, like an evening without a cloud.

Wesley biographer, John Hampson, remarked that, "his style was the calm, equal flow of a placid stream," and his eyes, "the brightest and most piercing that can be conceived." "Few have seen him," Hampson continued, "without being struck by his appearance; and many, who have been greatly prejudiced against him, have been known to change their opinion the moment they were introduced to his presence."

Charles, on the other hand, had a meekness and unfeigned humility. Commented his family after his death:

His most striking excellence was humility; it extended
to his talents as well as virtues; he not only acknowledged
and pointed out but delighted in the superiority of another;
and if there was a human being who disliked power, avoided
pre-eminence and shrunk from praise, it was Charles Wesley.
He desired to please others, particularly John, but was often
determined to follow his own course.

John Gambold said of Charles Wesley that he "was a man made
for friendship, who, by his cheerfulness and vivacity, would refresh his
friend's heart; with attentive consideration, would enter into and settle
all his concerns; so far as he was able, would do anything for him, great
or small, and by a habit of openness and freedom, leave no room for
misunderstanding."

It seems that Charles was a compliant, submissive individual who
out of genuine affection for his brother and others often chose agreement over conflict. Gambold was surprised at Charles' deference to
John during their time at Oxford: "I have never observed any person
have a more real deference for another than [Charles] had for his
brother. . . . He followed his brother entirely. Could I describe one of
them, I could describe both." Charles' willingness to obey John may
have been partly due to his mother viewing his brother after the rectory
fire as specially chosen by God and the fact that she vowed "to be more
particularly careful of the soul of this child." Charles recognized that
he was a compliant person who hated confrontation, revealing to his
wife Sally on December 24, 1755: "You know my principle. I sacrifice
all, even my own brother, to peace and quietness. Rather than hazzard
a quarrel I would run away from every human creature, including you."
Bishop Latrobe, the head of the Moravian Church in England, commented scathingly about John and Charles' relationship in the 1780s:
"His brother Charles has been attached to him in a manner that has
made him unsteady in all his connections with other persons, being his
implicit follower in all things." According to John R. Tyson: "There was,
deep in Charles' personality, something that made him willing to be
led by his brother, just as there was something in John that made him
prone to lead. Things went along smoothly with their shared ministry

when each man settled into his unspoken but well established role."[31] Charles was to write despondently in 1735 after John had pressured him into accompanying him to Georgia that his brother "always had the ascendant over me."

Despite this, Charles occasionally sought to establish his independence from his brother: he intervened in John's proposed marriage to Grace Murray; he refused to forsake his family in Bristol, despite John's urgent requests to return to itinerant evangelism; then there was his unqualified conception of Christian perfection (which John said was "set too high") and his single-minded determination to keep Methodism from separating from the Church of England.

Curiously, despite his great learning, intellect, and granite-like stubbornness and determination, John could be astonishingly naive and a poor judge of character, particularly when it came to women. John was renowned for his lack of discretion and would usually reveal everything he knew. Charles said in a letter to a mutual friend about John, "You expect he will keep his own secrets; let me tell you, he never could do it since he was born; it is a gift which God has not given him." Following the disaster in Georgia, Charles described John as being "born for the knaves." After his experience of dealing with the colonists, Charles had resolved to be more cautious in the future: "For my part, I will never imitate [him], I will ever beware of men, as he who best knows them advises. I will not think all men rogues till I find them otherwise . . . but I will insist upon a far different probation from what my brother requires before I take any one into my confidence." When Charles received John's account of his grappling with an enraged Mrs. Hawkins in Georgia, he reported wryly, "All this will teach him a little of the wisdom of the serpent, of which he seems as utterly void as his dear friend Mrs. H[awkins] is of the innocency of the dove." John vigorously defended his trusting nature, asserting, "I believe in everybody. Charles believes in nobody, yet he is often more deceived than I."

John wrote home in 1723 that he was "seldom troubled with anything but bleeding at the nose, which I have frequently." One such

[31] John R. Tyson, *Assist Me to Proclaim: The Life and Hymns of Charles Wesley* (Grand Rapids, MI: William B. Eerdmans Publishing Co., 2007), 173.

occasion was on July 16, 1733, when he awoke to find himself spitting blood. "O Eternity . . . spare me for this company" (presumably the Holy Club). While at Oxford, when he was out walking, he suffered a nose bleed, which refused to stop. "I stripped myself and leapt into the river, which happened luckily not to be far off." The shock of the cold water contracted the muscles and the bleeding stopped.

John loved bathing and exercise. He swam and went boating, played "real tennis," and rode regularly. When he was at Charterhouse, he promised his father that he would run three times around an open space called Green before breakfast, and he kept his promise. John attributed his excellent health to "constant exercises and change of air." He, like Charles, was a vegetarian, but after being stricken by a "violent flux" in Ireland, he decided to resume eating meat. In a letter to his mother in November 1724, John mentioned a book called an *Essay on Health and Long Life,* by Dr. Cheyne. Cheyne's theory was that good health and long life depended on temperance in eating and drinking combined with plenty of exercise. Cheyne was against eating highly salted food and recommended drinking two pints of water and one pint of wine every twenty-four hours. He also advocated eating only a small amount of meat and a slightly larger amount of vegetables each day. Wesley wrote in his *Journal* that, "in consequence of reading Dr. Cheyne, I chose to eat sparingly and drink water. This was another great means of continuing my health."

In June 1766, when John Wesley was sixty-three, he was still physically fit, his hair was still predominantly dark, and his vigor and determination were undiminished. He remarked: "If it pleases God that I, who am now in my sixty-third year, find no disorder, no weakness, no decay, no difference from what I was at five and twenty, only that I have fewer teeth and more grey hairs." John Wesley had remarkable endurance and stamina and continued to travel throughout Britain on horseback, reading voraciously as he went, until he was seventy. He then traveled in a chaise [a small carriage] or a horse and trap.

Despite having an incredibly robust constitution, John suffered from bouts of ill health. During the winter of 1741–2, he became ill riding in the rain and then preaching in Wales with what was probably a severe attack of "the ague," or malaria. In 1745, John had what he described as his worst ever journey, traveling to Newcastle through "wind, and hail, and rain, and ice, and snow, and driving sleet, and piercing cold. . . . Oh for ease and a resting place! Not yet. But eternity is at hand!" This and his heavy workload may have contributed to a breakdown when he suddenly felt overwhelmed: "One, and another, and another, hurrying me continually, it seized upon my spirit more and more, till I found it necessary to fly for my life."

He regained his composure, but in October 1753, he became seriously ill again, suffering from fever, headache, shivering, cramp, and coughing. Convinced that he was dying, he wrote his own epitaph for his tombstone:

> Here lieth
> The body of John Wesley,
> A brand plucked out of the burning,
> who died of consumption in the fifty-first year
> of his age,
> not leaving, after his debts are paid,
> ten pounds behind him:
> praying,
> God be merciful to me, an unprofitable servant!

But John applied one of his own remedies, placing powdered brimstone mixed with the white of an egg on brown paper and putting it on his afflicted side. According to Wesley, the pain subsided in five minutes. He recovered and wrote to those who prayed for his recovery, thanking his "best friends . . . who have been the greatest instruments, in God's hands, of my recovery thus far."

In 1775, John contracted an illness during a tour of Ireland and it was feared again that he might die, with Lady Huntingdon writing to Charles to express her condolences: "I do grieve to think his faithful labours are to cease on earth." Yet following this brush with death, John was to comment in April 1776: "Since I recovered my strength after my late fever, I have scarcely known what pain or weakness or weariness meant. My health is far better and more uninterrupted than it was when I was five-and-twenty. I was then much troubled with a shaking hand. But all that is over."

This was not his last brush with death, for in the spring of 1783, at the age of nearly eighty, he developed a fever and racking cough, confessing, "the wheel of life seems scarcely able to move." As always he recovered and lived for another eight years.

Charles battled with ill health for much of his adult life, which may have been due to being born two months prematurely and the demands of itinerant ministry. He frequently suffered from headaches and nose bleeds; and successive bouts of pleurisy, gout, lumbago, and dysentery left him weakened physically. The deprivation of his years at Oxford and the primitive living conditions he was forced to endure in Georgia seemed to have had a detrimental effect on his respiratory system. Writing to his wife Sally, Charles lamented: "Next Monday my brother sets out for Bristol by Oxford and etc. I dare not accept his offer and venture with him. His way of travelling would kill a younger man. Now I know not when I shall see Bristol, or at all."

Charles' powerful preaching and ministry to the sick, dying, and imprisoned also affected his health. It often left him physically and emotionally exhausted. There were times when he could barely speak or walk because he was so drained. According to John Telford, "Charles Wesley never spared his strength, five services a day were by no means unusual." Charles recorded: "When my work is over, my strength, both bodily and spiritual, leaves me. . . . God by me strengthens the weak hands and confirms the feeble knees; yet am I myself as a man in whom is no strength. I am weary and faint in mind, longing continually to be discharged."

In August 1740, with the controversy over the doctrine of predestination raging, Charles became seriously ill and it was thought he might not live. Charles recalled: "I was taken with a shivering and then the fever came. The next morning I was bled. . . . My pain and disease increased for ten days; so that there was no hope for my life. . . . It was reported I was dead, and published in the papers." Charles, however, recovered, aided by the careful attention of Dr. Middleton, though characteristically he gave thanks to God for his survival—he who "made all things work for my recovery."

Despite his physical frailty, Charles proved to be a more attractive preacher than his brother. He had a fine musical voice and a poet's way with words, combining sermon and song to form a blended form of spontaneous worship. George Whitefield considered Charles to be England's greatest preacher. He could attract larger crowds than even the best of the Methodist preachers. In Bristol during the 1740s, John Nelson tried for three weeks to gain an audience preaching, "spending his strength in vain," but when Charles preached there he drew an immense crowd that "filled the valley and side of the hill . . . [like] grasshoppers."

In spite of such successes, Charles was still racked by doubt and was concerned that constant preaching might damage his frail health: "I am continually tempted to leave off preaching and hide myself . . . [to] have leisure to attend to my own improvement. God continues to work by me, but not in me, that I can perceive. Do not reckon on me, my brother, in the work God is doing; for I cannot expect He should long employ one who is ever longing and murmuring to be discharged." Yet, Charles was to report after preaching in Bristol in 1741: "The Spirit of power came down, the fountain was set upon, my mouth and heart enlarged, and I spoke such words as I cannot repeat. Many sank under the love of Christ crucified, and were constrained to break out, Christ died for all."

John's sermons, in contrast, had a tendency to be too focused on theological issues. John was also convinced that he had to offend those who listened to hold their attention. His first biographer, John Hampson, who heard both John and Charles preach, regarded Charles' sermons as more "awakening and useful" and less "dry and systematic." According to Hampson, Charles had "a remarkable talent of expressing the most important truths with simplicity and energy; and his discourses were sometimes truly apostolic, forcing conviction on his hearers in spite of the most determined opposition." Similarly, Howell Harris remarked that whenever he heard Charles preach that "I thought my soul was drawn out of my body to Christ."

After preaching in Bristol, Charles records in his journal how he spoke "with great freedom and power." Joseph Williams witnessed Charles preaching and wrote an account of the experience:

> I found him standing on a table, in an erect posture, with hands and eyes lifted to heaven in prayer, surrounded with, I guess, more than a thousand people; some few of them persons of fashion, both men and women, but most of them of the lower rank of mankind. . . . He prayed with uncommon fervency, fluency and variety of proper expression. He then preached about an hour . . . in such a manner as I have seldom, if ever, heard any Minister preach . . . to convince his hearers that . . . God is willing to be reconciled to all; even the worst of sinners.
>
> Although he used no notes, nor had anything in his hand but a Bible, yet he delivered his thoughts in a rich, copious variety of expressions, and with so much propriety that I could not observe anything incoherent or inaccurate thro' the whole performance.

A lay preacher called John Valton who heard Charles preach in London in July 1764 recalled "His word was with power; and I thought my Saviour was at hand, never being so sensibly affected under a discourse before. In the evening I heard him again at the Foundery and all seemed to be comforted and affected by his word." Another observer, James Sutcliffe, said that Charles, although appearing frail, once he began preaching, "he was on his high horse [and] age and infirmities were left behind. It was a torrent of doctrine, of exhortation and eloquence bearing down all before him."

John made it clear that he deliberately spoke in a simple way so he could be easily comprehended by all:

> I design plain truth for plain people. Therefore . . . I abstain from all nice and philosophical speculations, from all perplexed and intricate reasonings, and, as far as possible, from even the show of learning, unless in sometimes citing the original Scriptures. I labour to avoid all words which are not easily understood . . . and in particular those kinds of

> technical terms that so frequently occur in bodies of divinity
> . . . but which to common people are an unknown tongue.

Although John's preaching was dry and unemotional, he could hold the attention of vast audiences. "The sweet, crystal clear voice," according to Green, "even in tone and yet now and again raised in emphasis, held the congregation spell-bound." Wesley estimated that he could be heard up to a distance of 140 yards, and on one occasion he addressed around 32,000 people at Gwennap Pit in Cornwall. His stamina and capacity to preach were immense. On Sunday, November 28, 1742, for example, John preached at five and at eight in the morning in Newcastle; he then walked seven miles to Tanfield Lea, and after preaching there returned to preach in Newcastle again at four. During the week of April 20, 1747, Wesley preached fifteen times in thirteen different locations.

Commentary on his preaching style varied somewhat. For example, Johan Liden heard John preach to more than 4,000 people at the Methodist chapel in Spitalfields in London in 1769. He said about John's approach: "The sermon was short but eminently evangelical. He has not great oratorical gift, no outward appearance, but he speaks clear and pleasant." Horace Walpole remarked on John's preaching style after hearing him speak in 1766: "He spoke his sermon, but so fast and with so little account, that I am sure he has often uttered it. . . . There were parts and eloquence in it, but towards the end he exalted his voice and acted very ugly enthusiasm." John Nelson, one of the first Methodist lay preachers, described the first time that he heard John preach: "As soon as he got upon the stand, he stroked his hair and turned his face towards where I stood and I thought fixed his eyes upon me. His countenance struck such an awful dread upon me, before I heard him speak, that it made my heart beat like the pendulum of a clock; and, when he did speak, I thought his whole discourse was aimed at me." An Elizabeth Hinton described the same affect that John's preaching had on her: "He told me my heart. . . . And when I looked at him I thought he spoke to me only."

As early as the 1740s, Charles began to chafe at John's determination to always get his own way, remarking: "I find it is utterly in vain to write to you upon anything whereon we are not already agreed. Either you set aside the whole by the short answer that I am in an ill humour, or take no notice at all of my reasons, but plead conscience. . . . I have so little success in my remonstrances that I have many times resolved never to contradict your judgement as to any thing or person." According to author Gary Best, Charles was no longer willing to obediently acquiesce to John's requests:

> Charles made it clear he only wanted to work in the Bristol area, although he conceded he was willing to preach in London whenever John was absent. The truth was that Charles was tired of playing second fiddle to the dictatorial John and felt it was time to surrender to his physical infirmity. Successive bouts of pleurisy, gout, lumbago and dysentery had weakened his constitution. In addition, he was no longer prepared to spend such large amounts of time away from Sally.[32]

On June 15, 1758, Charles confided to Sally: "I believe I shall quite come over to you, and never stir from home—except to visit the sick or to preach. . . . My love of retirement increases with my business: and I should not be sorry, if all the religious world cast me off." Often confronted with a conflict of loyalties, with his wife and family on one side and John on the other, Charles began to refuse his brother's requests and resented his demands that he join him in itinerant preaching, once inscribing on one of John's directives: "Trying to bring me under HIS yoke."

Yet John insisted on Charles doing what he, John, wanted rather than following the advice of his wife Sally or anyone else, including Lady Huntingdon. Wrote John:

> Take one side, or the other. Either act really in connection with me, or never pretend it. Rather disclaim it, and openly avow you do not. . . . Take counsel with me once or twice a year, as to the places where you will labour. Hear my advice before you fix whether you take it or no. . . . I am a better judge in this matter than either Lady Huntingdon, Sally . . . or any other; indeed, than your own heart.

---

[32] Gary Best, *Charles Wesley* (London: Epworth Press, 2006), 245.

"How apt you are to take the colour of your company!" wrote John in 1766. "When you and I [talked] together you seemed at least to be of the same mind with me and now you are all off the hooks again! . . . unless you only talk [so] because you are in the humour of contradiction; if so I may as well blow against the wind as talk with you."

The disagreements between the two men had nothing to do with a rivalry for leadership over the Methodist movement. Charles never had any desire to replace John as the leader. When John became seriously ill in 1753 and appeared to be dying, many, including George Whitefield, assumed that Charles would take on the mantle, but he maintained that he had "neither a body, nor a mind, nor talents, nor grace for it."

Moreover, Charles' impetuous and ill-conceived intervention to stymie Grace Murray's marriage to John proved to be a turning point in his relationship with his brother. Never again would they be on such intimate terms. Indeed, when John married Mary Vazeille a year later, he chose not to inform Charles when it would take place. John and Charles' relationship cooled still further after John's disastrous marriage and Charles' decision to conclude his itinerant ministry and concentrate on preaching in London and Bristol. On October 30, 1753, John expressed his annoyance at Charles' reluctance to share the burden of itinerant ministry:

> What I have desired any time these last ten years is, either you would really act in connexion [with me] or that you would never say you do. Either leave off professing, or begin per-forming. . . . O brother, pretend no longer to the thing that is not. You do not, will not act in concert with me. Not since I was married only (the putting it on that is a mere finesse), but for ten years last past, and upwards, you have no more acted in connexion with me than Mr. Whitefield has done. Would to God you would begin to do it now; or else, talk no more as if you did.

John wrote again to Charles in July 1755 stressing the same point: "I should wonder if Wales or Margate or something did not hinder you [from] taking any step which I desire, or which might save my time or strength. Then I will go to Cornwall myself, that is all. . . . For a wife and a partner I may challenge the world! But love is rot!"

On July 28, 1755, Charles wrote to Lady Huntingdon when Sally was pregnant, suggesting that John was still trying to persuade him to resume his ministry as an itinerant evangelist: "My brother has gathered much displeasure against me. 1. Because I was not pleased with his Conference, neither can I yet see [it] with his eyes. 2. Because I am not in Cornwall. He cannot feel my Reasons for staying with my wife. I sent him more as soon as she was delivered." The child subsequently died with Charles' grief turning to resentment against John and his wife Molly.

From the 1750s onward, John and Charles often had disagreements about the direction of the Methodist movement. John's insistence that Methodist preachers give up their jobs to travel extensively angered Charles, who proposed to John that all preachers should only be expected to preach part-time while pursuing their original occupations. He confided to Lady Huntingdon that he hoped his proposal would weaken John's authority: "It will break his power, their not depending on him for bread, and reduce his authority within due bounds, as well as guard against that rashness and credulity of his, which has kept me in continual awe and bondage for many years. . . . If he refuses, I will give both preachers and society to his sole management, for this ruin shall not be under my hands." John somehow saw the letter and replied, shocked: "In what respect do you want to 'break my power' and 'to reduce my authority within due bounds'? I am quite ready to part with the whole or any part of it. It is no pleasure to me, nor ever was."

As the century wore on, Charles was apt to annotate his brother's demanding letters "Trying to bring me under his yoke" and file them unanswered. At times their partnership became severely strained, but crucially it was never broken. And it was John who was desperate for a reconciliation, particularly as those he hoped would stand by him deserted or betrayed him, including his right-hand man at the Foundery, Thomas Maxfield. John wrote in a melancholic tone, "By the mercy of God I am still alive and following the work to which He has called me, although without any help, even in the most trying times, from those of whom I might have expected it." In a letter to Charles in 1766, John lamented their deteriorating relationship: "Why do we keep at such a distance?" Two years before, John had pleaded with Charles for a reconciliation: "I think vainly there is no need that you and I should be such strangers to each other. Surely we are old enough to be wiser."

Whatever their differences of opinion or periods of estrangement, blood proved thicker than water for John and Charles Wesley. Charles wrote to a friend in 1771, "Take it for granted that I am fixed, resolved, determined, sworn, to stand by the Methodists and my Brother, right or wrong, through thick and thin." And Charles commented towards the end of his life: "Thus our Partnership here is dissolved, but not our Friendship. I have taken him for better or worse, till death do us part; or rather, re-unite us in love inseparable. I have lived on earth a little too long—who have lived to see this evil day. But I shall very soon be taken from it, in steadfast faith, that the Lord will maintain his own cause."

"Friendship was crucial to Charles Wesley," Tyson has commented. "Only his relationship to his brother mattered more."[33] Thus it was that when Lady Huntingdon, a staunch friend of Charles and his wife, urged him to publicly denounce John, it effectively ended their relationship and he filed her letter with a note in capital letters stating, "Lady Huntingdon's last. UNANSWERED BY JOHN WESLEY'S BROTHER."

[33] Tyson, *Assist Me to Proclaim*, 134.

8

THE WESLEYS
AND WOMEN

Both John and Charles Wesley are dangerous
snares to many young women.

—JOHN HUTTON

When John was four years old, his regular companions were girls aged sixteen, twelve, eleven, ten, and five. Thus his early life was dominated by women, particularly as Susanna refused to allow her offspring to play with the children in the parish. Green has said:

> There was a decisive streak of femininity in John's character (and to some extent in that of Charles also). His neatness, his meticulous, at times fussy, concern with detail, his personal sensitivity, his histrionic approach, must have been in part conditioned at this early age. While he was well-liked by his fellow men, he seems always to be more at home in female society. The influence of the sisterhood was without doubt pervasive.[34]

John Wesley grew up in an overwhelmingly female household. His eldest brother Samuel (born 1690) left for Westminster school a year after John was born, and his father was a distant figure, teaching John ancient languages but nothing much else. That left John surrounded

---

[34] Green, *The Young Mr. Wesley*, 56.

by his mother and five elder sisters (nine other siblings had died or were to die in childhood or infancy): Emilia (1692, nicknamed Emily), Susanna (1695, nicknamed Sukey), Mary (1696, nicknamed Molly), Hetty (1697, short for Mehetabel), Ann (1702, nicknamed Nancy), and the maid. Samuel and Susanna would go on to have another son, Charles in December 1707, and two daughters, Martha (1706, nicknamed Patty or Pat) and Kezziah (1709, nicknamed Kezzy). As Susanna prohibited them from playing with other children or talking to the servants, John grew up without a strong male influence, which may explain his tortuous relationships with women in later life. John said that he had not married "because I should never find such a woman as my father had." The women John met apparently never matched the qualities of his mother. According to Green: "The figure of his mother was never far from his mind in Oxford and Georgia. His inability to make a proposal of marriage to the women with whom he was in love represented the psychological impact of all this; none of them reached the standards he associated with her. When he was face to face with the need for a decision he could not take the step which seemed to savour of a betrayal."[35] John's fear of marriage may also have had its roots in his parents' own stormy marriage, with their frequent bickering and stand-offs.

Green has suggested that John in many areas of life "remained astonishingly naive for so intelligent and observant a man; he was also emotionally immature. Moreover it has been long recognized that he compared his female friends with the figure of his mother, and found them wanting. They would be his confidantes but would not provide the support he wanted."[36] His father Samuel warned him to "burn romances, shut his eyes and heart against any sexual urges," and never marry because "there was never a truly great man who could bridle his passions." And Gary Best has suggested that "Fear of the consequences of marriage was to be instilled into . . . John . . . with disastrous consequences."[37] One of John's sisters commented incisively that her brother

---

[35] Ibid.

[36] Ibid., 203.

[37] Best, *Charles Wesley*, 11.

liked a woman "merely for being a woman." And Best has commented: "John Wesley's Achilles heel was that he liked the company of women, but believed any sexual feelings were a sign of an inadequate Christian commitment. This meant that he appeared to women to court their attention only to reject them."[38]

When John left Epworth for Charterhouse School in January 1714, Charles Wesley also had a predominantly feminine upbringing for the next two years until he entered Westminster and stayed with his brother Samuel and his wife.

Charles entered Christ Church College, Oxford in the autumn of 1726 and described his first year at university as "lost in diversions," one of which was his dalliances with women, including a number of actresses. He had a particularly narrow escape from the clutches of a London actress called Molly Buchanan, who was appearing in *The Virgin Queen* at the Theatre Royal in Lincoln's Inn. Charles had formed an attachment to Molly, and her mother seemed intent on forcing his hand into marriage. Charles later confided somewhat callously to John:

> To do the Old Lady justice, she did give us opportuni-
> ties enough could I have had the Grace to have laid hold of
> them. . . . Hints were lost upon so dull and stupid a Fellow
> as I was; and as such no doubt I have been since sufficiently
> laughed at. . . . From henceforth . . . I shall be less addicted to
> gallantry . . . and liking women simply for being women. . . .
> But enough of her—I'll blot my brain and paper no longer
> with her. . . . I can't imagine, by the by and by, why you should
> mistrust her abilities; she's never the less qualified for the
> stage for being a whore, sure.

Both the Wesleys became friendly with Robert Kirkham at Oxford and through him his sisters, Sarah (or Sally), Elizabeth (or Betty), and Damaris and their friends, Anne Granville and her sister Mary Pendarves. John, Charles, and the women adopted classical nicknames.

It appears that Damaris loved John, much to the chagrin of her suitor who resented Wesley's presence. But John fell in love with Sally Kirkham, "Varanese," and may have thought about marrying her. He

[38] Ibid., 82.

even discussed the possibility of marriage with his Oxford friend Robin Griffiths the day after his ordination (Griffiths died of tuberculosis not long after). But John had no money and numerous debts; Sally was four years his senior (he was twenty-two) and marriage would have excluded him from becoming a Fellow of an Oxford College. As Green has commented, "the full consummation of marriage was something of which he felt and fought shy." So no proposal came forth, and in December 1725, Sally married a schoolteacher, John Chapone. John attended her wedding and wished her happiness, writing in his diary, "May God give her the happiness she deserves." But even after her marriage, she and John still wrote to each other and met to discuss religion and theology. John remained in love with Sally and probably she him, although she had a happy marriage and bore five children. Sally told John, "I would certainly tell you if my husband should ever resent your freedom, which I am satisfied he never will: such an accident as this would make it necessary to restrain in some measure the appearance of esteem I have for you, but the esteem as it is grounded on reason and virtue and entirely agreeable to us both, no circumstance of life will ever make alter." One evening John sat with Sally and her sister and leaned on her breast, while clasping both her hands in his as she said many "obliging things" to him. Green has suggested that John regarding the Kirkham sisters "lacked the strength of will, perhaps the genuine desire, to go further than friendship."

When John returned to Epworth from Oxford in April 1726, he fell in love with a local girl named Kitty Hargreaves, but as happened later, he could not decide whether to take the final step into matrimony. His father disapproved of his romance with Kitty and, according to John, sent "Miss Kitty away in suspicion of my courting her." John wrote in his diary, lamenting the end of his romance: "As we would willingly suffer a little pain or forgo some pleasure for others we really love, so if we sincerely love God we should readily do this for him. For this reason one act of self-denial is more grateful to our Master than the performance of many lesser duties . . . begin in small things first." And then in cipher, "Never touch Kitty's hand again." He later resolved "never to touch any woman's breast again."

In 1730, John embarked on a relationship with Mrs. Mary Pendarves, a thirty-year-old widow who had been a part of the Kirkham circle in the Cotswolds. John had given her the Greek nickname "Aspasia," while, other than "Cyrus," she referred to him as "Primitive Christianity." John's feelings for Mary grew stronger, but he also had a sense they would never, like his relationship with Sally, be fulfilled when he wrote an impassioned letter to Mary and Anne Glanville, which was most likely really directed at Aspasia:

> I perceive that I am making another avenue for grief, that I am laying open another part of my soul, at which the arrows of fortune may enter. . . . Should one to whom I was united by the tenderest tie, who was as my own soul, be torn from me, it would be best for me. . . . Surely if you were called first mine ought not to overflow because all tears were wiped from your eyes. . . . Tell me, Aspasia; tell me, Selima, if it be a fault that my heart burns within me when I reflect on the many marks of regard you have already shown.

Later, he revealed to Mary tenderly, "I have a thousand things to say. I cannot say half of what I feel."

Although Mary found his correspondence spiritually exciting and attentions flattering, she was not in love with John. By July 1734, their relationship had cooled. By that time, Mary had not written to him for more than a year, and when she eventually did, John perhaps feeling humiliated, brought their relationship to a close, writing a final letter: "Alas Aspasia, experience has shown how far my power is short of my will. For some time I flattered myself with the pleasing hope, but I grow more and more ashamed of having indulged it. . . . Doubtless you acted upon cool reflection; you declined the trouble of writing not because it was a trouble, but because it was a needless one. . . . I sincerely thank you for what is past."

John believed that when he went to America as a missionary that there would be few eligible women and that he would not have to confront sexual temptation. However, he soon realized after his arrival in Georgia that he was likely to fall in love, for he wrote to his brother in Greek so that it could not be read by others: "I stand in jeopardy every hour. Two or three women here, young and pretty, God fearing. Pray for me that I know not one of them after the flesh."

One of those was Sophy Hopkey, the attractive, seventeen-year-old niece of Mrs. Thomas Causton, whose husband was Savannah's chief magistrate and Georgia's storekeeper. John began to give her religious instruction and teach her French, while Sophy dressed in white, knowing he liked it, and nursed him when he became ill. In July 1736, John found himself alone with Sophy in the parsonage: "I took her by the hand, and before we parted I kissed her. And from this time, I fear there was a mixture in my intention, though I was not too soon sensible of it."

Shortly afterwards she left Savannah to stay with a family in Frederica. John joined General Oglethorpe in Frederica and then returned to Savannah with Sophy by boat, with only his boy servant and the crew. The weather forced them to land on the southern tip of the uninhabited St. Katherine's Island. One night as they lay awake by the fire, John asked Sophy about her engagement to Thomas Mellichamp.

"I have promised him either to marry him or no one at all," she replied.

Overcome by emotion, John then blurted out, "Miss Sophy, I think myself happy if I was to spend my life with you."

At this, Sophy wept and declared: "I am very unhappy. I won't have Tommy, for he is a bad man. And I can have none else." She asked him to speak no more of the matter, and John "ended our conversation with a psalm."

Yet by Sunday, February 26, 1737, their relationship had progressed further with John commenting: "Unless I prayed without ceasing . . . [I] could not avoid some familiarity or other which was not needful. Sometimes I put my arm round her waist, sometimes took her by the hand, and sometimes kissed her."

When John called at the Caustons a few days later, he found her alone, recalling, entranced, "Her words, her eyes, her air, her every motion and gesture, were full of such a softness and sweetness." At that point, if he had proposed, she probably would have accepted. They met again the following day, but again John could not bring himself to take the final step:

> Finding her still the same, my resolution failed. At the
> end of a very serious conversation, I took her by the hand, and,
> perceiving she was not displeased, I was so utterly disarmed,
> that that hour I should have engaged myself for life, had it not
> been for the full persuasion I had of her entire sincerity and
> in consequence of which I doubted not but she was resolved
> (as she had said) "never to marry while she lived."

Immediately afterwards he regretted his actions and, although
he saw her every day, he did not touch her again. John consulted the
Moravian pastor John Töeltschig, who recommended that he should
marry Sophy. Charles Delamotte and Benjamin Ingham, however, did
not think she was a suitable bride. In a quandary, John even cast lots
marked "Marry," "Think not of it this year," and "Think of it no more"
in an attempt to come to a decision. The problem was that he believed
that celibacy was essential for his quest for personal perfection: "I
cannot take fire into my bosom and not be burnt," while battling with
"the weight of unholy desires."

Sophy, who had now rejected Mellichamp, gave the undecided
Wesley time to propose formally, but when he did not, she announced
her engagement to William Williamson. But even then she gave John
one last chance, for when she and Williamson came to see Wesley she
said, "Sir I have given Mr. Williamson my consent—unless you have anything to object." Sophy and Wesley were then left alone. Wesley almost
brought himself to the point of asking her to marry him. Recalled
John, "I sat there with the words on my tongue, 'Miss Sophy, will you
marry me?'" but he just could not bring himself to say it. Instead, he
asked if Williamson was a religious man. She repeated that she had
given her consent, unless Wesley objected. They both shed tears, but
when Williamson returned, John asked them both to assist each other
in serving God, then he kissed them both and turned away. Comments
Green regarding John's indecision:

> He [Wesley] wanted to remain a fellow of his Oxford
> college, but marriage would not allow it. He wanted his own
> sanctification, but sex interfered with it. At times he thought
> that Miss Sophy was in every way suited to be his bride; but at

other times he was less sure. He never seems to have doubted his own fitness to be her husband. He sought to be fair and judicial but he was unwise and even unjust.[39]

On Friday, March 11, 1737, Sophy Hopkey and Williamson set out for Purrysburg where they were married the following day. When Wesley heard about their departure, he felt physically ill. He tried to begin the day as usual with prayer and singing, but then recorded in his *Journal* that he was in pain. By mid-morning he was experiencing "much more pain" and recorded that he "Tried to pray, lost, sunk."

The relationship between Wesley and the Williamsons became more tense over the following weeks when it became apparent that Sophy had been seeing Williamson at least two weeks before their sudden engagement. John then discovered that Sophy had been in love with Thomas Mellichamp and had lied when she claimed that she wanted to be rid of him. Shortly after, a hurt and angry John wrote to the now pregnant Sophy, stating, "what I dislike about your past and present behaviour." He then excluded her from Holy Communion on the grounds that she was guilty of wrongdoing and had not openly declared herself to have truly repented. An enraged Williamson secured a warrant for John's arrest, claiming £1,000 damages for defamation. Fearing that he would be framed by Causton, who had hand-picked a Grand Jury in his determination to get a conviction, John made his escape to England in December 1737.

John seemed relieved to have escaped what now appeared an imprudent marriage. From then on he made a virtue out of not having a wife and children, claiming he had more time to serve God. He warned his followers: ". . . on this and every occasion, avoid all familiarity with women. This is a deadly poison both to them and to you. You cannot be too wary in this respect."

In 1743, John published his *Thoughts on Marriage and A Single Life* in which he propounded the virtues of remaining single and celibate, claiming, "We may safely say, 'Blessed are they who abstain from things lawful in themselves, in order to be more devoted to God.'" He was

---

[39] Green, *John Wesley*, 47.

still heralding the virtues of the single life in 1751, four days before he informed Charles that he was "resolved to marry." When challenged later about this apparent hypocrisy, he could only lamely reply that he married "for reasons best known to myself." In 1790, when asked again why he married, he could only answer, "Because I needed a home and to recover my health."

John considered that no Methodist preacher, including himself, should "preach one sermon or travel one day less in a married than in a single state." According to Stanley Ayling, "He had long ago linked his wiry body and ardent soul in a indissoluble union with the cause of Methodism."[40] Charles appeared to agree; he and John had made a pact that neither would marry without the other's permission. But he had a different, more emotional temperament than John, a fact discerned by General Oglethorpe, who advised Charles before he left Georgia for England in July 1736: "On many accounts I should recommend to you marriage, rather than celibacy. You are of a social temper and would find in a married state the difficulties of working out your salvation exceedingly lessened and your helps as much increased."

Charles was already in his forties when he met and fell madly in love with the attractive and shy twenty-one-year-old Sarah "Sally" Gwynne, daughter of Methodist converts Marmaduke Gwynne, a local magistrate, and Sarah, a rich heiress, while staying at their house in Garth, South Wales. Charles later revealed to Sally that "at first sight my soul seemed pleased to take acquaintance with you." The feelings were mutual, yet neither he nor Sally said anything to her parents because Charles was poor and nearly twice her age.

Charles revealed his marital intentions to John in November 1748, and to his surprise, his brother was delighted, believing Sally was an ideal choice. Charles then sought the approval of her family. While her father gave his blessing, her mother was not convinced that Charles had the means to comfortably support her daughter, so Charles had to prove that he was earning at least £100 per annum before she would give her consent. His only hope of securing a regular income was through the sale of his hymnbooks, but then John came forward and offered to

---

[40] Ayling, *John Wesley*, 217.

provide £100 a year from his own means. When Mrs. Gwynne was still unconvinced, the Wesleys' friend, Vincent Perronet, assured her that Charles and John's publications "will last and sell while any sense of true religion and learning still remain among us." Mrs. Gwynne finally gave her approval, but just when all appeared to be agreed, John seemed to have second thoughts about the marriage and spoke of withdrawing his offer of financial support. This may have been due to his fears that Sally's mother would try and prevent Charles' itinerant evangelism, but she assured him she would not interfere. John, then, relented and agreed to the marriage.

Charles was married on April 8, 1749, recording with delight: "At eight I led my Sally to church. . . . Mr. Gwynne gave her to me, under God. My brother joined our hands. It was a most solemn season of love! I never had more of the divine presence at the sacrament. My brother . . . prayed over us in strong faith. We walked back to the house, and he joined us again in prayer. Prayer and thanksgiving was our whole employment. We were cheerful without mirth, serious without sadness. . . . My brother seemed happiest among us."

The newlyweds took up residence in a modest, rented house on Charles Street in Bristol and later moved to more spacious accommodation in London when the family was given a house in Marylebone by a wealthy Methodist supporter in 1777. However, despite the annual stipend of £100, there were times when Charles was short of money and unable to pay his creditors, even having to pawn his coat at one point. John was unsympathetic. He even suggested that it was unreasonable for Charles to receive any money from Methodist funds. John insensitively wrote: "I could not do it, if it were my own case. I should account it robbery. I have often wondered how either your conscience or your sense of honour could bear it. . . . I desire only to spend and be spent in the work which God has given me to do."

John's indecision regarding the financial support he promised to Charles may also have been influenced by the fact that he had fallen in love himself and was considering marriage to the thirty-two-year-old housekeeper of the Orphan House in Newcastle, Grace Murray. She has been described as "Wesley's last love." John said of her that she was "such a person as I had sought in vain for many years, and determined not to part with." He may also have been influenced by the Methodist Conference in 1748, where the delegates challenged his negative view of marriage by claiming "that a believer might marry, without suffering loss in his soul."

Grace, the widow of a seaman named Alexander Murray, had become one of John's class leaders and then oversaw the Orphan House in Newcastle. She had traveled around the northern societies with him and proved her worth questioning and counseling the women members. On August 1, 1748, John was in Newcastle when he was taken ill and Grace attended to him. While she was nursing him back to health, he observed her, commenting: "I esteemed and loved her more and more. And when I was little recovered I told her, sliding into it I know not how, 'If ever I marry, I think you will be the person.'" History was repeating itself, for these were virtually the very words he had spoken to Sophy Hopkey twelve years before.

John later spoke more directly to Grace, and she replied, "This is too great a blessing for me, I can't tell how to believe it. This is all I could have wished for under Heaven, if I had dared to wish for it." He was now sure that they were engaged. The night before he left Newcastle he said to her: "I am convinced God has called you to be my fellow labourer in the Gospel. I will take you with me to Ireland in the spring. Now we must part for a time. But, if we meet again, I trust we shall part no more." Grace implored John to take her with him, and he relented. She accompanied him on a tour throughout Yorkshire and Lancashire. However, the situation was complicated by the fact that Grace had been courted by Methodist lay preacher John Bennet when she had nursed him during a long illness in 1746. Although Grace had not agreed to marry Bennet, he believed he was first in line and considered that John was abusing his position as Methodism's leader to pursue Grace even though he was unaware of their attachment.

When the party arrived in the town of Chinley, they met Bennet and then went on to Astbury in Cheshire. Wesley then made the fatal error of leaving Grace with Bennet with, according to Green, "an ignorance of human nature astonishing in one so widely traveled (an ignorance which he never outgrew)."[41] John went on to preach in Derbyshire, declaring, "I left her in Cheshire with John Bennet and went on my way rejoicing." Bennet subsequently asked Grace to marry him. Grace was unconvinced that John wanted to marry her, but she gave no answer to Bennet.

The following morning, Bennet asked Grace directly: "Is there not a contract between you and Mr Wesley?"

"There is not," she replied.

Two days later, Grace accepted his proposal and both wrote to John seeking his approval, with Grace adding that "she believed that it was the will of God." A devastated John, believing there was nothing that he could do to stop the union, gave them his consent, but Grace changed her mind and sent an affectionate letter to John who assumed her marriage to Bennet had been called off. She, John, and one of his lay preachers, William Tucker, then embarked for Ireland in April 1749. John wrote of Grace as they traveled throughout the country:

> I saw the work of God prosper in her hands. She lightened my burden more than can be expressed. She examined all the women in the smaller Societies and the believers in every place. She settled all the women-bands; visited the sick; prayed with the mourners; more and more of whom received remission of sins during her conversation on prayer. Meantime she was to be both a servant and friend, as well as a fellow-labourer in the Gospel. She provided everything I wanted. She told me with all faithfulness and freedom, if she thought anything amiss in my behaviour.

The success of Charles' marriage may have led to John questioning his own commitment to celibacy, for it was while they were in Dublin that he and Grace decided to enter into what was known as a spousal de praesenti, a marriage that had not been consummated. He declared solemnly, " I do take thee as my wife," and Grace replied, "I do take thee as my husband."

When they returned to Bristol, however, Grace was angered by John's affectionate behavior toward a society member called Molly

---

[41] Green, *John Wesley*, 95.

Francis, and "in a sudden fit of jealousy," she sent a love letter to Bennet, but then repented and informed John of her actions.

On August 30, 1749, John and Grace arrived in Epworth where they were met by John Bennet who claimed Grace "as his right." John left the room, convinced that Grace loved Bennet and that they "should marry without delay." But when he wrote her a note ending their relationship, she declared in a flood of tears: "My dear sir, how can you possibly think I love any other than you? I love you a thousand times better than I loved John Bennet in my life. But I know not what to do. I am afraid if I don't marry him he will run mad." John was troubled by the thought that if one of them did not withdraw Grace might die, recording, "So I again determined to give her up." However, John was in a quandary, "As I now knew she loved me, and as she was contracted to me before, I knew not whether I ought to let her go." When John and Grace set off for Newcastle, he insisted that Grace choose. She replied, "I am determined by conscience, as well as inclination to live and die with you."

Convinced that Bennet was manipulating Grace, John wrote him a long and accusing letter. He sent it by messenger, but inexplicably it was never delivered. Charles, however, received a copy of it. In part it read: "Was this consistent with gratitude or friendship? Indeed, with common justice? . . . Oh that you would take scripture and reason for your rule instead of blind and impetuous passion! . . . You may tear her away by violence. But my consent I cannot, dare not give: nor, I fear, can God give you his blessing." In the meantime, John and Grace moved on to Hindley Hill in Northumberland, where at her request they renewed their vows in the presence of Methodist lay preacher Christopher Hooper. John then left to fulfill a preaching engagement in Whitehaven, leaving Grace with friends.

When Charles found out about the proposed marriage, he was determined to stop what he was convinced was an unsuitable union. He considered Grace to be little better than a domestic servant; he was concerned that their marriage would jeopardize John's leadership of the movement and undermine "the whole work of God;" and he may have believed that Grace was in fact betrothed to Bennet first. Charles may have also felt that if John was discredited, he might be expected to do more or even assume the leadership of the movement. Charles went straight to Newcastle to speak to John, who by this time had moved on to Whitehaven. He found instead the agitated members of the Newcastle society, one of whom declared vehemently, "If John Wesley be not damned then there is no God." Charles' prejudice against Grace was further hardened when a woman named Jane Keith, who was jealous of Grace, informed him that "all the societies were ready to fly into pieces" if John went ahead with his unsuitable marriage.

Charles rode hard on to Whitehaven to confront John, warning, "All our preachers would leave us, all our Societies disperse, if you married so mean a woman." John responded by telling Charles: "As I knew she was pre-engaged to me, as I regarded not her birth, but her qualifications, and as I believed those consequences might be prevented, could see no valid objection yet."

Not satisfied with his brother's response, Charles galloped as fast as he could to Hindley Hill, where Grace was residing, burst in on her and proclaimed: "Grace Murray, you have broken my heart," and then promptly fainted. Charles gave her a letter that he had written which suggested that John had given her up and then took her by pillion to Newcastle, although Grace believed that he was taking her to John. Once at Newcastle, Charles and a number of the society members convinced her that she could never have John and that he had behaved in a dishonorable way towards her, with one declaring, "Good God, what will the world say? He is tired of her, and so thrusts his whore into a corner. Sister Murray, will you consent to this!" Reluctantly, Grace agreed to marry John Bennet, and they were married on October 3, 1749 at St Andrew's Church in Newcastle.

John arrived at Hindley Hill to be told that Grace had left with Charles two hours previously. He reacted passively, merely commenting, "The Lord gave and the Lord has taken away: blessed be the name of the Lord." But later, when John realized that he had lost Grace, he was heartbroken and sank into a state of depression, lamenting "in great heaviness, my heart was sinking in me like a stone." Only preaching was able to alleviate his distress.

The following day, John was told by George Whitefield, whom he met in Leeds, that Grace and Bennet were now married. Whitefield "wept and prayed" over Wesley, but John was too stunned even to shed a tear. Whitefield opposed the marriage and in his opinion believed Grace was John's wife, but Charles' "impetuosity prevailed and bore down all before it."

When Charles arrived, John was initially reluctant to see him until Whitefield persuaded him to do so. But there was a tense standoff, with Charles storming out, shouting: "You villain! I renounce all intercourse with you, but what I would have with a heathen man or publican." However, urged on by a weeping Whitefield and John Nelson, the brothers embraced silently. Then Bennet arrived, and both he and John kissed and wept in silence. As John quietly related the facts to Charles, his brother realized that he had mortally wounded his brother. Wrote John: "He seemed utterly amazed. He clearly saw I was not what he had thought, and now blamed her only." John was to write about Charles: "I can forgive, but who can redress the wrong? If I have any strength at all (and I have none but what I have received) it is in forgiving injuries."

A few days later, a grief-stricken John wrote to his friend Thomas Bigg in Newcastle: "Since I was six years old I never met with such a severe trial as for some days past. A wonderful train of providences had been preparing a fellow labourer. I fasted and prayed and strove all I could, but the sons of Zeruiah were too hard for me. The whole world fought against me; but above all my own familiar friend."

When John realized the full extent of Charles' betrayal, he vowed never to see him again. Charles, knowing of his brother's bitter resentment, descended into a deep depression. According to Green, "[John's] intimacy with his brother was never the same again. He forgave an action that seemed as treacherous as it was mean; but he would never again consult Charles on a matter of similar import." Tragically, it might have been better if John had done so, for within eighteen months he had contracted the worst of all possible marriages. As Gary Best says, "Though Grace Murray's name was never mentioned again, the ghost of what might have been if John had married her instead of Molly Vazeille continued to cast a permanent shadow over the relationship between the two brothers." John never trusted Charles to the same extent that he had before the Grace Murray affair. A coldness descended on their relationship that lasted a number of years, with Charles excluded from his brother's counsel.

Charles, for his part, clearly believed that he had acted in the best interests of his brother and the Methodist movement, writing, "God knows, as I told him [John], that I had saved him from a thousand false steps." And Charles had written to Grace at the height of the drama:

> Fain would I hope that you can say something in your defence (when I come to talk with you) which now I know not. But the case appears thus to me: You promised J[ohn] B[ennet] to marry him—since which you engaged yourself to another. How is that possible? And who is that other? One of such importance that his doing so dishonest an action would destroy himself and me and the whole work of God. It was on the very brink of ruin; but the snare is broken, and we are delivered.

In a letter to John Bennet, dated December 15, 1750, Charles claimed that he was attempting to rescue "the whole work of God," but acknowledged that it had ruined his relationship with John: "If the Lord Himself had not been on our side, well may we both and all Israel say, 'They had swallowed us up quick, and by us ourselves destroyed the whole work of God.' It is all over with our friend [John]. Only me he cannot love as before. But I must have patience and suffer all things that the gospel be not hindered."

Despite their estrangement, Charles was convinced that his relationship with John would recover eventually, confiding to Vincent Perronet, "I am persuaded we shall stand or fall together." But the strain of the affair had seriously depleted Charles' strength. He told Perronet that he was "next to useless. . . . For when I preach my word is without power or life. My spirit is that of the whole people. All are faint and weary. All seem on the brink of desperation."

Initially, John gave his blessing to the newly married couple and told Grace he would attempt to forgive her, but later he accused Bennet of behaving dishonorably:

> I was never yet convinced that your marrying Grace
> Murray was according to the will of God. . . . you proposed
> marriage without either my knowledge or consent. Was this
> well done? God warned you the same night that I had took her
> first. . . . I think you have done me the deepest wrong which
> I could receive on this side of the grave. But I will spare you.
> "Tis but a little time, and I shall be where the weary are at rest."

The rift between the two men never healed, particularly as John suggested that Bennet was too influenced by George Whitefield.

Bennet left the Methodist movement in 1751, taking with him more than a hundred members of the Bolton society and all but one of the society in Stockport. In 1754, he became pastor of a Calvinistic chapel in Warburton and died at the age of forty-five in 1759. Grace bore him five children, returned to the Wesleyan fold after her husband's death, and lived until 1803. John and Grace did not meet again for nearly forty years. When their paths crossed in 1788 at Moorfields where her son was preaching, he was eighty-five and she seventy-two. They had a short, cordial conversation and never saw each other again.

According to a Dr. Fitchett, "[John] Wesley was always ready to propose to the particular face that at that moment was bending over him in sickness." And so it was that in January 1751, John damaged his ankle in a fall on the ice-covered road over London Bridge and was nursed to recovery by one of Charles and Sally's acquaintances, Mary Vazeille, at her home in Threadneedle Street, London. She was a forty-one-year-old widow of Huguenot descent who was known as "Molly,"

On February 2, 1751, Charles recorded in his journal that: "My brother, returned from Oxford, sent for me and told me he was resolved to marry! I was thunderstruck and could only answer, he had given me the first blow, and his marriage would come like the coup de grace. Trusty Ned Perronet followed, and told me the person was Mrs. Vazeille! One of whom I had never had the least suspicion." Dismayed and disappointed at John's choice of wife, Charles wrote: "I refused his company to the chapel, and I retired to mourn with my faithful Sally. I groaned all the day and several following ones, under my own and people's burden. I could eat not pleasant food, nor preach, nor rest, either by night or by day."

John had given his "apology" for his pending marriage on February 17 at the Foundery society, but Charles was still staggered when he discovered that John had married Molly probably the following day without consulting him, particularly as he believed that she was "a woman of a sorrowful spirit" who had nothing in common with his brother. Wrote Charles: "At the Foundery, I heard my brother's apology. Several days afterwards I was one of the last that heard of his unhappy marriage." On February 27, John apologized again. Charles commented: "My brother came to the chapel-house with his wife. I was glad to see him; saluted her, stayed long enough to hear him preach, but, ran away when he began his apology."

One preacher said about John's marriage, an event that Green describes as "the worst mistake of John's life,"[42] that "Had he searched the whole kingdom he would scarcely have found a woman more unsuitable to the prospects of a happy marriage. There never was a more preposterous union. It is pretty certain that no love lighted their torches." And Ayling said of John Wesley that "By temperament and conviction, and long habit, he was a nomad. There was small prospect of him settling down at home, as Charles was beginning to do so."[43]

As soon as his foot had healed, John resumed traveling throughout Britain, writing frequent tender letters to his wife: ". . . you have surely a right to every proof of love I can give. . . . I feel you every day nearer to my heart. . . . I shall never love any creature better than I love you." He also gave her permission, unwisely as it turned out, to open letters addressed to him.

All seemed to go well at first, with Molly accompanying John on his ministry tours, despite considerable danger and discomfort. On July 6, 1752, she rode all day with John to Manchester and on to Whitehaven, while in Hull they were attacked by a mob. John wrote proudly of Molly: "Your name is precious among the people. They talk of you much and know not how to commend you enough, even for those little things, your plainness of dress, your sitting among the poor at the preaching, your using sage-tea and not being delicate in your food. Their way of

[42] Ibid., 104.

[43] Ayling, *John Wesley*, 216.

mentioning you often brings tears into my eyes. Bless God for all his benefits."

Within months of their union, however, Molly was complaining about being in a loveless marriage and of the rigors of sharing John's preaching campaigns, lacking his passion for mission. John struggled with this: "All my patience was put to the proof again and again. To hear persons at my ear fretting and murmuring at every thing is like tearing the flesh off my bones." In a letter written in the 1750s to his friend and supporter Ebenezer Blackwell, John tried to put on a brave face about his crumbling marriage: "My wife is at least as well as when we left London: the more she travels the better she bears it. It gives us yet another proof that whatever God calls us to be he will fit us for. . . . I was at first afraid she would not so well understand the behaviour of a Yorkshire mob; but there has been no trial: even the Methodists are now at peace throughout the kingdom."

Those close to John disliked Molly, with Vincent Perronet believing her to be "an angry, bitter spirit" and Charles revealing that he could only bear talking to her for two minutes at the Foundery without quarreling. Molly had never forgiven Charles for his negative reaction to her marrying John, even though he made every effort to convince her that he was "perfectly reconciled with her." In April 1755, Charles wrote to Sally, revealing his thoughts about Molly: "What shall you and I do to love her better? 'Love your enemies' is with man impossible: but is anything too hard for God? I fear you do not constantly pray for her. I must pray for her or sink into the spirit of revenge."

After more than nine years of marriage and years of complaining and arguments, John made it clear to Molly what he expected of her in a harsh and severe letter:

> Alas, that to this hour you should neither know your duty nor be willing to learn it! Indeed, if you are wise, whether a good woman or not, you would long since have given me a carte blanche: you would have said, "Tell me what to do and I will do it; tell me what to avoid and I will avoid it. I promised to obey you, and I will keep my word. Bid me to do anything, everything. In whatever is not sinful, I obey. You direct, I will follow the direction."

> This it had been your wisdom to have done long ago, instead of squabbling for almost these ten years. This it is both your wisdom and your duty to do now; and certainly better late than never. This must be your indispensable duty, till (1) I am an adulterer; (2) you can prove it. Till then I have the same right to claim obedience from you as you have to claim it from Noah Vazeille [her son]. Consequently, every act of disobedience is an act of rebellion against God and the King, as well as against Your affectionate Husband.

Even when their marriage had disintegrated, Wesley was still willing to express his admiration of her virtues: "I still love you for your indefatigable industry, your exact frugality, your uncommon neatness and cleanliness, both in your person, your clothes and all things around you."

Molly began opening all his letters before forwarding them and even broke into his bureau at home and showed his private letters to more than twenty different persons on purpose to make them have an ill opinion of him, with John commenting indignantly, "My wife picks my lock and steals my papers." Wesley complained to Blackwell while in Ireland, "And I have no friend or servant where she is who has honesty or courage to prevent it." In an attempt to stop the contents of his letters being revealed, John had a bureau constructed with secret compartments. Infuriated by her behavior, John wrote to Molly in November 1759: "You totally lose my esteem; you violently shock my love: you quite destroy my confidence. You oblige me to lock up everything, as from a thief. . . . You cut yourself off from joint prayer. For how can I pray with one that is daily watching to do me hurt. . . . O Molly, throw the fire out of your bosom! Shun as you would a serpent those that stir it up."

John had always had a habit of writing in an intimate, effusive, though innocent, manner to the female members of the societies, and this inflamed his wife's jealousy and her fears of his infidelity. She even accused him of having an affair with Charles' wife, Sally. To Sarah Ryan, the attractive housekeeper he appointed at Kingswood school in 1757, John wrote affectionately:

> You have refreshed my bowels in the Lord. . . . I not only
> excuse but love your simplicity; and whatever freedom you
> use, it will be welcome. . . . What can I do to help you? . . .
> The conversing with you, either by speaking or writing, is an
> unspeakable blessing to me. I cannot think of you without
> thinking of God. Others often lead me to him; but it is, as
> it were, going round about; you bring me straight into his
> presence.

Molly opened and read these letters. Consumed with rage and
jealousy, she appeared unexpectedly at a conference in Bristol when
Ryan was helping to serve dinner to John and sixty to seventy Methodist
preachers and exclaimed, "The whore now serving you has three husbands living!"

John Hampson witnessed an astonishing incident while traveling
with Wesley in Ireland:

> I was once on the point of committing murder. Once,
> when I was in the north of Ireland, I went into a room, and
> found Mrs.Wesley foaming with fury. Her husband was on the
> floor, where she had been trailing him by the hair of his head.
> She herself was still holding in her hand venerable locks which
> she had plucked up by the roots. I felt as though I could have
> knocked the soul out of her.

An angry John countered Molly's accusations by telling her:
"Suspect me no more, asperse me no more, provoke me no more. Do
not any longer contend for mastery, for power, money, or praise. . . .
Leave me to be governed by God and my conscience."

In January 1758, John revealed to Sarah Ryan that "Last Friday,
after many severe words, my wife left me, vowing she would see me
no more." She returned but she left home again in 1769 and again in
1771, vowing this time would be her last. Wesley reported in his *Journal*
laconically on January 23 of that year: "For what cause I know not, my
wife set out for Newcastle, purposing 'never to return'. [In Latin] I have
not left her. I have not sent her away. I shall not ask her to come back."

There were attempts at reconciliation, including a brief moment of
joy in 1772, but these failed to last. In 1775, Molly left for the final time,

taking with her some of his letters (which presumably were not hidden by Wesley), extracts of which she had shown to his doctrinal opponents and, suggested Luke Tyerman, to the *Morning Post* newspaper. Molly claimed that his last words to her as she was leaving him were, "I hope I shall see your wicked face no more," although he denied it.

Life was certainly not easy for Molly. Apart from marital strife, she suffered from a number of debilitating illnesses, was defrauded of much of her money, had a son who died, another who proved to be a "grievous cross," and a daughter who was in poor health. Typically, John suggested whether her misfortunes were sent by God "to break the impetuosity and soften the hardness" of her spirit.

Two years later in September 1777, when Molly expressed a desire to return to him, Wesley informed her that "The water is spilt and cannot be gathered up again": "All you can do now . . . is to unsay what you have said. For instance, you have said over and over that I lived in adultery these twenty years. Do you believe this, or do you not? If you do, how can you think of living with such a monster? If you do not, give it me under your hand. Is not this the least you can do?"

In contrast to John's disastrous liaison, Charles' marriage to Sally, whom he often described as "my best friend," proved happy and enduring: "I look back with delight on every step, every circumstance, in that whole design of providential love. I rejoice with great joy at our blessed union . . . [and] desire to thank my great Benefactor for giving you to my bosom." And in another letter Charles wrote, "Every hour of every day you are laid upon my heart; so that I make mention of you in all my prayers."

From the 1750s onward, Charles focused ever more attention on his wife and family. Sally had been stricken with smallpox in 1753, and when he was informed of this, he traveled immediately to Bristol to be by her side. With great faith and fortitude, Charles agreed to take with him a mentally ill man, John Hutchinson, whom he had been helping, for Hutchinson was threatening to commit suicide if Charles left without him. It was a nightmare of a journey, with Hutchinson ranting and raving and attacking Charles who tried to stop him from killing himself: "My flesh shrank at taking him in, a miserable comforter to me in my lowest distress. . . . Instead of comforting me all the way [he] insulted my sorrow and spoke against my wife. I was so hindered and distracted by him that I could pray very little."

Charles was exhausted by the time he reached Bristol and shocked when he saw his beloved Sally: "I found my dearest friend on a restless bed of pain, loaded with the worst kind of disease. . . . From the sole of the foot, even unto the head, there is no soundness in her; but wounds and putrefying sores." When Charles suggested to Hutchinson that it might be better if he found alternate lodgings and left him to look after his wife, the latter flew into a rage. Fortunately, Charles was able to persuade Hutchinson to stay elsewhere.

Sally survived but was left horribly scarred. Charles, however, declared that he loved her even more.

Their sixteen-month-old son John, however, died of the disease. Four other children—John James, Martha Maria, Susanna, and Selina—died in infancy, increasing Charles' unwillingness to be apart from his wife and children. Three children—Charley (Charles, 1757), Sally (Sarah, 1759), and Sammy (Samuel, 1766)—survived, with the two sons becoming talented musicians, while Sally sang and played the harpsichord. In July 1755, Charles and Sally's second child, Martha Maria, died. When Sally became pregnant again in 1757, Charles was determined not to cause her any anxiety by traveling too great a distance: "My heart is with you always, or not at all; for no one can supply your place." Their third child, christened Charles, was born on December 11, 1757.

Charles' beloved wife Sally and his children were at his bedside when he died on March 29, 1788. Sally was granted an annual pension of £50 by the Methodist movement and lived to the age of ninety-six, dying in December 1822. His daughter, Sally, died six years later, while Charles junior died in May 1834 and Samuel in October 1837.

In October 1778, John wrote to Molly for the last time:

> You have laid innumerable stumbling blocks in the way, both of the wise and the unwise. You have served the cause and increased the number of rebels, deists, atheists and weakened the hands of those that love and fear God. If you were to live

a thousand years twice told you could not undo the mischief
which you have done. And until you have done all you can
towards it, I bid you Farewell!

John and Molly never met again. When she died in London on
October 8, 1781, he was not informed for several days of the details
concerning her funeral. He recorded in his *Journal*, without a trace of
emotion: "I came to London and was informed that my wife died on
Monday. This evening she was buried, though I was not informed of
it till a day or two after." In her will she bequeathed him the wedding
ring he had given her thirty years before.

John's paternal relationships with women continued into his old
age. A large circle of young Methodist women received his exhortations,
inquiries into their thoughts and feelings, and expressions of his concern and affection. He always tried to dissuade them from marriage.
The class leader Nancy Bolton, for example, was saved from three
suitors by his intervention and only married after his death. Yet John
also sought to keep his male preachers unattached, which may have
reflected his own disastrous marriage.

A small number of women preachers played a significant role in
John's Connexion—the Methodist group that he led. He wrote to John
Peacock of Grimsby in March 1780, demanding "a final stop to the
preaching of women in this circuit. If it were suffered it would grow, and
we know not where it would end." Yet, he supported them at other times.
John Fletcher, a close friend of both John and Charles, married Mary
Bosanquet in 1781, and they operated in his Madeley parish virtually as
joint ministers until his death in 1785. In 1787, John went a step further
and recognized Sarah Mallet as a preacher in Norwich, warning her,
"You must expect to be censured, [but] go on and fear nothing but sin."
After John's death, the opponents of female preachers in the Methodist
movement had his policy reversed, despite the successful evangelistic
campaigns of women such as Elizabeth Evans during the 1790s.

9

BE PERFECT AS YOUR FATHER IN HEAVEN IS PERFECT

Christian perfection is the goal of our religious race; the stand whereon our crown of reward is placed.

—CHARLES WESLEY

There was no other doctrine that caused more strife and controversy within the Methodist movement than Christian perfection, but it was a doctrine beloved by John Wesley and one that he refused to relinquish, although he did moderate his views over the years. Even John admitted that it caused division: "There is scarcely any expression in Holy Writ which has given more offence than this. The word perfect is what many cannot bear; the very sound of it is an abomination to them. And whoever preaches perfection (as the phrase is) that is, asserts that it is attainable in this life, runs great hazzard of being counted by them worse than a heathen or a publican."

On January 1, 1733, John preached the first of numerous sermons on Christian perfection at St. Mary's Church in Oxford, in which he preached that striving for perfection was a natural response to the call of Christ to "be perfect as your Father in Heaven is perfect." In the preface of *Hymns and Sacred Poems*, published jointly by John and Charles Wesley in 1739, they defined their belief in Christian perfection as: "Faith working by love in us is the length and breadth and depth and height of Christian perfection. This commandment have we from Christ, that he who loves God, loves his neighbour also; and that we manifest our love by doing good unto all men, especially to them that are of the household of faith."

In 1729, Charles read Henry Scougal's devotional classic *The Life of God in the Soul of Man* (and then lent it to George Whitefield). Scougal described genuine religion as a "union of the soul with God, a real participation in the Divine nature, the image of God drawn upon the soul, or in the Apostle's phrase, it is Christ formed within us." In October 1735, while on his way to Georgia, Charles wrote: "Christian perfection is the goal of our religious race; the stand whereon our crown of reward is placed. Hitherto therefore must all our desires be bent; hitherto must all our desires tend. To this are all the promises of the gospel made."

During his time at Oxford and in Georgia, John strove for perfect holiness through fasting, prayer, self-examination, and the sacraments, drawing ideas from the Early Fathers and medieval mystics. In 1725, he read Bishop Jeremy Taylor's *Rule and Exercises of Holy Living and Dying*, published in the 1650s, and was particularly affected by the part that spoke of the purity of intention. Of this Wesley wrote, "I instantly resolved to dedicate all my life to God; all my thoughts and words and actions, being thoroughly convinced there was no middle way; but that every part of my life (not some only) must either be a sacrifice to God or myself; that is, in effect, to the devil." This need for dedication to God was reinforced a year later when he read Thomas à Kempis' *The Christian Pattern or the Imitation of Christ*. Concerning this book's impact, John said:

> The nature and extent of inward religion, the religion of the heart, now appeared to me in a stronger light than ever it had done before. I saw that giving even all my life to God (supposing it possible to do this and to go no further) would profit me nothing unless I gave my heart, yes, all my heart, to Him. . . . I began to see that true religion was seated in the heart, and that God's law extended to all our thoughts as well as words and actions.

Interestingly, John was also annoyed by *The Imitation*'s strictness. As he expressed to his mother: "I can't think that when God sent us into the world he had irreversibly decreed that we should be perpetually miserable in it . . . that all mirth is vain and useless, if not sinful. Why then does the Psalmist so often exhort us to rejoice in the Lord?"

John followed this book by reading the former Anglican clergyman William Law's *A Practical Treatise on Christian Perfection*, which "convinced me more than ever of the absolute impossibility of being half a Christian." According to John, in 1729, he "began not only to read but to study the Bible as the one and only standard of truth, and the only model of pure religion. From this I saw in a clearer and clearer light the indispensable necessity of having the mind which was in Christ and of walking as Christ also walked." In 1741, John came across a rare seventeenth-century theological work by the former Archbishop of Canterbury's chaplain Robert Gell, who claimed that God's perfection could be achieved while a person still lived and that it was possible to be dead to sin. In that year John published a sermon on Christian perfection, although he may not have preached it, after receiving the blessing of the Bishop of London, Edmund Gibson, in which he attempted to clarify his position on Christian perfection and sinless perfection, a term he claimed he never used and regarded as unattainable while on earth:

> Christian perfection, therefore, does not imply (as some seem to have imagined) an exemption either from ignorance or mistake, or from infirmities or temptations. Indeed, Christian perfection is only another term for holiness. They are two names for the same thing. Thus everyone who is perfect is holy; and everyone who is holy is, in the scripture sense, perfect. Yet we may, lastly, observe, that neither in this respect is there any absolute perfection on earth. There is no Perfection of degrees, as it is termed—none which does not admit of a continual increase. So that, however much anyone has attained or in however high a degree one is perfect, he or she still has need to grow in grace and advance daily in the knowledge and love of God his Saviour.

In conformity, therefore, both to the doctrine of St. John and to the whole tenor of the New Testament, we fix this conclusion—a Christian is so far perfect as not to commit sin.... This is the glorious privilege of every Christian; indeed though he be but a babe in Christ.

At the first Methodist conference in 1744, John was asked what he meant by Christian perfection.

Question. What is implied in being a perfect Christian?

Answer. The loving God with all our heart, soul and might.

Q. Does this imply that all inward sin is taken away?

A. Undoubtedly, or how can we be said to be "saved from all our uncleanesses.

Then at the 1759 conference, he was again questioned on the subject:

Question. What is Christian perfection?

Answer. The loving God with all our heart, mind, soul and strength. This implies that no wrong temper, none contrary to love, remains in the soul; and that all the thoughts, words and actions are governed by pure love.

Q. Do you affirm that this perfection excludes all infirmities, ignorance and mistake?

A. I continually affirm quite the contrary, and always have done so.

Q. But how can every thought, word and work be governed by pure love and the individual be subject at the same time to ignorance and mistake?

A. I see no contradiction here: One may be filled with pure love and still be liable to mistake. Indeed, I do not expect to be freed from actual mistakes till this mortal puts on immortality. I believe this to be a natural consequence of the soul's dwelling in flesh and blood.

Wesley went on to explain what he believed to be the difference between what he termed voluntary and involuntary sin:

> To explain myself a little further. . . . Not only sin properly so called (that is, a voluntary transgression of a known law) but sin, improperly so called (that is an involuntary transgression of a divine law, known or unknown) needs the atoning blood. I believe there is no such perfection in this life as excludes these involuntary transgressions which I apprehend to be naturally consequent on the ignorance and mistakes inseparable from mortality. Therefore sinless perfection is a phrase I never use lest I should seem to contradict myself. I believe that a person filled with the love of God is still liable to these involuntary transgressions. Such transgressions you may call sins, if you please; I do not, for the reasons above-mentioned.

In a letter to the Methodists in Otley, dated July 7, 1761, John described his belief in perfection:

> The perfection I teach is perfect love; loving God with all the heart: receiving Christ as Prophet, Priest and King, to reign alone over all our thoughts, words and actions. . . . To say that Christ will not reign alone in our hearts, in this life, will not enable us to give Him all our hearts. This, in my judgement, is making Him half a Saviour; He can be no more, if He does not quite save us from our sins.

In another letter to a Dorothy Furly in September 1762, John emphasized that Christian perfection is "an instantaneous deliverance from all sin," that is compatible "with living in a corruptible body; for this makes it impossible 'always to think right.' While we breathe we shall more or less mistake. If, therefore, Christian perfection implies this, we must not expect it till death."

John Wesley's belief in Christian perfection remained constant, if not consistent, throughout his life, despite severe criticism within the Methodist movement and by his opponents. In old age he commented, "Forty years ago I knew and preached every Christian doctrine which I preach now." He was convinced, as he explained to one of his preachers in 1766, that "When Christian perfection is not strongly and explicitly preached, there is seldom any remarkable blessing from God." His doctrine of perfection was reinforced by the publication of *A Plain Account Of Christian Perfection* in the same year. Wrote John:

> But whom do you mean by one who is perfect? We mean one in whom is the mind that was in Christ and who so walks as Christ also walked; one who has "clean hands and a pure heart" or that is cleansed from all filthiness of flesh and spirit; one in whom is no occasion of stumbling and who, accordingly, does not commit sin. To declare this a little more particularly: we understand by that scriptural expression a perfect man is one in whom God has fulfilled His faithful Word, "I cleanse you from all your filthiness and from all your idols. . . . I will deliver you from all your uncleannesses."

Further Thoughts on Christian Perfection followed a year later to strengthen confidence in perfection as a goal for all Christians. John made it clear that no human could be truly perfect because of "unavoidable defects of human understanding" and "humanity's innate capacity to make mistakes." He also argued against "that daughter of pride, enthusiasm," which encouraged people to assume that "dreams, voices, impressions, visions, or revelations" must be from God when they "may be from the devil."

> By perfection I mean the humble, gentle, patient love of God, and our neighbour: ruling our tempers, words, actions. I do not include an impossibility of falling from it, either in part or in whole. Therefore, I retract several expressions in our Hymns that partly express, partly imply, such an impossibility. And I do not contend for the term sinless, though I do not object against it. As to the manner, I believe this perfection is always wrought in the soul by a simple act of faith; consequently, in an instant. But I believe a gradual work, both preceding and following that instant.
>
> As to the time. I believe this instant generally is the instant of death, the moment before the soul leaves the body. But I believe it may be ten, twenty, or forty years before. I believe it is usually many years after justification; but that

it may be within five years or five months after it, I know no conclusive argument to the contrary. If it must be many years after justification, I would be glad to know how many. And how many days or months, or even years, can anyone allow to be between perfection and death? How far from justification must it be; and how near to death?

But whereas John always spoke of a qualified but instantaneous perfection, Charles stressed an unqualified, gradual perfection that continued throughout a Christian's life until death, when it was experienced in full. Whereas John believed that God never deserted a true believer, Charles argued that God sometimes deliberately withdrew his presence from people in order to test them, so periods of "spiritual darkness" were to be expected by all, however strong their faith. John believed perfection was possible as soon as a believer's faith was strong enough; Charles repeated his opinion that it was only achievable after death. John disagreed, believing that "to set perfection too high (so high as no man that we ever heard or read of attained) is the most effectual . . . way of driving it out of this world."

Determined to provide living proof of his doctrine, John held up as an example of Christian perfection John Fletcher, his friend and heir-apparent, who had become vicar of Madeley in Shropshire in 1760. But Fletcher refused to accept being made out to be a saint, declaring: "My perfection is to see my imperfection; my comfort to feel I have the world, flesh and devil to overthrow through the Spirit and merits of my dear Saviour; and my desire and hope is to love God with all my heart, mind, soul and strength, to the last gasp of my life. This is my perfection. I know no other."

Charles also believed that he had come across an example of his perception of Christian perfection when he visited a Mrs. Hooper several times and was present when she died. "My soul was tenderly affected for her sufferings, yet the joy swallowed up the sorrow. How much more then did her consolations bound! . . . I asked her whether she was not in great pain. 'Yes,' she answered, 'but in greater joy. I would not be without either.' 'But do you prefer life or death?' She replied,

'All is alike to me; let Christ choose; I have no will of my own.' This is that holiness, or absolute resignation, or Christian perfection."

Disquiet was growing among the Methodist societies at what was seen as John's naivety and how easily he could be deceived, particularly when a number of Methodists in Otley, Yorkshire, claimed that they had been entirely sanctified, "being saved from all sin." In January 1760, John wrote in his *Journal*: "I desired those who believed they were saved from sin (sixteen or seventeen in number) to meet me at noon, to whom I gave such cautions and instructions as I judged needful." In March, John met with others "who believed they were saved from sin," reporting "that they feel no inward sin and, to the best of their knowledge, commit no outward sin . . . they see and love God every moment and 'pray, rejoice and give thanks evermore' . . . have constantly as clear a witness from God of sanctification as they of justification." A year later in 1761, John met with around forty people in London "who believe God has delivered them from the root of bitterness. The number increases daily."

However, Charles contended that the shallow lifestyles of these self-proclaimed perfectionists stood in stark contrast to their arrogant boasts. He argued that the nature of perfect love was only fully understood and appreciated by the saints. For that reason anyone truly worthy of the name Christian accepted perfection as achievable only after death.

The Methodist preacher Peter Jacko wrote to Charles in September 1761 regarding the discussions at that year's conference, reporting:

> It is determined that there are no texts of Scripture which will absolutely support instantaneous Perfection; that there is no state in this world which will absolutely exempt the person in it from sin and that therefore they have need of caution and etc. These are some of the conclusions we came to. The rest, I suppose, your Brother will tell you soon. . . . Whether he and the rest of the contenders on the other side of the question will abide by these conclusions time will determine.

To restore a sense of propriety and reason within the movement, Charles pleaded with John to expel any of those who claimed to be perfect and were clearly not by their lifestyle, but John hesitated, informing Charles in January 1762 that he needed to be gentle with the perfectionists: "There is need of a lady's hand, as well as a lion's heart." John ignored Charles' and others' misgivings and made the fatal error of giving one of his longest-serving lay preachers, Thomas Maxfield, the task of promoting perfection among the London societies. Maxfield came under the influence of an ex-soldier and self-proclaimed prophet named George Bell who claimed that the world was going to end on February 28, 1763. Maxfield, Bell, and others were preaching that by faith a person could become "as perfect as an angel." When Bell claimed that he had cured a woman who was terminally ill with breast cancer, John declared it to be a miracle, even though many in the movement denounced Bell's claim as deception.

However, with around a hundred Methodists quitting the movement in disgust over Bell and with ever more absurd claims of perfection threatening to undermine the movement, John was reluctantly forced to moderate his earlier enthusiasm for Christian perfection. He warned those who claimed to be perfect that they could easily lose their state of perfection if sin reentered their hearts:

> To expect deliverance from wandering thoughts, occasioned by evil spirits, is to expect that the devil should die or fall sleep. To expect deliverance from those [temptations] which are occasioned by other men, is to expect either that all men should cease from the earth, or that we should be absolutely secluded from them. And to pray for deliverance from those [temptations] which are occasioned by the body, is, in effect, to pray that we may leave the body.

On November 2, 1762, John wrote to Thomas Maxfield warning him about his preaching on perfection:

> I disliked your supposing man may be perfect "as an angel"; that he can be absolutely perfect; that he can be infallible, or above being tempted; or that the moment he is pure in heart he cannot fall from it. . . . I dislike something that has the appearance of enthusiasm, overvaluing feelings and inward impressions; mistaking the mere work of imagination

for the voice of the Spirit; expecting the end without the means; and undervaluing reason, knowledge and wisdom in general. . . . But what I most dislike is your littleness of love . . . your bigotry and . . . your divisive spirit.

By December, John went further, describing Maxfield as "inimitably wrong-headed" and criticized as unedifying the meetings held by the perfectionists: "[They are] like a bear garden; full of noise, brawling, cursing, swearing, blasphemy and confusion. . . . Those who prayed were partly the occasion of this, by their horrid screaming and unscriptural, enthusiastic expressions." And of George Bell he commented, "He now spoke as from God what I knew God had not spoken."

For many, however, John's rebukes were woefully insufficient: they wanted decisive action and were shocked at his vacillation over the issue. Among these critics was Methodist preacher John Downey:

I consider the follies and extravagance of the witnesses as the devices of Satan to cast a blemish on the real work of God. . . . As to the folly of the enthusiasts, Mr. Charles hears every week less or more. Why his brother suffers them we cannot tell. He threatens, but cannot find in his heart to put execution. The consequence is the talk of all the town and entertainment for the newspapers.

William Romaine, one of Lady Huntingdon's preachers, observed: "I pity Mr. John from my heart. His societies are in great confusion; and the point, which brought them into the wilderness of rant and madness, is still insisted on as much as ever. I fear the end of this delusion. . . . Perfection is still the cry . . . and brotherly love is almost lost in our disputes."

As far back as the early 1740s, Whitefield had been an opponent of Christian perfection. He wrote to John criticizing him for believing that sinless perfection was possible in this life: "I cannot agree that the inbeing of sin is to be destroyed in this life. . . . What a fond conceit is it to cry up perfection and yet cry down the doctrine of final perseverance." He also questioned John's doctrine of sin and mocked his practice of casting lots.

Stung by the criticism, particularly from among his own preachers, John published a letter in the January 8, 1763 edition of the *London Chronicle* newspaper in which he made it clear that George Bell and his followers were not part of the Methodist movement:

> One Bell, said to be a Lifeguardsman, holds forth to an assembly, near Hanover Square. He is supposed to belong to the Methodists; but he advances things which many Methodists abhor. Nevertheless his delusions spread. Many of his followers think themselves perfect and declare they shall never die, "because," as they say, "our dear Lord, who will certainly come a second time, is at the door and we shall see him come."

Charles bitterly resented that John had ignored his advice for four years, writing to Joseph Clowney, a Methodist preacher on February 11, 1763, lamenting: "Sad havoc Satan has made of the flock, since you and I were first acquainted. . . . I had a warning four years ago of that flood of enthusiasm which has now overflowed us, and of the sect of ranters that should arise out of the Perfect witnesses. My late hymns are a farther standing testimony."

The debate continued to rage over the doctrine of Christian perfection. In February 1766, John Fletcher wrote to John Wesley to explain his concept of perfection:

> I think we must define exactly what we mean by the perfection which is attainable here. In so doing we may, through mercy, obviate the scoffs of the carnal, and the misapprehension of the spiritual world, at least, in part. . . . The light that I now see the thing in, is this: as the body is not capable of perfection on this side of the grave, all those powers of the soul whose exertion depends, in part, of the frame and well being of the body, or the happy flow of the animal spirits, will not, cannot be perfected here. . . . The one power, that I see can be perfected here, because it is altogether independent from the body, is the will, of course the affections so far as they work on the will.

John replied to Fletcher's letter the following day:

> What I mean by perfection, I have defined both in the
> first, and in the farther thoughts upon that subject. "Pure
> love, rejoicing evermore, praying always, in everything giving
> thanks." And I incline to think, the account you give will
> amount to the same thing. . . . But we may observe, that,
> naturally speaking, the animal frame will affect more or less
> every power of the soul; seeing, at present, the soul can no
> more love that it can think any otherwise that by the help of
> bodily organs. If, therefore, we either think, speak, or love
> aright, it must be by power from on high.

Despite all the controversies, John still clung tenaciously to his view
of Christian perfection, writing to Charles on July 9, 1766:

> That perfection which I believe, I can boldly preach;
> because, I think, I see five hundred witnesses of it. Of that
> perfection which you preach, you think you do not see any
> witness at all. I wonder you do not, in this article, fall in plumb
> with Mr. Whitefield. For do you not, as well as he, ask, "Where
> are the perfect ones?" I verily believe there are none. . . . I
> cordially assent to his opinion, that there is no perfection here
> such as you describe; at least, I never met with an instance
> of it, and I doubt I never shall. Therefore, I still think, to set
> perfection so high is effectually to renounce it.

But the damage had already been done. Even John was forced to admit
that "They made the very name of Perfection stink in the nostrils of
those who loved and honoured it before."

By May 1768, John revealed to Charles that he was at the end of
his tether and feeling isolated: "I am at my wits end with regard to two
things—The Church [meaning the Church of England] and Christian
perfection," and he urged his brother to stand by him on both issues:
"Unless both you and I stand in the gap in good earnest, the Methodists
will drop them both [the Church and Christian perfection]. Talking
will not avail. We must do, or be borne away. Will you set shoulder to
shoulder? If so think deeply upon the matter, and tell me what can be
done." John finished with an exhortation in Latin: "Come, be a man!

Stretch your nerves." A few week later, John wrote again to Charles, this time in a state of indecision: "What shall we do? I think it is high time that you and I at least should come to a point. Shall we go on asserting Perfection against the world? Or shall we quietly let it drop? . . . I am weary of intestine [sic] war, of preachers quoting one of us against the other. At length let us fix something for good and all."

10

DIABOLICAL STILLNESS

. . . swallowed up in the dead sea of stillness . . .

—CHARLES WESLEY

At the beginning of May 1738, John Wesley joined with Peter Böhler and James Hutton to establish the statutes for a new religious society which met first at Hutton's house and then moved to a room in Fetter Lane off Fleet Street in London. Both John and Charles agreed to act as pastors of the society, although in reality it was John who became its real leader due to Charles' poor health. Eight individuals were identified as potential members, six of whom were former Oxford Methodists, including Benjamin Ingham and George Whitefield. It was decided that members would meet together on a weekly basis in small bands for mutual confession and prayer, together with the occasional fast and love feast (Eucharist). It is likely that Böhler hoped that the Fetter Lane gathering would become the first Moravian society in Britain, but he had to leave for America on May 4 and urged John and Charles to continue to avoid the "sin of unbelief."

In June 1738, John left for Germany with Benjamin Ingham, without informing Charles. Over the next three months, they visited the University of Jena and the Moravian Brethren communities in Herrnhut and Marienborn, where they stayed with their leader, Count Nikolaus von Zinzendorf. Initially, John was enamored by the Christian community. "I am with a Church whose conversation is in heaven," he gushed to his brother Samuel. He wrote to Charles the same day: "The spirit of the Brethren is beyond our highest expectation. Young and old, they breathe nothing but faith and love at all times and places."

The experience transformed Ingham into a committed Moravian, but John began to have reservations about their doctrine and the dictatorial Zinzendorf himself, whom he felt had too much authority: "Is not the Count all in all? Are not the rest mere shadows; calling him Rabbi; almost implicitly both believing and obeying him?" Much to John's concern he discovered that the Moravians did not consider the Bible as divinely inspired but rather as a collection of ancient texts. They believed that the process of God's revelation was without end and ongoing. They also had an almost obsessive focus on the sufferings of Christ, which they referred to as "blood and wounds teaching." However, there were three aspects of Moravian life that John would adopt and employ when establishing the Methodist societies: the importance of education, love feasts, and occasional all-night vigils that had been common in the early, first-century church.

John returned to England in September 1738. Then he and Charles spent most of their time in Bristol where they established two new preaching houses: one was built on the site of the proposed miners' school at Kingswood and the other in the center of Bristol. The latter became known as the "New Room," which was funded by contributions from the ninety members of the two societies that met at Nicholas Street and Baldwin Street, later forming one United Society in Bristol. Another United Society was formed by combining the societies in London.

In October 1739, Philip Henry Molther arrived in London from Germany en route to the Moravian settlement in Pennsylvania and ended up staying a year, before Zinzendorf recalled him to Germany. Like Böhler, Molther came from the Alsace region of France, had studied theology at the University of Jena, and had been a tutor to Zinzendorf's son. When he visited the Fetter Lane Society when John and Charles were away in Bristol, he was shocked at how animated and noisy the meetings in London were. He described being "almost terror-stricken at hearing their sighing and groaning, their whining and howling, which strange proceeding they call the demonstration of the Spirit and power."

John returned to London on November 1, 1739 and was disturbed to discover that Molther had been teaching his Quietest doctrines to the Fetter Lane congregation. One member in particular had been convinced by Molther that she had no faith and should stop doing good works until she received the gift of faith. Molther believed that there were no degrees of faith, only full assurance, and that could only be achieved by waiting in stillness for Christ to impart it. Therefore, worship, fasting, private prayer, attending communion, or engaging in social outreach were unnecessary for those who knew they were saved, a doctrine Charles scathingly called "diabolical stillness." Both the Wesleys believed that communion was one of the most important means by which God's grace was experienced. And they believed it was essential that Christians should express their faith by faithfully obeying the commands of Christ. Molther claimed John and Charles must lack proper faith if they did not understand that, once assured of salvation, any activity became pointless.

While in London, two businessmen called Watkins and Ball approached John to establish a preaching house similar to the one in Bristol. They recommended a large, derelict brick building in Windmill Street called the Foundery, which had been used to cast cannon until a massive explosion in 1716 had reduced it to a "vast, uncouth heap of ruins." It was cheap at only £150, but the required extensive renovations increased the bill to more than £800. Its greatest significance was that it providentially provided John and Charles with an alternative meeting place to Fetter Lane after it became clear that no compromise with the Moravians could be reached. It became the Methodist movement's headquarters until the City Road Chapel was established in 1778. It also would provide a home to John and Charles' mother, Susanna, until she died in 1742 at the age of seventy-three.

John and Charles returned to Bristol, but an anonymous letter from London, dated December 4, 1739, warned them about what was happening at Fetter Lane in their absence:

> This day I was told by one that does not belong to the
> bands, that the society would be divided. . . . I believe Brother
> Hutton, Clark, Edmonds and Bray are determined to go
> on, according to Mr. Molther's directions and to "raise up
> a church," as they term it; and I supposed above half our
> brethren are on their side. But they are so very confused they
> don't know how to go on; yet are unwilling to be taught, except
> by the Moravians.

It was painful for Charles to discover that two of his closest
friends—James Hutton and John Bray, who would be joined by Charles
Delamotte—could be counted among the "still brethren." After disputing with Bray and others, Charles wrote, "I laboured for peace, but
only the Almighty can root out those cursed tares of pride, contempt
and self-suffiency with which our Moravianised brethren are overrun."

Convinced now that John was driven by ambition, Hutton complained to Count Zinzendorf that Wesley should be content "to waken
souls in preaching, but not to lead them to Christ. But he will have
the glory of doing things." George Stonehouse, vicar of Islington, was
another of Charles' friends who sided with the Moravians. Observed
Charles, "He is now taught to teach, that there are no degrees of faith;
no forgiveness or faith, where any unbelief remains; any doubt or fear
or sorrow." Such was the Moravians' influence on Stonehouse that he
refused to pray and read the Bible with or bring the sacrament to an
elderly dying woman. He informed her daughter that "These outward
things must be laid aside. She has nothing to do but be still." When
John protested, Stonehouse announced that he was going to leave the
Church, declaring "no honest man can officiate as a minister in the
Church of England."

"The Philistines have been upon him and prevailed," wrote Charles
Wesley of Charles Delamotte, but Delamotte urged Charles not to make
the adherence to Methodist spiritual disciplines an issue. Remarked
Delamotte: "They are mere outward things. Our brethren have left
them off. It would only cause divisions to bring them up again. Let them
drop, and speak of weightier matters of law." Charles reported sadly in
his journal of an unfortunate visit to the Delamotte residence: "I went
straight to Blendon; no longer Blendon to me. They could hardly force

The parents of John and Charles Wesley

Samuel Wesley (1662–1735)

Susanna Wesley (1669–1742)

John Wesley by John Faber Jr., published by and after John Michael Williams, published 10 September 1743 © National Portrait Gallery, London

CHARLES WESLEY, A.M.
Presbyter of the Church of England, and late Student of Christ Church.
LONDON
Publish'd 20.th March 1786, by John Atlay at the New Chapel, City Road.

Born 1708. Died 1788. Aged 80.

Charles Wesley by Jonathan Spilsbury, published 1786 © National Portrait Gallery, London

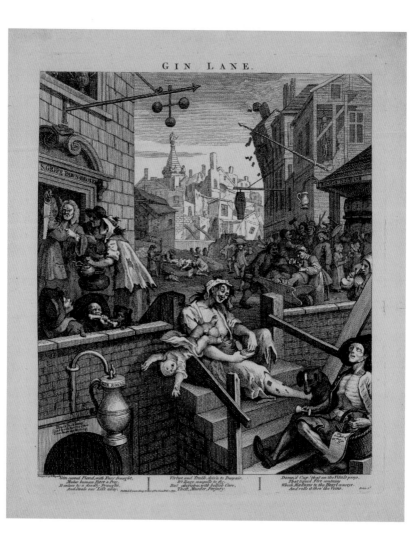

Gin Lane in London, by William Hogarth, painted in 1751

George Whitefield

THE OXFORD METHODISTS.

The Oxford Methodists, otherwise known as The Holy Club. John Wesley stands at the head of the table. To his immediate right (in the background) is George Whitefield. Seated at the table to Whitefield's right are James Hervey, Robert Kirkham (wearing glasses), Benjamin Ingham in conversation with Charles Wesley, followed by William Morgan. John Gambold is seen removing a book from the shelf on the left.

John Wesley preaching to the Native Americans

John Wesley preaching to the mob at Wednesbury in October 1743

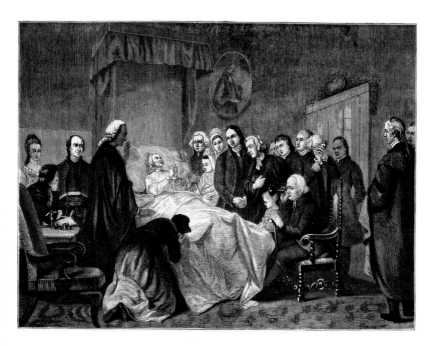

The death of John Wesley on 2 March 1791

John Wesley, painted in 1788 by William Hamilton
© National Portrait Gallery, London

Early portrait of Charles Wesley © Alamy

themselves to be barely civil. I took an hasty leave, and with a heavy heart, weighed down by their ingratitude, returned to Bexley."

It was a member of the Fetter Lane Society, John Simpson, who was of most concern to Charles. Simpson urged the Fetter Lane members to embrace the "stillness" doctrine. Charles described him in his journal as "poor, perverted Mr. Simpson." When John attempted to put a stop to the controversy that had broken out in London, he found to his dismay that the society was in a state of disarray: "Here I found every day the dreadful effects of our [still] brethren's reasonings and disputing with each other. Scarce one in ten retained the first love and most of the rest were in the utmost confusion, biting and devouring one another." Simpson continued to sow seeds of division among the London Methodists, declaring "Believers are not subject to ordinances; and unbelievers have nothing to do with them. They ought to be still; otherwise they will be unbelievers as long as they live." Charles reported: "Simpson and the rest have dissuaded them, and indeed all our friends from ever hearing my brother or me, or using any of the means. They condemn all doing good, whether soul or body. 'For unless you trust in them,' say they, 'you would not do good works, so called.'"

Charles discovered that Simpson was claiming that "No soul can be washed in the blood of Christ, unless it be first brought to a true believer, or one in whom Christ is fully formed." When confronted by Charles on the issue, Simpson admitted he knew of only two such ministers: Philip Molther and the mystic and false prophet George Bell. Charles wrote in his journal: "First perish Molther and Bell and all mankind, and sink into nothing, that Christ may be all in all." Charles also confronted Moravian members of the Fetter Lane Society who claimed there was no Christian priesthood and that they were as qualified to administer the sacrament as anyone else. Charles described one of them as the "self-ordained priest," and both declared that they were no longer members of the Church of England.

These confrontations took their toll on a frail Charles: "I got home, weary, wounded, and bruised, and faint, through the contradiction of sinners; poor sinners, as they call themselves; these heady, violent, fierce contenders for stillness. I could not bear the thought of meeting them again."

At Easter 1740, Charles preached at the Foundery: "I strongly preached Christ and the power of his resurrection. My intention was not to mention one word of the controverted points, till I had spoke with each of the seducers." But when Charles started preaching, he felt strongly led "into the very line of battle and struggle. My mouth was opened to ask, 'Who has bewitched you, that you should let go of your Saviour? That you should cast away your shield and your confidence and deny you ever knew him?' . . . The whole congregation was in tears. I called them back to their Saviour, even theirs, in words which were not mine; pressed obedience to the divine ordinances." Two days later when Charles was again preaching at the Foundery, he was challenged by Simpson and other Moravians for "preaching up the ordinances." Simpson informed him that "if I recommended the ordinances, he must preach against me." But Charles made it clear his "resolution never to give them up, as he and our poor deluded brethren had done."

When John again returned to London in April 1740, he found that the society was becoming ever more influenced by Molther's Quietest theology. John challenged the Moravians regarding their rejection of the means of grace: "As to the way of faith, you believe: that the way to attain it is to wait for Christ and be still. i.e. Not to use (what we term) 'the means of grace'; Not to go to church; Not to communicate; Not to fast; Not to use so much private prayer; Not to read the Scriptures . . . Not to do temporal good; Nor to attempt doing spiritual good." John observed that the meetings at the Fetter Lane Society had become "cold, weary, heartless, dead. . . . I found nothing of brotherly love among them now; but a harsh, dry, heavy stupid spirit. For two hours, they looked one at another, when they looked up at all, as if half of them was afraid of the other." John was prevented from speaking at Fetter Lane even though he was forced to sit patiently through an hour of "dumb show" as Charles described it. On another occasion, John wrote: "I went to Fetter Lane and plainly told our poor, confused, shattered society where they had erred from the faith. It was as I feared; they could not receive my saying." Charles, for his part, was convinced that

Molther was appealing to mankind's "lazy, corrupt nature". Concluded Charles:

> A separation I foresee unavoidable. All means have been taken to wean our friends of their esteem for us. They say God never used us as instruments to convert one soul . . . and George Whitefield . . . [is condemned as] an unbeliever. . . . I think it safest not to converse with such of our misled, misleading brethren. . . . My brother came most critically. The snare, we trust will now be broken and many simple souls delivered. Many here insist that a part of their Christian calling is liberty from obeying, not liberty to obey. The justified, say they, are to be still; that is, not to season the scriptures, not to pray, not to communicate [take the Lord's Supper], not to do good, not to endeavour, not to desire; for it is impossible to use the means without trusting in them. Their practice is agreeable to their principles. . . . Lazy and proud themselves, bitter and censorious towards others, they trample upon the [Church] ordinances and despise the commands of Christ. I see no middle point wherein we can meet.

On June 5, 1740, John returned from another period of ministry in Bristol. The following day, accompanied by Charles and Howell Harris, John met with Molther and suggested it might be better to divide the Fetter Lane Society into Wesleyan and Moravian groups. Molther rejected this plan and accused John of being a "child of the devil [and] a servant of corruption."

John and Charles agreed that there was now no alternative but to withdraw from Fetter Lane and take whomever they could to their new meeting place at the Foundery. Wrote Charles:

> The noisy "still-ones" well knew that they had carried their point by wearying out the sincere ones scattered among them . . . [but] Benjamin Ingham seconded us. . . . We gathered up our wreck . . . for nine out of ten are swallowed up in the dead sea of stillness. O why was this not done six months ago! How fatal was our delay and false moderation. . . . I tremble at the consequence, will they submit themselves to every ordinance of man, who refuse subjection to the ordinances of God? . . . I told them plainly, "I should continue with them

so long as they continue in the Church of England." My every word was grievous to them, I am a thorn in their sides and they cannot bear me.

In July 1740, John decided to act and visited Fetter Lane for the last time: "Finding there was no time to delay without utterly destroying the cause of God, I began to execute what I had long designed—to strike at the root of the grand delusion." John Wesley first read out a statement to the congregation:

> About nine months ago, certain of you began to speak contrary to the doctrine we had till then received. The sum of what you asserted is this:
>
> That there is no such thing as weak faith; that there is no justifying faith where there is any doubt or fear, or where there is not, in the full, proper sense, a new, clean heart.
>
> That a man ought not to use those ordinances of God which our Church terms "the means of grace," before he has such a faith as excludes all doubt and fear, and implies a new, clean heart.
>
> You have often affirmed that "to search the Scriptures," to pray, or to communicate before we have this faith, is to seek salvation by works, and that till these works are laid aside no man can receive faith.

John concluded by declaring: "I have warned you hereof again and again and besought you to turn back to the law and the testimony. I have borne with you long, hoping you would return. But as I find you more and more confirmed in the error of your ways, nothing now remains but that I should give you up to God. You that are of the same judgement follow me!" He then left the meeting without uttering another word, followed by eighteen or nineteen members of the society. Almost all the female members of the Fetter Lane Society joined the Wesleys at the Foundery, but only a third of the men. It is possible that more would have followed John if one of the Moravians had not hidden his hat. While he was searching for it, some of his would-be followers were persuaded to remain at Fetter Lane.

Charles was disappointed that among those who did not join them were Martha Claggett and her daughters who had been some of his first converts in June 1738. Even though Martha had found Charles' preaching inspirational, Molther's promise of a guaranteed place in heaven apparently proved a more powerful inducement.

The following Wednesday, John wrote, "our little company met at The Foundery instead of Fetter Lane." Around twenty-five Methodists formed the basis of a new society, including Susanna Wesley and Lady Selina Huntingdon. James Hutton described the departure of the Wesleys from Fetter Lane:

> . . . he formed his Foundery society, in opposition to the one which met at Fetter Lane and which had become a Moravian society. Many of our usual hearers consequently left us, especially the females. We asked his forgiveness, if in anything we had aggrieved him, but he continued full of wrath, accusing the Brethren that they by dwelling exclusively on the doctrine of faith, neglected the law and zeal for sanctification. In short, he became our declared opponent and the two societies of the Brethren and Methodists thenceforward were separated and became independent of each other.

In September 1740, Charles became seriously ill, which he documented in a letter to George Whitefield that same month: "For this month past [God] has visited me with a violent fever. There was no possibility of my surviving it; but I knew in my self I should not die. I had not finished my course, and scarce begun it. The prayer of faith prevailed. Jesus touched my hand and immediately the fever departed from me." Charles also related the events surrounding the stillness controversy: "The most violent opposers of all are our own brethren of Fetter Lane, that were, for we have gathered up between twenty and thirty from the wreck and transplanted them to the Foundery. The remnant has taken root downward and bore fruit upwards. A little one is become a thousand. They grow in grace, particularly humility and in the knowledge of our Lord Jesus Christ."

The rancorous separation of the Wesleyan Methodists and the Moravians appeared to draw a line under the affair, but surprisingly both John and Charles started to have doubts about their hardline stance when they met Peter Böhler, who had returned from America. Charles, in particular, seemed to be moderating his views on the Moravians, and James Gambold and Westley Hall did all they could to encourage him to join them. In early 1741, Charles met Peter Böhler who convinced him that a union with the Moravians was not only possible but desirable. He even contemplated going to Germany with Böhler. Charles wrote to John on March 10, 1741, questioning his motives for opposing the Moravians:

> My dear brother, I fear all is not right in your own breast, otherwise you would not think so hardly of them [the Moravians]. Is not there envy, self love, emulation, jealousy? Are you not afraid lest they should eclipse your own glory, or lessen your own praise? Do you not give too much credit to all that you only hear of them? . . . I am sure they are a true people of God. There is life and power amongst them.

Charles was also impressed by the reverence the Moravians seemed to have for the ordinances, which was his main bone of contention: "This I know, the Brethren have the greatest respect for the ordinances of the Lord. Four times I received the Lord's Supper with them, and I never saw that sacred mystery so solemnly celebrated any where else. Neither did I ever feel so great power and grace."

John also met Böhler in April 1741, and like Charles felt conflicted about the Moravians. "I had a long conversation with Peter Böhler. I marvel how I refrain from joining these men. I scarce ever see any of them but my heart burns within me. I long to be with them. And yet I am kept from them." In his reply to Charles' letter on April 21, John made it clear that the Moravians' false doctrines made continued separation essential and expressed his concern that Charles' determination to resist the Moravians may have weakened: "O my brother, my soul is grieved for you. The poison is in you. Fair words have stole away your heart."

The division in the Fetter Lane Society was a cause of great concern among the Moravian community as a whole, most of whom did not share Molther's adversarial approach to the Wesleys. Count Zinzendorf dispatched August Spangenberg to try to reconcile the two parties, without success, and even visited London himself in September 1741. But he was critical of the Wesley's emphasis on good works, so no agreement could be reached.

Zinzendorf, however, urged the Moravian societies to remain in the Church of England, but Molther was unmoved. In 1742, the Fetter Lane Society was formally constituted as a society of the (Moravian) Church of the United Brethren, which was later licensed in England as a Dissenting body. This betrayal, as he perceived it, by the Moravians was anathema to Charles, and John was equally implacable, writing the following year: "My belief is that the present design of God is to visit the poor Church of England." In 1745, Zinzendorf placed an advertisement in the *Daily Advertiser* declaring that the Moravians had no connection with the Wesleys. Even in the 1780s it appeared that the wounds still had not healed, for in 1785 the Moravian Bishop Latrobe commented scathingly of John, "It is very doubtful, whether John Wesley knew himself as a sinner or the Lord as his Saviour."

11

THE CALVINIST
CONTROVERSY

. . . the hellish, blasphemous, explosive lie . . . the
foulest tale . . . that has ever hatched in Hell.

— CHARLES WESLEY

While the "stillness" debate was continuing to rage at Fetter Lane, the Wesleys plunged headfirst into a new and potentially more damaging controversy regarding their opposition to the doctrine of predestination and its most famous exponent, George Whitefield. John and Charles Wesley believed in Arminianism, the doctrine expounded by the sixteenth-century, anti-Calvinist Dutch theologian Jakob Arminius. He believed that salvation was available to all but not necessarily accepted by all since God had given humankind a free will to choose. At least two generations of Wesleys, including their father and mother, had been Arminian, and their elder brother Samuel was a staunch Anglican and Arminian.

Throughout their lives, John and Charles Wesley remained fervent opponents of predestination. Their mother, Susanna, influenced John while he was at Oxford. She recorded, "The doctrine of predestination, as maintained by the rigid Calvinists, is very shocking, and ought to be abhorred, because it directly charges the most high God with being the author of sin." Commented Green, "To the end of his days [John] Wesley remained an unrepentant Arminian."[44]

---

[44] Green, *John Wesley*, 113.

Charles believed that the doctrine of predestination was like "a millstone round the neck" to many who heard the gospel. He described Calvinists as "Priests of Moloch." When he summarized "the two great truths of the everlasting gospel" from a Wesleyan perspective, he claimed they were "universal redemption and Christian Perfection."

Concerning John Wesley, Green says: "Wesley was temperamentally and intellectually opposed to the doctrine which made nonsense of his own fervent conviction that God willed all men to salvation. It contravened the logic of the Christian faith, sabotaged the pursuit of true holiness and divested good works of any function in the Christian scheme of things."[45] John Wesley's tract "What is an Arminian?" described the Wesleyan position on salvation as the "undeniable difference" between absolute and conditional predestination: "The Arminians hold God has decreed, from all eternity, touching all that have the written word, 'He that believes shall be saved; he that believes not shall be condemned.'" Declared John to Calvinists: "You say, Christ died only for the elect; and these must and shall be saved. I say, Christ died for every man and he wills all men to be saved." The Wesleys believed in conditional election, that God has eternally decreed to save all those who profess faith in Jesus Christ, as opposed to their Calvinist opponents who believed that God preordained or elected some individuals for salvation and some for damnation before the foundation of the earth and that the elect could never lose their salvation. It was a belief that Charles described as the "injustice of reprobation." Arminians believed that salvation could be lost if the saved did not persist in their faith, as confirmed by how they lived and conducted themselves, a view that infused many of Charles' hymns. John declared emphatically: "The fundamental doctrine of the people called 'Methodists' is Whosoever will be saved, before all things it is necessary that he hold the true faith; the faith which works by love; which, by means of the love of God and our neighbour, produces both inward and outward holiness." The Wesleys also believed in the doctrine of original sin and did not think it was possible for sinful people to turn to God without His prevenient grace, which was a necessary precondition for salvation.

---

[45] Ibid., 112.

As early as September 1738, Charles was debating predestination with the group that met at John Bray's house. Charles stated: "At Bray's, I expounded Eph. 1:4. A dispute arising about absolute predestination, I entered my protest against that doctrine." In June 1739, Charles reported in his journal that arguments concerning predestination had become more frequent among the Methodists: "The sower of tares is beginning to trouble us with disputes about predestination." Continued Charles: "My brother was wonderfully owned at Wapping last week, while asserting the contrary truth. To-night I asked in prayer, that if God would have all men to be saved, he would show some token for good upon us. Three were justified in immediate answer to that prayer. We prayed again; several fell down under the power of God, present to witness his universal love."

Yet Charles was always torn between his friendship with Whitefield, his opposition to predestinarianism, and his loyalty to his brother, writing to Whitefield in 1740:

> Many, I know, desire nothing so much as to see George Whitefield and John Wesley at the head of different parties, as is plain from their truly devilish pains to effect it, but be assured, my dearest brother, our heart is as your heart. O may we always thus continue to think and speak the same things. . . . I do not think the difference [between us] considerable. . . . I shall never dispute with you touching election, and if you know not yet to reconcile that doctrine with God's universal love, I will cry unto him, "Lord what we know not, show you us;" but never, offend you by my different sentiment. . . . My soul is set upon peace, and drawn out after you by love stronger than death.

Still, Charles' growing dislike of predestination, what he described as the "poison of Calvin," was based not just on his belief that God was willing to save all people who turned to him, but also the haughty pride that he had observed in those who believed that they were members of the "elect." Charles reported in his journal one such individual: "In the afternoon I spoke a word of caution to one who seems strong in the faith and begins to be lifted up; the sure effect of her growing acquaintance with some of Calvin's followers." And he wrote to his wife Sally in 1747:

"To urge that doctrine on unawakened souls, is to stop them at the very threshold and to infuse into those who are unconvinced, is to drive them either into presumption or despair."

Charles wrote about those who he believed were deluded into a false sense of security. He reported one case in which a man who "came home elect" felt such moral freedom that he beat his wife, informing her that "if he killed her he could not be damned." Charles was appalled to see how many people he encountered who were dying and dreading the prospect of death because they were terrified of being among those who were damned. In another case, Charles tried to comfort a dying woman, but was rejected because she was convinced she was going to hell. However, she permitted him to pray with her, and she changed her mind before she died. Charles said, "God gave us a faint spark of hope." In the same month he came across a woman who believed herself to be one of the elect. He remarked that never before had he met anyone so "Full of pride, and self, and the devil." He concluded, "I cannot allow them Christ's righteousness for a cloak to their sins."

Charles' experience of caring for the dying who had such a fear of death and the arrogant confidence of Calvinists convinced him that there could be no compromise on the issue of predestination. When John showed evidence of softening his stance on the doctrine in the hope of a reconciliation with George Whitefield in September 1741, Charles was implacable, warning his brother:

> [He] wraps up . . . [his Calvinist views] in smoother language than before, in order to convey the poison more successfully. Our Society, on this account, go to hear him, without any scruple or dread. We have sufficiently seen the fatal effects of this devillish doctrine already, so that we cannot keep at too great a distance from it. . . . Do you know the value of souls! Precious, immortal souls! Yet trust them within the sound of predestination? . . . Stop the plague just now, or it will be too late. Send me word, first post, that you have warned our flock from going to hear the other's gospel. . . . Send me word, I say, by next post, that you have restrained the unwary, or I shall on the first preaching night renounce George Whitefield on the house-top.

John also was appalled by his own experience of encountering extreme Calvinism—a view that could more accurately be described as Antinomianism. John described its adherents as "the firstborn children of Satan." In his *Journal* on March 23, 1744, he records with horror a conversation he had with one who claimed he was not bound by moral laws governing the non-elect. Enquired Wesley:

> "Do you believe you have nothing to do with the law of God? "I have not; I am under no law; I live by faith." "Have you, as living by faith, a right to everything in the world?" "I have; all is mine, since Christ is mine." "May you, then, take anything you will anywhere? Suppose out of a shop. . .?" "I may if I want it, for it is mine. Only I will not take offence." "Have you also a right to all the women in the world?" "Yes, if they consent." "And is not that a sin?" ". . . Not to those whose hearts are free."

There were even reports of diehard Calvinists worshipping naked, declaring that since clothes were only worn as a consequence of sin, they, being free from sin, did not need to wear any.

On April 26, 1739, when John was preaching at Newgate jail in Bristol, he felt strongly that he should preach vehemently against predestination to reveal what he believed to be the falsehood of Calvinism. After doing so, he prayed aloud that God would send a sign that would confirm his inner feeling. Recalled Wesley: "Immediately, the power of God fell upon us. One, and another, and another, sunk to the earth. You might see them, dropping on all sides as thunderstruck. One cried out aloud. I went and prayed over her, and she received joy in the Holy Ghost. A second falling into the same agony, we turned to her, and received for her also the promise of the Father."

John criticized George Whitefield for his adherence to Calvinism, claiming it was inappropriate for a Church of England minister to believe in predestination. In a heated exchange between the two, Whitefield declared to John: "I am ten thousand times more convinced of the doctrine of election . . . than when I saw you last. You think otherwise. Why, then, should we dispute, when there is no probability of convincing? Will it not, in the end, destroy brotherly love, and insensibly take from us that cordial union and sweetness of soul, which I pray God may always subsist between us?" Whitefield made it clear where he stood doctrinally: "I embrace the Calvinistic scheme not because Calvin, but Jesus Christ has taught it to me. . . . God chose us from eternity, He called us in time, and I am persuaded will keep us from falling finally, till time shall be no more."

Among the members of the Foundery were many who agreed with Whitefield, including John Acourt, who proved to be so disruptive that Charles ordered his exclusion. Acourt, supported by Howell Harris, appealed to John for reinstatement: "What, do you refuse admitting a person into your Society, only because he differs from you in opinion?"

Wesley replied, "No; but what opinion do you mean?"

Acourt then said: "That of election. I hold a certain number is elected from eternity. And these must and shall be saved. And the rest of mankind must and shall be damned. And many of your society hold the same." They disputed further until Acourt declared: "Because you are all wrong and I am resolved to set you right."

Replied John, "I fear your coming with this view would neither profit you nor us."

Acourt concluded: "Then I will go and tell all the world that you and your brother are false prophets. And I tell you, in one fortnight you will all be in confusion."

John made it clear to Acourt that it would better for all involved if he kept away from the society.

In June 1740, John decided "to strike at the root of the grand delusion" by preaching a sermon on "Free Grace" to expose Calvinism "in all its naked, hideous deformity" and which Charles described as "the hellish, blasphemous, explosive lie . . . the foulest tale . . . that has ever hatched in Hell." The Wesleys published John's sermon "Free Grace" as a pamphlet. In it John set forth a fierce denunciation of predestination:

> It is a doctrine full of blasphemy; of such blasphemy as I should dread to mention, but that the honour of our gracious God, and the cause of truth, will not suffer me to be silent. . . . This doctrine represents our blessed Lord, Jesus Christ the righteous . . . as a hypocrite, a deceiver of the people, a man

void of common sincerity. . . . This the blasphemy clearly
contained in the horrible decree of predestination. And there
I fix my foot. On this I join issue with every assertor of it. You
represent God as worse than the devil. But you say, you will
prove it by Scripture. Hold! What will you prove by Scripture?
That God is worse than the devil? It cannot be.

John was later to write of the evil of believing that God con-
signed "unborn souls to hell [and] damned them from their mother's
womb. . . . I would sooner be a Turk, a deist, indeed an atheist, than I
could believe this. It is less absurd to deny the very being of God than
to make him an almighty tyrant." Charles reinforced this message by
composing a thirty-six-verse hymn entitled "Universal Redemption."
According to John R. Tyson, "Charles [like John] considered the notion
of a eternal decree of 'reprobation' to be unworthy of the God of the
Bible, whom they viewed as a God of love."[46]

George Whitefield was bewildered why the Wesleys would want to
stir up the debate about election and predestination. Whitefield wrote
to John in June 1740: "For Christ's sake, let us not be divided amongst
ourselves. Nothing will so much prevent a division as our being silent
on this head." And to a mutual friend he wrote: ". . . for Christ's sake
desire dear Brother Wesley to avoid disputing with me. I think I would
rather die than see a division between us; and yet how can we walk
together if we oppose each other?" Whitefield wrote again to John on
February 14, 1741, during his return trip from America to England:

> My dear brethren, why did you throw out the bone of
> contention? Why did you print that sermon against predesti-
> nation? Why did you in particular, my dear brother Charles,
> affix your hymn, and join in putting out your late hymn book?
> How can you say you will not dispute with me about election,
> and yet print such hymns, and your brother send his sermon
> over against election to . . . America? Do you not think, my
> dear brethren, I must be as much concerned for truth, or
> what I think truth, as you? God is my judge. I always was, and
> I hope always shall be, desirous that you may be preferred

---

[46] Tyson, *Assist Me to Proclaim*, 103.

> before me. But I must preach the Gospel of Christ, and this
> I cannot now do without speaking about election. . . . O my
> dear brethren, my heart almost bleeds within me! Methinks
> I would be willing to tarry here on the waters forever, rather
> than come to England to oppose you.

When John's sermon "Free Grace" was published, Methodist lay preacher and one of John's "sons of the gospel," John Cennick, sided with Whitefield, accusing John of acting like a pope and Charles as behaving like Satan "making war on the saints." Kingswood school, on the outskirts of Bristol, where Cennick had been appointed a master on John's recommendation, proved to be a hotbed of predestinarianism when it was revealed that Cennick was a closet Calvinist. Lamented Charles, "The poison of Calvin has drunk up their spirit of love. . . . Alas! we have set the wolf to keep the sheep! God gave me moderation toward him, who, for many months, has been undermining our doctrine and authority."

In December 1740, Charles warned John what was happening at Kingswood society. "Things are come to a crisis at Kingswood. They tell me plainly they will separate from me if I speak one word against final perseverance, or hint at the possibility of a justified person's falling from grace. . . . All the bands, they say, are of their opinion; and no one who is not can love Christ. . . . I condescended to say that I would not speak against final perseverance, if he [Cennick] would not speak for it. But he would not agree even to this." Eventually the Methodist societies in Bristol and Kingswood would split first into Arminian and Calvinist bands and then into separate Wesleyan and Calvinist Methodist societies.

Cennick believed that it was impossible for the justified to fall from grace and, while an advocate for living according to the Scriptures, refused to accept the Wesleyan view that the saved still had to seek holiness or risk losing their salvation. When Charles returned to Bristol in November 1741, he was appalled by what Cennick was preaching and countered it by proclaiming that Christ died for all, leading Cennick to publicly challenge him. Concerned that Cennick might be planning a coup to take control of the Bristol societies, as Molther had done in

London, Charles confronted him when they dined together. According to Cennick, Charles "began to dispute election. He fell into a violent passion and affrighted all at the table and arising from the table, he said he would go directly and preach against me, and accordingly did. He called Calvin the first-born son of the devil and set all people against me." When he had calmed down, Charles tried to be concil-iatory, meeting with Cennick and offering "to drop the controversy if he would." But Cennick refused any compromise regarding universal redemption. Charles then rebuked him for his disloyalty:

> You came to Kingswood upon my brother sending you.
> You served under him in the gospel as a son. I need not say
> how well he loved you. You used the authority he gave you
> to overthrow his doctrine. You everywhere contradicted it
> . . . [and] you have stolen the people's hearts from him. . . .
> We deserved [more] at your hands. I say "we" for God is my
> witness how condescendingly loving I have been toward you.

John liked Cennick and was concerned about the impact on the society in Bristol if he was expelled. John still hoped that there could be a reconciliation between Cennick and Charles. He met with Cennick at Kingswood to try to repair "the breaches which had been made . . . [and] heal the jealousies and misunderstandings which had arisen." But Cennick was cold and unresponsive and had already written to George Whitefield urging him to return from America to take charge of the revival:

> How glorious did the gospel seem once to flourish in
> Kingswood! Now brother Charles is suffered to open his
> mouth against the truth, while the frightened sheep gaze and
> fly, as if no shepherd was among them. . . . Brother Charles
> pleases the world with universal redemption and brother
> John follows him in everything. No atheists can preach more
> against predestination than they; and all who believe election
> are counted enemies of God, and called so. . . . If God gives
> you leave, make haste.

In reply to Cennick's letter, Whitefield wrote to the Wesleys defend-ing Calvinism, claiming that "dooming millions to everlasting burnings is not an act of injustice, because God, for the sin of Adam, might justly have thus doomed all." This private letter was somehow published and printed as a pamphlet entitled "A Letter to the Reverend John Wesley . . . by the Reverend George Whitefield" and was distributed to members of the Methodist society at the Foundery on February 1, 1741. After preaching, John announced: "A private letter, wrote to me by Mr. Whitefield, has been printed without his leave or mine. I will do just what I believe Mr. Whitefield would do were he here himself." He then symbolically tore up the letter and everyone in the congregation did the same. John then issued a rebuttal in print, proclaiming the letter to be "one of the greatest absurdities and impositions that folly or impudence could invent . . . a correspondence of evil." However, Cennick, Howell Harris, and Joseph Humphreys wrote defending the letter and, probably as a precaution, John introduced the issuance of tickets of membership for society members, dependent on their acceptance of his views.

On Feburary 22, 1741, Cennick, along with twenty supporters, made his move, challenging John after he had finished preaching at the New Room in Bristol, to reconsider his opinion about Calvinism, but Wesley rebuked him for deceitfully going behind his back and causing division: "You have not done right in speaking against me behind my back. . . . You should have told me this before, and not have supplanted me in my own house, stealing the hearts of the people, and by private accusations, separating friends." A few days later, John announced that he was expelling Cennick and his close associates from the movement, not because of his Calvinism but "for talebearing, backbiting, and evil speaking" and "for dissembling, lying, and slandering." John asserted that he acted with "the consent and approbation of the band-society in Kingswood." Cennick was stunned, but said nothing, writing later in his diary: "I was a little surprised, yet I showed little of it to the souls, only they saw me weep as I went out." Joseph Humphreys, another of John's "sons of the gospel," was asked to replace Cennick as his chief lay assistant. Humphreys refused and publicly burned a copy of one of John's anti-predestinarian tracts, "Treatise on Predestination," and left the movement. The final break occurred on March 8, 1741, when

Cennick and fifty-one others withdrew from the Kingswood society, which was mainly composed of converted colliers, while ninety decided to stay with John Wesley.

When Whitefield returned from America in that month, he complained that many of his former followers rushed by with their fingers in their ears whenever he was preaching because they had been urged to do so by the Wesleys to prevent them from hearing heretical doctrine.

> Many, very many of my spiritual children who at my last departure from England would have plucked out their own eyes to have given them to me, are so prejudiced by the dear Messrs. W's dressing up the doctrine of election in such horrible colours, that they will neither hear, see, nor give me the least assistance: Yes, some of them send threatening letters that God will speedily destroy me.

Initially, John refused to see Whitefield and Charles went instead, but it became evident, despite their friendship, that the theological divide remained. Whitefield wrote poignantly, "It would have melted any heart to have heard Mr. Charles Wesley and me weeping after prayer that, if possible, the breach might be prevented." John and Whitefield eventually met. But under pressure from his Calvinist supporters, Whitefield refused to shake hands with Wesley and threatened to oppose him openly. In response, John banned him from preaching at the Foundery and the New Room in Bristol. Whitefield was devastated by this rejection, and Harris found him "sick and vomiting, he wept with strong crying and weeping."

Howell Harris persuaded John to meet Whitefield in November 1741 and the latter wrote to John ecstatically: "Reverend and Dear brother . . . I humbly ask pardon. I love you as much as ever. . . . May God remove all obstacles that now prevent our union! . . . May all disputings cease, and each of us talk nothing but Jesus, and Him crucified! This is my resolution." John was ill and their discussions were limited, but they met again in April 1742, and according to John, "I spent an agreeable hour with Mr. Wh. I believe he is sincere in all he says concerning his desire of joining hands with all that love the Lord Jesus Christ." However, they could not come to a consensus regarding their theological differences, with John concluding granite-like: "But if (as some would persuade me) he is not, the loss is all on his side. I am just as I was. I go on my way, whether he goes with me or stays behind." For his part, Whitefield wrote to his assistant in Georgia: "What is most cutting of all, I am constrained, on account of our differing principles, publicly to separate from . . . my old friends." And later, Whitefield confessed privately that John's cutting remarks affected him deeply: "I have been supplanted, despised, censured, maligned, judged by and separated from my nearest and dearest friends."

Nevertheless, whatever their doctrinal differences, George Whitefield and the Wesleys remained friends and preached for each other on occasion. There were also regular attempts at reconciliation. John remarked that he desired that they might "trample on bigotry." When Whitefield visited him in 1755, he rejoiced that "disputings were no more; we love each other." As a mark of Whitefield's respect for John, when a Calvinist asked him whether they would see John Wesley in heaven, he replied: "I fear not because he will be so near the throne and we shall be at such a distance, that we shall hardly get sight of him." As late as 1766, when Whitefield again returned from America, John recorded: "Mr. Whitefield called on me. He breathes nothing but peace and love. Bigotry cannot stand before him, but hides its head wherever he comes."

✠ ✠ ✠

Initially, Lady Selina Huntingdon supported the Wesleys against Whitefield and the predestinarians. A young relation of Lady Huntingdon, Fanny Cowper, was dying of tuberculosis and had expressed a desire to see both John and Charles before she died. Lady Huntingdon had to implore them to come: "I beg you will set out as soon as may be after receiving this, as every day she has lived this past fortnight seems a fresh miracle, wrought for some purpose not yet known."

John set out for her Yorkshire estate, and on the way passed someone he described as a "serious man" who was probably a Presbyterian Dissenter determined to press his arguments for predestination. When he demanded to hear John's views on the matter, the latter replied, "I told him over and over, 'We had better keep to practical things, lest we should be angry at one another.' And so we did for two miles, till he caught me unawares, and dragged me into the dispute before I knew where I was. He then grew warmer and warmer, told me I was rotten at heart, and supposed I was one of John Wesley's followers. I told him, 'No, I am John Wesley himself.'" Startled, the man shot forward like "one who unawares has trodden on a snake. . . .[But] being the better mounted of the two, I kept close to his side, and endeavoured to show him his heart, till we came into the street of Northhampton."

By 1748, however, Lady Huntingdon had embraced Calvinist doctrines. She appointed Whitefield as her personal chaplain and became one of his main patrons and figures in the Calvinistic Methodist movement. The relationship between Huntingdon and the Wesleys would become even more strained when she became convinced that John had forsaken justification by faith and was teaching salvation through works. She wrote to Charles: "I find it difficult to blame your brother to you, while as an honest man I must pity and not less regard you, as you must suffer equal disgrace and universal distruct [sic] from the supposed union with him."

⊞ ⊞ ⊞

At the Methodist Conference in August 1769, John announced that he was no longer going to pursue his efforts to work with the Calvinists and unite the evangelicals behind Methodism, commenting dismissively, "They are a rope of sand: and such they will continue." At the conference the following year, he produced a detailed statement of what "the old Methodist doctrines" were and damned all connections with the Calvinists, thus ending any chance of a rapprochement.

With Whitefield's death in 1770, a second generation of Calvinists, including Anglican vicar Augustus Toplady, renowned for composing the hymn "Rock of Ages," Richard and Rowland Hill, William Cadogan, and John MacGowan, came to prominence. These Calvinists were not deferential to the Wesleys as Whitefield had been. Indeed, they would become highly hostile.

When John preached at Whitefield's funeral, he spoke of reconciliation and deliberately omitted any mention of predestination. This
led to an outpouring of anger from extreme Calvinists who wrote in
the Calvinist inspired *Gospel Magazine*: "Are not the very doctrines of
popery, yes, of popery, unmasked. Is it not awful that 29,406 souls, who
are in Mr. Wesley's societies, should be so dreadfully seduced from the
Protestant doctrines, and deluded into a belief of the doctrines of the
mother of harlots, the whore of Babylon, the Church of Rome?"

In March 1770, John inflamed the controversy by condensing and
distorting Toplady's 134-page book *Absolute Predestination* into a 12-page
tract, concluding: "The sum of all is this: One in twenty (suppose) of
mankind are elected; nineteen in twenty are reprobated. The elect
shall be saved, do what they will; the reprobate will be damned, do
what they can. Reader believe this or be damned. Witness my hand,
A-T-." A furious Toplady responded to John's abridgement, accusing
him of being "guilty of Satanic shamelessness . . . a lurking, sly assassin"
and "endeavouring to palm on his credulous followers his pernicious
doctrines with all the sophistry of a Jesuit and the dictatorial authority
of the pope." He concluded by saying, "I would no more enter in a
formal controversy with such a scribbler, than I would contend, for the
wall, with a chimney sweeper." Wesley did not reply but disdainfully
dismissed Toplady's arguments: "I do not fight with chimney-sweepers.
He is too dirty a writer for me to meddle with. I should only foul my
fingers."

One Calvinist declared that he "abhorred John Wesley as much
as he did the pope and ten times more than he did the devil." Others
described Wesley as a papalist, heretic, and an atheist, as a "venal
profligate," a "wicked slanderer," an "apostate miscreant," and a "grey-
headed enemy of all righteousness." Richard Hill pronounced, "Popery
is about midway between Protestantism and Mr J. Wesley," while his
brother Rowland sneeringly said of John, "Wesley has been a proverb
for his contradictions for about thirty years." Another attack on Wesley
launched by Toplady proclaimed: "Time, sire, has already whitened
your locks; and the hour must shortly come, which will transmit you to
the tribunal of that God on whose sovereignty a great part of your life

has been one continued assault." Toplady viewed Wesley's doctrine as a blend of virtually every false religion on earth "mingled with as much palpable atheism as could possibly be scraped together."

When John did a volte-face and opposed American demands for no taxation without representation in his *A Calm Address to Our American Colonies* (1775), which was essentially an abridgement of a pro-government pamphlet entitled *Taxation No Tyranny*, by Dr. Samuel Johnson, Toplady exploded in anger. He lampooned Wesley in a publication called *An Old Fox Tar'd and Feather'd*: "Whereunto shall I liken Mr. John Wesley? and with what shall I compare him? I will liken him unto a low and puny TADPOLE in Divinity, which proudly seeks to disembowel an high and mighty WHALE in politics." In response, John claimed that "As soon as I received new light myself, I judged it my duty to impart it to others."

In 1777, Rowland Hill remarked savagely about John's sermon marking the opening of the City Road Chapel: ". . . a wretched harangue, from which the blessed name of Jesus is almost totally excluded [preached by the] lying apostle of the Foundery . . . unprincipled as a rook and as silly as a jackdaw, first pilfering his neighbour's plumage and then going proudly forth, displaying his borrowed tail to the eyes of the laughing world." John commented wryly on this vitriolic attack, "Compared to him [Hill], Mr. Toplady himself is a very civil, fair spoken gentleman."

In 1778, John established the bimonthly *The Arminian Magazine* as a means of countering the views expressed in the *Gospel Magazine* and to promote his opinions. Said Wesley:

> Thousands have been poisoned already. . . . To guard those who are not poisoned yet (not to get money), I fight them at their own weapons. I oppose magazine to magazine, though of a different kind. . . . This magazine not only contains no railing, but (properly speaking) no controversy. It proves one point: "God wills all men to be saved and to come to the knowledge of the truth." It goes straight forward, taking notice of no opponents, but invariably pursuing the one point. And this is the only way to preserve the Methodists and to make the Calvinists quiet.

Regardless of the invective that poured forth against him, John Wesley was unmoved from his theological perspective. As late as 1783 he wrote: "Of Calvinism, Mysticism and Antinomianism have a care for they are the bane of true religion; and one or other of them has been the great hindrance of the work of God wherever it has broke out."

12

THE HOLY SPIRIT AND THE SUPERNATURAL

*I do not recollect any scripture wherein
we are taught that miracles were to be confined within
the limits of the apostolic or Cyprianic age . . .*

—JOHN WESLEY

On New Year's Day 1739 at Fetter Lane, sixty believers, including John and Charles Wesley and George Whitefield, who had just returned from Georgia, gathered for a "love feast" of bread and water. They prayed through the night until 3.00 a.m. and experienced an extraordinary outpouring of the Holy Spirit. As John Wesley recorded: "The power of God came mightily upon us, insomuch that many cried out for exceeding joy, and many fell to the ground. As soon as we were recovered a little from that awe and amazement at the presence of His Majesty, we broke out with one voice, 'We praise you, O God; we acknowledge you to be the Lord.'" The same manifestations occurred six months later, which John recorded in his *Journal*: "June 16, 1739. In that hour, we found God with us at the first. Some fell prostrate upon the ground. Others burst out, as with one consent into loud praise and thanksgiving. And many openly testified there had been no such day as this since January the first proceeding."

Despite George Whitefield describing the former meeting as "the happiest New Year's Day that I ever saw," he opposed these experiences and spoke forthrightly to John Wesley about them:

> I cannot think it right in you to give so much encouragement to these convulsions. . . . Was I to do so, how many would cry out every night? I think it is tempting God to require such signs. That there is something of God in it, I doubt not. But the devil, I believe, interposes. I think it will encourage . . . people . . . [to] depend on visions, convulsions, etc more than on the promises and precepts of the gospel.

Charles Wesley also disliked any extreme emotional response to his preaching and was skeptical about the origin of these manifestations, describing them as "the fits" and those who displayed such signs were either told forcefully to stop or were removed from his meetings. Just to emphasize his opposition to these incidents, Charles always kept a large bucket of water in plain view of the congregation, ready to dowse anyone who made such utterances. Claimed Charles:

> Many counterfeits I have already detected. Today one who came from the ale-house drunk was pleased to fall into a fit for my entertainment, and beat himself heartily. I thought it a pity to hinder him, so . . . we left him to recover at his leisure. Another girl, as she began to cry, I ordered to be carried out. Her convulsion was so violent as to take away the use of her limbs, till they laid and left her without the door. Then immediately she found her legs and walked off.

Preaching in Newcastle in 1743, Charles was determined to put a stop to any outbursts, writing in his journal:

> The first night I preached here, half my words were lost through their outcries. Last night, before I began, I gave public notice whoever cried, so as to drown my voice, should be carried to the farthest corner of the room. But my porters had no employment the whole night; yet the Lord was with us, mightily convincing of sin and righteousness. I am more and more convinced the fits were a device of Satan to stop the course of the gospel. Some very unstill sisters, who always took

care to stand near me, and tried which should cry loudest, since I had them removed out of my sight, have been as quiet as lambs.

As a staunch adherent to Church of England doctrine, Charles was not in favor of overt enthusiasm. His viewpoint may have been prejudiced by an incident that occurred to him and John during their time in the Holy Club. One Sunday, they went for a walk and had a supernatural experience, as John recalled: "Just as we were beginning to sing, he [Charles] burst into a loud laughter. I asked him, if he was distracted and began to be very angry, and presently after to laugh as loud as he. Nor could we possibly refrain, though we were ready to tear ourselves to pieces, but we were forced to go home without singing another line." John was convinced that this event was demonic in origin and was later to equate it with an incident that occurred in 1740 when his followers were influenced "by a spirit of laughter as they could in no wise resist." Wesley interpreted this phenomenon as being "buffeted by Satan, . . . violently and variously torn of the evil one."

Yet John Wesley was convinced that, on many occasions, such incidents were indeed the Holy Spirit at work, with people being convicted of their sins, delivered from demonic oppression, and healed physically and emotionally. Luke Tyerman in *The Life and Times of the Rev. John Wesley* reported that there were beds at the Foundery for those in the congregation who had a "fit" and "were carried out and laid upon these beds, that Wesley might pray the evil spirit out of them and the good spirit into them, and thus convert them." To one strident critic John replied:

> You deny that God does now work these effects; at least, that He works them in this manner. I affirm both; because I have heard these things with my own ears, and have seen them with my eyes. . . . I have seen (as far as a thing of this kind can be seen) very many persons changed in a moment from the spirit of fear, horror, despair, to the spirit of love, joy, and peace; and from sinful desire, till then reigning over them, to a pure desire of doing the will of God. . . . I will show you him that was a lion till then, and is now a lamb; him that was a drunkard, and is now

exemplarily sober; the whoremonger that was, who now abhors the very "garment spotted by the flesh." These are my living arguments.

Wesley recorded in his *Journal* a number of incidents that he believed were the work of the Spirit, including the following:

> Many of those that heard began to call upon God with strong cries and tears. Some sunk down, and there remained no strength in them; others exceedingly trembled and quaked; some were torn with a kind of convulsive motion in every part of their bodies, and that so violently that often four or five persons could not hold them. I have seen many hysterical and epileptic fits, but none of them were like these in many respects.
>
> I have seen . . . very many persons changed in a moment from the spirit of fear, horror, despair, to the spirit of love, joy and peace and from sinful desire till then reigning over them, to a pure desire of doing the will of God. These are matters of fact . . . .
>
> Great numbers wept without any noise; others fell down as dead, some sinking in silence, some with extreme noise and violent agitation. I stood on the pew seat, as did a young man in the opposite pew, an able bodied, fresh, healthy countryman. But in a moment, while he seemed to think nothing less, down he dropped with a violence inconceivable. The adjoining pews seemed shook with his fall. I heard afterward the stamping of his feet, ready to break the boards, as he lay in strong convulsions at the bottom of the pew. Among several that were struck down in the next pew, was a girl who was as violently seized as him.

Despite vehement opposition from the majority of the Church of England clergy and the skepticism of brother Charles and George Whitefield, John robustly defended miracles and supernatural manifestations, proclaiming:

> I do not recollect any scripture wherein we are taught that miracles were to be confined within the limits either of the apostolic or Cyprianic age, or of any period of time, longer or shorter, even till the restitution of all things. . . . Perhaps

the danger is to regard them (miracles) too little, to condemn them altogether; to imagine they had nothing of God in them and were an hindrance to his work.

It was not by faith by which St. Paul was saved, another by which he wrought miracles. Even at this day in every believer faith has a latent miraculous power (every effect of prayer being really miraculous) although in many, both because of their own littleness of faith, and because the world is unworthy, that power is not exerted. Miracles, in the beginning, were helps to faith; now also they are the object of it.

John was convinced that doubt, unbelief, and religious formality were the reasons that miracles and the gifts of the Holy Spirit were rarely witnessed in his day:

The cause of this was not (as has been vulgarly supposed) "because there was no more occasion for them," because all the world was become Christians. This is a miserable mistake; not a twentieth part of it was then nominally Christian. The real cause was, "the love of many," almost all Christians so called, was "waxed cold." The Christians had no more of the Spirit of Christ than the other heathens. The Son of Man, when he came to examine his Church, could hardly "find faith upon earth." This was the real cause why the extraordinary gifts of the Holy Ghost were no longer to be found in the Christian Church; because the Christians were turned Heathens again, and had only dead form left.

That the grand reason why the miraculous gifts were so soon withdrawn, was not only that faith and holiness were well-nigh lost, but that dry, formal, orthodox men began even then to ridicule whatever gifts they had not themselves and to decry them all as either madness or imposture.

✠ ✠ ✠

Throughout the fifty-three years that John Wesley wrote his famous *Journal,* he recorded numerous incidents of miracles, deliverances, divine intervention, people raised from the dead, and even those who opposed his ministry being struck down.

A remarkable case was that of a weaver called John Haydon, a regular church-goer. He heard that people were being affected by unusual "fits" at Methodist meetings and came to see for himself. After the meeting, he stayed with his friends until one o'clock in the morning, trying to persuade them that it was all a satanic delusion.

The following day he sat down to dinner but then decided to finish reading "a sermon which he had borrowed on 'Salvation by Faith.'" As he read the last page, he changed color, fell from his chair, and began screaming terribly and beating himself against the ground, causing the neighbors to flock to the house. John Wesley was told in the street of this occurrence and came immediately to the house, which was full of people. Haydon's wife would have kept them outside, but the weaver said, "No, let them all come; let all the world see the just judgement of God." Haydon was lying on the floor, held by two or three men, when Wesley entered, but immediately stared transfixed at him. Stretching out his hand, he cried, "Ay, this is he who, I said, was a deceiver of the people. But God has overtaken me. I said it was all a delusion; but this is no delusion." He then roared out, "O you devil! You cursed devil! Yes, you legion of devils! You can't stay. Christ will cast you out. I know His work is begun. Tear me to pieces, if you will; but you cannot hurt me." No sooner had he spoken than he began to beat himself on the ground. His chest heaved and great drops of sweat rolled down his face. Wesley and his friends prayed earnestly until Haydon's writhing ceased, and he was delivered of demonic possession. In the evening Wesley visited him again. His voice was gone and he was as weak as a child, but he was full of peace and joy. This experience was only one of many that he recorded in his *Journal*:

> October 23, 1739: I was pressed to visit a young woman at Kingswood. I found her on the bed, two or three persons holding her. Anguish, horror and despair, above all description, appeared in her pale face. The thousand distortions of her whole body showed how the dogs of hell were gnawing at her heart. The shrieks intermixed were scarce to be endured.

She screamed out, "I am damned, damned; lost for ever! Six days ago you might have helped me. But it is past. I am the devil's now, I have given myself to him: his I am, him I must serve, with him, I will go to hell. . . ." She then began praying to the devil. We began, "Arm of the Lord, awake, awake!" She immediately sank down as asleep; but as soon as we left off, broke out again, with inexpressible vehemence: ". . . You need not be damned, though I must." She then fixed her eyes on the corner of the ceiling and said, "There he is. Come, good devil, come. You said you would dash my brains out: come, do it quickly. I am yours, I will be yours."

We interrupted her by calling upon God; on which she sunk down as before and another young woman began to roar out as she had done. My brother now came in, it being about nine o'clock. We continued in prayer till past eleven; when God, in a moment, spoke peace into the soul, first of the tormented and then of the other. And they both joined in singing praise to Him who had stilled the enemy and the avenger.

October 25, 1739. I was sent for to one in Bristol, who was taken ill the evening before. (This fact too I will simply relate, so far as I was an ear or eye witness of it.) She lay on the ground, furiously gnashing her teeth, and after a while roared aloud. It was not easy for three or four persons to hold her, especially when the name of Jesus was named. We prayed; the violence of her symptoms ceased, though without a complete deliverance.

In the evening, being sent for to her again, I was unwilling, indeed, afraid, to go: Thinking it would not avail, unless some who were strong in faith were to wrestle with God for her. I opened my Testament on those words, "I was afraid and went and hid your talent in the earth." I stood and reproved and went immediately. She began screaming before I came into the room, then broke out into a horrid laughter mixed with blasphemy, grievous to hear.

One who from many circumstances apprehended a preternatural agent to be concerned in this, asking, "How did you dare to enter into a Christian?" was answered, "She is not a Christian. She is mine." Q. "Do you not tremble at the name of Jesus?" No words followed, but she shrunk back and trembled exceedingly. Q. "Are you not increasing your own damnation?" It was faintly, "Yes, yes." Which was followed by fresh cursing and blaspheming.

My brother coming in, she cried out, "Preacher! Field preacher! I don't love field-preaching." This was repeated two hours together, with spitting, and all the expressions of strong aversion. We left her at twelve, but called again about noon Friday, 26. And now it was that God showed He heard our prayer. All her pangs ceased in a moment. She was filled with peace and knew that the son of wickedness was departed from her.

October 27, 1739: I was sent for to Kingswood again, to one of those who had been so ill before. A violent rain began just as I set out. Just at that time, the woman (the three miles off) cried out, "Yonder comes Wesley, galloping fast as he can." When I was come, she burst into a horrid laughter and said, "No power, no power; no faith, no faith. She is mine; her soul is mine. I have her and will not let her go." We begged of God to increase our faith. Meanwhile, her pangs increased more and more, so that one would have imagined, by the violence of the throes, her body must have been shattered to pieces. One who was clearly convinced this was no natural disorder said, "I think Satan is let loose. I fear he will not stop here," and added, "I command you in the name of the Lord Jesus to tell if you have commission to torment another soul." It was immediately answered, "I have. L--y C--r and S--h J--s." We betook ourselves to prayer again and ceased not till she began, with a clear voice and composed cheerful look, to sing, "Praise God, from whom all blessings flow." The reader must be told that L--y C--r and S--h J--s lived at some distance, and, at the time were in perfect health. The day after, they were affected in the same way as the poor creature just delivered.

December 15, 1742. I preached at Horsley-upon-Tyne, eight (computed) miles from Newcastle. It was about two in the afternoon. The house not containing people, we stood in the open air, in spite of the frost. I preached again in the evening, and in the morning. We then chose to walk home, having each of us catched a violent cold by riding the day before. Mine gradually wore off; but Mr. Meyrick's increased, so that, on Friday, he took to his bed.

Mon. 20. – When I came home, they told me the Physician said, he did not expect Mr. Meyrick would live till the morning. I went to him, but his pulse was gone. He had been speechless and senseless for some time. A few of us immediately joined in prayer: (I relate the naked fact:) Before we had done, his sense and his speech returned. Now, he that will account for this by natural causes, has my free leave: But I choose to say, this is the power of God . . . .

Sat. 25. – The Physician told me he could do no more; Mr. Meyrick could not live over the night. I went up and found them all crying about him; his legs being cold, and (as it seemed) dead already. We all kneeled down, and called upon God with strong cries and tears. He opened his eyes and called for me, and from that hour, he continued to recover his strength, till he was restored to perfect health. – I wait to hear who will either disprove this fact, or philosophically account for it.

January 13, 1743. I rode to Stratford-upon-Avon. I had scarce sat down before I was informed that Mrs K., a middle-aged woman, of Slattery, half a mile from Stratford, had been for many weeks past in a way which nobody could understand; that she had sent for a Minister, but almost as soon as he came, began roaring in so strange a manner, (her tongue at the same time hanging out of her mouth and her face being distorted into the most terrible form) that he cried out, "It is the devil, doubtless! It is the devil!" and immediately went away. I suppose this was some unphilosophical Minister, else he would have said, "Stark mad! Send her to Bedlam."

I asked, "What good do you think I can do?" One answered, "We cannot tell, but Mrs K. . . . earnestly desired you might come, if you was anywhere near, saying she had seen you in a dream and should know you immediately. But the devil said, (those were her own expressions) "I will tear your throat out before he comes." But afterwards she said, his words were, "If he does come, I will let you be quiet and you shall be as if nothing ailed you, till he is gone away."

A very odd kind of madness this! I walked over about noon, but when we came to the house, desired all those who came with me to stay below. One showing me the way, I went straight to her room. As soon as I came to the bedside, she fixed me with her eyes, and said, "You are Mr. Wesley. I am very well now, I thank God. Nothing ails me, only I am weak." I called them up and we began to sing,

> Jesus, thou hast bid us pray,
> Pray always and not faint:
> With the word a power convey
> To utter our complaint.

After singing a verse or two we kneeled down to prayer. I had just begun (my eyes being shut) when I felt as if I had been plunged into cold water and immediately there was such a roar, that my voice was quite drowned, though I spoke as loud as I usually do to three or four thousand people. However, I prayed on. She was then reared up in bed, her whole body moving at once, without bending one joint or limb, just as if it were one piece of stone. Immediately after it was writhed into all kind of postures, the same horrid yell continuing still. But we left her not till the symptoms ceased, and she was (for the present, at least) rejoicing and praising God.

August 24, 1743. I make it my business to inquire concerning the truth of a strange relation which had been given me and found there was no possibility of doubting it. The plain fact was this: The Rev. Mr. – (I use the words of a gentleman of Bristol, whose manuscript lies by me) preached at two or three churches on these words, "Having the form of godliness, but denying the power thereof." After showing the different sorts of Dissenters from the Church of England, who (as he said) had only the form of godliness, he inveighed very much against the novel sect, the upstart Methodists (as he termed them) which indeed he was accustomed to do, more or less, in almost all his sermons. "These are the men," said he, "whom St. Paul foretold, who have the form, the outward show of holiness, but not the power; for they are ravening wolves, full of hypocrisy within." He then alleged many grievous things against them, but without all colour of truth, and warned his flock to turn away from them and not to bid them God speed, lest they should be partakers of their evil deeds.

Shortly after he was to preach at St. Nicholas church. He had named the above-mentioned text twice, when he was suddenly seized with a rattling in his throat, attended with a hideous groaning. He fell backward against the door of the pulpit, burst it open and would have fallen down the stairs, but that some people caught him and carried him away, as it seemed, dead, into the vestry. In two or three days he recovered his senses and the Sunday following he died!

April 27, 1752. After preaching in the evening, I was desired to visit a person who had been an eminent scoffer at all religion, but was now, they said, "in a strange way." I found her in a strange way indeed; either raving mad or possessed by the devil. The woman herself affirmed that the devil had appeared to her the day before and, after talking some time, leaped upon and grievously tormented her ever since. We prayed with her. Her agonies ceased. She fell asleep and awaked in the morning calm and easy.

October 1, 1763. About half-hour after ten, ten of us came together, as we had agreed the day before. I said, "Is there any among you who does not believe that God is able and willing to deliver this soul?" They answered with one voice, "We believe he both can and will deliver her this day." I then fastened her down to the bed on both sides, and set two on each side to hold her if need were. We began laying her case before the Lord, and claiming his promise on her behalf. Immediately Satan raged vehemently. He caused her to roar in an uncommon manner; then to shriek, so that it went through our heads; then to bark like a dog. Then her face was distorted to an amazing degree, her mouth drawn from ear to ear, and her eyes turned opposite ways and starting as if they would start out of her head. Presently her throat was so convoluted that she appeared to be quite strangled; then the convulsions were in her bowels and her body swelled as if to burst. At other times she was stiff from head to foot, as an iron bar, being at the same time wholly deprived of her senses and motion, not even breathing at all. Soon after her body was so writhed, one would have thought all her bones must be dislocated.

We continued in prayer, one after another, till about twelve o'clock. One then said, "I must go; I can stay no longer." Another and another said the same, till we were upon the point of breaking up. I said, "What is this? Will you all give place to the devil? Are you still ignorant of Satan's devices?

Shall we leave this poor soul in his hands?" Presently the cloud vanished away. We all saw the snare and resolved to wrestle with God till we had the petition we asked of him. We began singing a hymn and quickly found his Spirit was in the midst of us; but the more earnestly we prayed, the more violently the enemy raged. It was with great difficulty that four of us could hold her down. Frequently we thought she would have been torn out of our arms. By her looks and motions we judged she saw him in a visible shape. She laid fast hold on Molly L--s and me with inexpressible eagerness and soon burst into a flood of tears, crying, "Lord, save or I perish! I will believe. Lord, give me power to believe; help my unbelief!" Afterwards she lay quiet for almost fifteen minutes. I then asked, "Do you now believe Christ will save you? And have you a desire to pray to him?" She answered, "I have a little desire, but I want power to believe." We bid her keep asking for the power and looking unto Jesus. I then gave out a hymn and she earnestly sang with us those words:

> O Son of Righteousness, arise,
> With healing in thy wing;
> To my diseased, my fainting soul,
> Life and salvation bring!

I now looked at my watch and told her, "It is half-hour past two. This is the time when the devil said he would come for you." But, blessed be God, instead of a tormentor, he sent a comforter. Jesus appeared to her soul and rebuked the enemy, though still some fear remained; but at three it was all gone and she mightily rejoiced in the God of her salvation. It was a glorious sight. Her fierce countenance was changed and she looked innocent as a child. And we all partook of the blessing, for Jesus filled our souls with a love which no tongue can express. We then offered up our joint praises to God, for his unspeakable mercies and left her full of faith and love and joy in God her Saviour.

June 15, 1769. Indeed there has not been hotter persecution of late years any where in the kingdom than here. The mob, encouraged by their superiors, beat and abused whom they pleased, broke open their houses, and did just what they listed. A wretched Clergyman confirmed therein, and applied to the Methodist Preachers 2 Timothy 3:6–7, the very text of that unhappy gentleman at Bristol, which he uttered, and dropped down in the pulpit. After he had painted them as black as devils, he added, "I have not time to finish now; next Sunday I will give you the rest." But the next morning he was struck in a strange manner. He could not bear to be a moment alone. He cried out, "Those hobgoblins; do not you see them? There, there! The room is full of them!"

Having continued thus some days, he screamed out, "See that hobgoblin at the bed's feet! O that roll, that roll which he holds up to me! All my sins are written therein." Not long after, without showing the least sign of hope, he went to his account.

June 5, 1772. In the following week, I preached in many towns round Newcastle and on Saturday went again to Sunderland. In the evening we mightily wrestled with God for an enlargement of his work. As we were concluding, an eminent backslider came strongly into my mind and I broke out abruptly, "Lord, is Saul also among the Prophets? Is James Watson here? If he be, show your power!" Down dropped James Watson like a stone and began crying aloud for mercy.

☩ ☩ ☩

John Cennick, who was preaching in London, in John and Charles' absence, wrote to John on September 12, 1739 to recount a supernatural incident:

On Monday night, I was preaching at the school on the forgiveness of sins, when numbers cried out with a loud and bitter cry. Indeed, it seemed that the devil and the powers of darkness were come among us. My mouth was stopped. The cries were terrifying. It was pitch dark; it rained much; and the wind blew vehemently. Large flashes of lightning and loud claps of thunder mingled with the screams and exclamations of the people. . . . The whole place seemed to resemble the habitation of apostate spirits; many raving up and down and crying, "The devil will have me; I am his servant! I am damned! My sins can never be pardoned! I am gone, gone for ever!"

A young man was in such horrors that seven or eight persons could scarce hold him. He roared like a dragon: "Ten thousand devils, millions, millions of devils are about me!" This continued three hours and what a power reigned amongst us! Some cried out with a hollow voice: "Mr. Cennick! Bring Mr. Cennick!" I came to all that desired me. They then spurned me with all their strength, grinding their teeth and expressing all the fury that heart can conceive. Their eyes were staring and their faces swollen and several have since told me that when I drew near, they felt fresh rage and longed to tear me to pieces. I never saw the like, nor even the shadow of it before. Yet I was not in the least afraid as I knew God was on our side.

Although John Wesley firmly believed in miracles, deliverances, and other supernatural experiences, he did not believe in speaking in tongues as the evidence of the baptism of the Holy Spirit. Commenting on Acts 2:38, John wrote: "Repent—And hereby return to God: be baptized—Believing in the name of Jesus—And you shall receive the gift of the Holy Spirit. . . . The gift of the Holy Ghost does not mean in this place the power of speaking with tongues. For the promise of [being able to do] this was not given to all that were afar off, in distant ages and nations." However, the Irish Methodist lay preacher Thomas Walsh wrote in his diary on March 8, 1750: "This morning the Lord gave me a language I knew not of, raising my soul to Him in a wondrous manner."

Wesley warned about placing too much emphasis on supernatural phenomena:

> Trust not in visions or dreams, in sudden impressions or strong impulses of any kind. Remember, it is not by these you are to know what is the will of God on any particular occasion, but by applying the plain scripture rule with the help of experience and reason and the ordinary assistance of the Spirit of God.
>
> . . . Not hastily ascribe things to God. Do not easily suppose dreams, voices, impressions, visions or revelations to be from God. They may be from him. They may be from nature. They may be from the devil. Therefore, "believe not every

spirit, but try the spirits whether they be of God." Try all things
by the written word and let all bow down before it. You are in
danger of enthusiasm every hour, if you depart ever so little
from Scripture.

John spoke against extreme practices that brought ridicule to
Christianity, and he sometimes reprimanded preachers who encouraged bizarre behavior, such as screaming in concert and the "Welsh
Jumpers" who would leap into the air and violently move their bodies
while singing the same verse of a hymn thirty or forty times until
exhausted. Wesley's explanation was that Satan took advantage of their
ignorance and simplicity "in order to wear them out and bring discredit
on the word of God."

Over the years, Wesley confronted a number of false prophets,
including John Adams and the so-called Shropshire Prophet George
Newans who, through numerous "prophecies," claimed he foresaw
the invasion of England and the destruction of the Roman Catholic
Church. One who had a significant influence on some in the movement
was former soldier George Bell who claimed that he was sinless and
foretold the end of the world on February 28, 1763. Bell was supported by Thomas Maxfield, one of Wesley's first lay preachers, his
deputy at the Foundery, and a man he described as being a "son of the
Gospel." Wrote Wesley in his *Journal*: "From the time that I heard of
George Bell's prophecy, I explicitly declared against it both in private
and in the society, in preaching, over and over; and, at length, in the
public papers." Bell was subsequently arrested for causing a public
disturbance. He lost his faith and turned to radical politics. However,
Maxfield left the movement, taking around two hundred of the society
with him to form an independent chapel and became a vociferous
opponent of Wesley.

John also had to contend with a group called the French Prophets
or "Camisards"—a Huguenot sect originating in France at the end of
the seventeenth century. The French Prophets believed in speaking in
tongues, claimed spiritual perfection, and prophesied the imminent
return of Jesus Christ. John believed their teachings were unbiblical,
while Charles was convinced that they were "pretenders to inspiration"

and had a sharp exchange with one of their prophetesses called Mary Lavington, a woman he described as having a "horrible, hellish laugh."

Signs, wonders, and miracles were an essential part of John Wesley's ministry, but he always emphasized that Christian love and the word of God were of greater importance. As early as May 1739, Wesley wrote in his *Journal*:

> But in the meantime, I bless God that there is a more excellent gift than either the knowledge of languages or philosophy. For tongues and knowledge and learning will vanish away; but love never fails. . . . Another ground of these and a thousand mistakes, is, the not considering deeply, that love is the highest gift of God; humble, gentle, patient love; that all visions, revelations, manifestations whatever, are little things compared to love; and that all the gifts above-mentioned are either the same with, or infinitely inferior to, it.

John always saw himself as "a man of one book" and stated, "I receive the written Word as the whole and sole truth of my faith. . . . The Bible is my standard of language as well as sentiment. I endeavour not only to think but to speak 'as the oracles of God.'" He believed "the written word of God to be the only and sufficient rule of Christian faith and practice." Declared Wesley:

> My ground is the Bible. Yes, I am a Bible bigot. I follow it in all things, both great and small. The Scriptures are the touchstone whereby Christians examine all, real or supposed, revelations. In all cases they appeal "to the law and testimony," and try every spirit thereby. Receive nothing untried, nothing till it is weighed in the balance of the sanctuary. . . . Believe nothing they say, unless it is clearly confirmed by plain passages of holy writ. Wholly reject whatsoever differs therefore, whatever is not confirmed thereby. And, in particular, reject with the utmost abhorrence, whatsoever is described as the way of salvation that is either different from, or short of, the way our Lord has marked out.
>
> I am a spirit come from God and returning to God: just hovering over the great gulf; till a few moments hence, I am no more seen; I drop into an unchangeable eternity! I want to know one thing—the way to heaven; how to land safe on

that happy shore. God Himself has condescended to teach the way, for this very end He came from heaven. He has written it in a book. O give me that book! At any price, give me the book of God! I have it: here is knowledge enough for me. . . .

The Scripture, therefore, of the Old and New Testament is a most solid and precious system of divine truth. Every part thereof is worthy of God; and all together are one entire body, wherein they who are able to taste prefer to all writings of man, however wise or learned or holy.

In April 1786, the eighty-two-year-old John Wesley reaffirmed the importance of the Word of God when he wrote, "Scripture teaches us that the agreement of doctrines with truth, as taught in those Scriptures, is the only infallible rule."

13

MEN OF ONE BOOK

A skillful man, if the Bible were lost, might
extract it from Wesley's hymns.

—JOHN RATTENBURY

The first Methodist hymnbook, *Psalms and Hymns*, was published in 1737 in Charleston by John Wesley. It contained some of his own compositions, as well as adaptations of great English hymns, translations of hymns (mainly from the German Moravian hymnbook), slightly adapted verses by the Catholic John Austin, and some by his father and brother Samuel. *Psalms and Hymns*, however, did not contain any of Charles' compositions. It was the first hymnbook to be published in America and the first by an Anglican minister. After their return to England, the brothers jointly published five hymnals between 1739 and 1745. A sixth, *Moral and Sacred Hymns* (1744), appeared under John's name only.

But it was Charles rather than John Wesley who became the poet laureate of Methodism, composing more than nine thousand hymns and sacred poems, which amounts to, on average, a hymn a day every day for twenty-five years of his adult life. His talent for verse has been described by author John Rattenbury as "the greatest single gift which either brother possessed." More than four hundred of Wesley's hymns are still sung in churches and chapels worldwide today. Tyson has said: "Wesley's hymns reflected the emotional challenges of real life.

Certainly this has been a part of their staying power and continuing relevancy."[47]

Isaac Taylor, the writer and inventor, declared that there was no spiritual element that "does not find itself emphatically and pointedly and clearly conveyed in some stanzas of Charles Wesley's hymns." Charles' "Jesus, Lover of My Soul" has been described as the "finest heart hymn in the English language." Henry Ward Beecher declared: "I would rather have written that hymn of Wesley's, 'Jesus, lover of my soul, Let me to thy bosom fly,' than to have had the fame of all the kings that ever sat on earth. That hymn will go on singing until the last trumpet brings forth the angel band; and then, I think, it will mount up on some lip to the very presence of God."

Isaac Watts, the great hymn writer, declared that Charles' hymn "Come, O Thou Traveller Unknown" was worth all the verses he himself had written. Two of what are considered the four greatest Anglican hymns of all time were written by Charles Wesley: "Lo! He Comes with Clouds Descending" and "Hark the Herald Angels Sing" with the latter Charles wrote in 1739 as a hymn for Christmas Day, and it originally began with the line "Hark how all the Welkin rings." It was adapted by George Whitefield and his friend Martin Madan who rewrote the first four of the opening eight lines to what we know today. So highly esteemed was Charles' hymn writing that the eminent composer George Frederic Handel himself set six of Wesley's hymns to music, although the most prolific composer of music for Charles' hymns was the German composer, bassoonist, and former Deist John Frederick Lampe.

Charles could play the harpsichord and flute, and was renowned for his solos on the latter at Oxford. But he composed no original music, although he may have adapted contemporary music to fit his compositions. He did not have a particularly good voice, with his son commenting that Charles "had not a vocal talent, but could join in a hymn or simple melody tolerable well in tune." However, he was a brilliant lyricist who not only expounded the central themes of the

---

[47] Ibid., viii.

Methodist movement but incorporated many of the issues facing Methodism into his hymns.

John once described Charles' verse as "the handmaid of piety" and as containing "all the important truths of holy religion." Charles himself commented, "Our hymns have helped spread the Gospel. God himself has own'd and applied them to many of your hearts." Swedish professor Johan Liden, who attended a service at the Foundery in 1769, wrote in his journal:

> The song of the Methodists is the most beautiful I ever heard. Their fine psalms have exceedingly beautiful melodies composed by great masters. They sing in a proper way, with devotion, serene mind and charm. It added not a little to the harmonious charm of the song that some lines were sung by only the women, and afterwards the whole congregation joined in the chorus.

Charles, even more so than John, was a "man of one book" and his main theological reference and resource was the Bible. Charles' approach to the Scriptures—what he called the oracles—was invariably Christ-centered. Regardless of where the biblical passage was, the focus was Jesus Christ and via this he preached justification and sanctification through his hymns. According to Tyson, Charles attempted to evangelize the Old Testament and treat it as though it were contemporary with Christ and the New Testament. Rattenbury has commented that "A skillful man, if the Bible were lost, might extract it from Wesley's hymns. They contain the Bible in solution." Author W. Garrett Horder wrote, somewhat hagiographically, in *The Hymn Lover* in 1889 that "Amongst Charles Wesley's writings are to be found some of the grandest hymns in the English language. For spontaneity of feeling, his hymns are pre-eminent. They are songs that soar. They have the rush and fervour which bear the soul aloft."

One historian has commented on Charles' hymn writing that "the hoof-beats hammered out the rhythm of the song as it shaped itself in his brain." Another who observed him called him an "evangelical centaur"—half man, half horse, who probably composed many of his hymns while riding from one preaching engagement to another. Said

Charles about one incident: "I crept on, singing or making hymns, till I got unawares to Canterbury." On at least one occasion, Charles surprised his friends by riding his horse through their garden and directly to the front door, through which he burst shouting, "Pen and ink! Pen and ink!" After having writing implements produced for him, he sat down and rapidly wrote down the hymn he had been composing in his head while he rode. After jotting down his composition on paper, Charles somewhat sheepishly greeted his hosts and politely apologized for bursting in on them in such a manner.

Composing hymns became so much a part of Charles' daily regimen that he was able to gauge the severity of an injury by its ability to interrupt that process, however slightly. Wrote Charles: "Near Ripley my horse threw and fell upon me. My [traveling] companion thought I had broken my neck, but my leg was only bruised, my hand sprained and my head stunned; which spoiled my making of hymns, or thinking at all, till the next day when the Lord brought us to New Castle."

Charles Wesley's hymns would change Christian worship, but his compositions were rarely sung in parish churches during his lifetime. They would instead be sung in market squares, on hillsides, and in Methodist preaching houses. Through his hymns, men and women of little or no education could learn essential scriptural truths. One convert, Elizabeth Downs, revealed to Charles that when she sang his hymns she felt her heart was being torn out of her body so strong was their impact on her. A typical Wesleyan practice was "lining out" the hymns—reading each line aloud to emphasize its meaning before singing it.

To assist Methodists to sing during times of individual and family prayer and in public worship, John issued a number of guides to music theory so that members could teach themselves to read musical notation. He also produced a study of music entitled *Thoughts on the Power of Music* in 1779. And John was not above intervening in the worship service if it failed to reach his expectations, as he did at the Methodist chapel in York in 1790: "During the singing some discordant notes grated harshly on Wesley's ear. . . . At the end of the verse, he said, 'Now listen to brother Masterman,' who was the leading singer. As this did not produce the desired effect, he stopped again and said, 'Listen to me.' But the cracked voice of the old man of nearly ninety [actually nearly eighty-seven] failed to do its office."

An example of Charles' extemporaneous talent as a hymn writer occurred when he was preaching at the docks in the coastal town of Plymouth. A mob of drunken sailors interrupted Wesley's preaching by half-singing and half-shouting a popular dance hall ditty. Charles remarked that he liked the melody but not the lewd lyrics and challenged the sailors to return later in the day, by which time he would have a song that they could all sing together. They returned, expecting to mock him still further, only to be deeply moved by the new lyrics of the song that Charles had composed, entitled "On the True Use of Musick."

By the 1750s, Charles realized that his deteriorating health and marital responsibilities would keep him from the mission field, writing in his journal on August 9, 1751: "Preaching, I perceive, is not my principal business. God knows my heart and all its burdens. O that He would take the matter into His hands, though He lay me aside like a broken vessel!" Charles continued to concentrate on composing hymns rather than itinerant ministry. The result was his magnum opus, *Short Hymns on Select Passages of Scripture*, published in 1762, which consisted of two volumes containing 2,030 hymns, with hundreds more remaining in manuscript form and only being published recently. In Charles' preface to the work, he comments, "God having graciously laid His hand upon my body, and disabled me for the principal work of the ministry, has thereby given me an unexpected occasion of writing the following hymns."

Charles Wesley's hymns were more than the background music of early Methodism; they were themselves vehicles of Wesleyan evangelism and expressions of Wesleyan theology. A thirty-six-verse hymn entitled "Universal Redemption," which supported John's sermon on free grace, was a rebuttal of what Charles viewed as "the poison of Calvin," the doctrine of predestination. In "A Funeral Hymn for Mrs. Hooper," which was published in his *Hymns and Sacred Poems* (1742), he celebrated Mrs. Hooper's death and what he believed to be her Christian perfection. Charles wrote hymns that expressed both the joys and the sadness of family life. *Hymns on the Death of a Child* was written when his son John died of smallpox. *Hymns and Sacred Poems* (the 1749 edition) was hastily put together from material in his notebooks collected over thirteen years while traveling and sold to give him some money to get married. "After Deliverance from Death by the Fall of an House" was written in 1743 after Charles had faced violent mobs while preaching. *Hymns and Sacred Poems* contained an entire section of "Hymns for the Persecuted." "The Prayer for the Church of England" (1780) expressed Charles' commitment to the Anglican Church and his determination that the Methodist movement remain in the "Old Ship" as he called it.

Charles' two series of *Hymns On God's Everlasting Love*, published in the 1740s, were a direct attack on the Calvinist doctrine of predestination, including a polemical hymn entitled "This Horrible Decree" in which predestination is described as a "hellish doctrine." George Whitefield complained to John, "dear brother Charles is more and more rash. He has lately printed some very bad hymns," and then he wrote to Charles himself: "Why did you in particular, my dear brother Charles, affix your hymn, and join in putting out your late hymn book? How can you say you will not dispute with me about election, and yet print such hymns?"

Hymns for Times of Trouble, produced in 1743–44, expressed Charles and John's patriotism, depicting their view that King George II was God's anointed vice-regent, responsible for upholding religious freedom and serving the needs of the British people. Charles repeatedly invoked God's protection for George II against the Jacobites.

However, John did not always agree with the sentiments that Charles expressed in his hymns. Some of his *Short Hymns on Select Passages of the Holy Scriptures* clearly reveal his feelings about the danger of the "loquacious, turbulent and bold perfectionists" and their false pride. John hit back by denouncing these hymns, claiming that he had seen "five hundred witnesses" to the truth of Christian perfection.

Joseph Williams witnessed a Methodist meeting where Charles prayed, preached, and expounded on the hymns they were singing:

Never did I hear such praying or such singing—never did I see and hear such evident marks of fervency of spirit in the service of God—as in that society. At the close of every petition, a serious Amen like a rushing sound of waters, ran through the whole society; and their singing was . . . the most harmonious and delightful I ever heard. . . . Indeed they seemed to sing with melody in their hearts. . . . if there be such a thing as heavenly music upon earth, I heard it there. . . . I do not remember my heart to have been so elevated, either in collegiate, parochial, or private worship, as it was there and then. . . . If therefore, any inquire . . . "Can any good come out of Methodism?" I can only answer . . . "Come and see".

In 1780, John Wesley compiled the best of many of the Methodist hymnbooks into one volume entitled *Collection of Hymns for the Use of the People Called Methodists.* It contained 480 of the 525 hymns Charles had written. John described it as "a little body of experimental and practical divinity . . . not so large as to be either cumbersome or expensive and . . . large enough to contain such a weight of hymns as will not soon be worn threadbare." According to John it contained "no doggerel, no botches . . . nothing turgid or bombast on the one hand, nor low and creeping on the other." It rather exemplified "the purity, the strength, and the elegance of the English language." It defined the essence of Wesleyan theology and spirituality. According to the philosopher James Martineau, it was "the grandest instrument of popular religious culture that Christendom has ever produced."

Charles Wesley's last published collection of hymns was *Prayers for Condemned Malefactors* (1778), a twelve-page pamphlet purposely composed for evangelistic visits to London's Newgate prison. Charles continued to compose hymns in the final years of his life, including *Hymns for the Methodist Preachers*, which he wrote in 1786, consisting of sixteen poems celebrating and praying for Methodist preachers. It was left in manuscript form. He wrote his last hymn just before he died in March 1788.

14

HELL UPON EARTH

*All Newgate rang with the cries of those whom
the word of God cut to the heart.*

—JOHN WESLEY

Prisons in eighteenth-century Britain were open-plan edifices of disorder, drunkenness, corruption, filth, and disease. Jailers were not paid but extracted fees from the incarcerated. A parliamentary inquiry led by Colonel (later General) James Oglethorpe in 1729–30 discovered starvation, neglect, torture, and even the murder of prisoners unable to pay fees to their jailers. Newgate prison in London was described as a "place of calamity [and a] habitation of misery." At the Marshalsea prison, also in London, inmates were dying daily from sickness and malnutrition in cells where prisoners were stacked on shelves, one tier above another. In 1728, the Marshalsea was contracted out to a local butcher for £400, and he went to extraordinary lengths to turn a profit: "To raise this rent oppression, extortion, cruelty and even torture were exercised, the prisoners being kept in close, crowded rooms, thirty to fifty being placed in each apartment not sixteen feet square, and three persons being allotted to each bed, each paying 2s 6p per week."

Thousands of debtors were thrown into prison, without trial, by their creditors so that by the 1770s almost half the entire prison population were debtors.

Virtually all inmates were infested with lice, and only a quarter of prisoners survived until their execution day. Infectious diseases such as typhus—the infamous "jail fever," which was transmitted by lice and fleas—killed more people than the gallows. Food was provided by the jailer for a fee and by charities to those who could not pay, but cooking was not included, so food was often eaten raw. Being released from prison was not simply a matter of completing a sentence and walking out. A departure fee had to be paid and until it was, prisoners remained behind bars. Those who died inside had to stay there as a rotting corpse until relatives could pay for them to be removed. The stench was overwhelming and unavoidable for the incarcerated, and even nearby shops were often forced to close in the summer because of the unbearable smell coming from the prison.

It was common for children to be conceived and born inside the prison, for men and women freely mingled, and the women found that they could swap sex for food. If they became pregnant, they could "plead the belly" in an attempt to avoid hanging. Prisoners often had their entire families inside the prisons with them, even their pets. Joseph Benardi's wife, for example, bore him ten children while he was imprisoned at Newgate. If their parents died in prison, surviving children were taken to the workhouse.

In 1776, Dr. William Smith described Middlesex prisons and their inmates:

> . . . few, accustomed to any degree of cleanliness, could bear the stench of such places, or stand the shock of such misery. Vagrants and disorderly women of the very lowest and most wretched class of human beings, almost naked, with only a few filthy rags almost alive with vermin, their bodies rotting with distemper, and covered with itch, scorbutic and venereal ulcers.
>
> In the morning, before the turn-keys attempt to open the doors of the different wards, which are . . . like the black hole in Calcutta, . . . they are obliged to drink a glass of spirits to keep them from fainting, for the putrid stream of myasma is enough to knock them down. They are very frequently seized

with such violent reachings, that nothing will lie upon their stomachs.

During the 1770s, the great prison reformer John Howard commented after visiting the Bridewell prison in Abingdon, Oxfordshire: "Two dirty day-rooms; and three offensive night-rooms: That for men eight feet square: one of the women's, nine by eight; the other four and a half feet square: the straw, worn to dust, swarmed with vermin: no court: no water accessible to prisoners. The petty offenders were in irons: at my last visit, eight were women."

John Wesley became a regular visitor to Newgate prison in Bristol, where he befriended the jailer, Abel Dagge. Dagge had become a committed Christian through George Whitefield's ministry in 1737. Encouraged by John, Dagge eradicated cheating, drunkenness, and prostitution, and disputes were settled on the spot without fighting or brawling. Dagge even introduced cottage-type industries, such as tailoring and shoe-making, to keep the inmates employed and give them a sense of self-respect. John wrote of Dagge's attempts to improve Newgate prison that it had become "as clean and sweet as a gentleman's house," and "By the blessing of God on these regulations, the whole prison has a new face. Nothing offends either the eye or the ear, and the whole has the appearance of a quiet serious family."

Charles recorded in his journal in July 1738 about visiting ten men in London's Newgate prison who were sentenced to death, one of whom was a black man found guilty of murdering his master. Daily, Charles offered him comfort by patiently explaining to him the gospel of Jesus Christ: "He listened with all the signs of eager astonishment. The tears trickled down his cheeks while he cried, 'What, was it for me? Did God suffer all this for so poor a creature as me?' I left him waiting for the salvation of God." Later, as the man was taken to Tyburn in London for execution, Charles was there to meet him: "The black spied me, coming out of the coach and saluted me with his looks. As often as his eyes met mine, he smiled the most composed, delightful countenance I ever saw."

Prepared to take their prison ministry further, Charles and his friend John Bray agreed to spend all night locked in the condemned cell, or the "condemned hole" as Charles described it, praying, teaching, comforting, singing, and observing the men going to the gallows as if to a wedding. Charles wrote about the experience in his journal:

> We wrestled in mighty prayer. All the criminals were present; and all delightfully cheerful. . . . Joy was visible in all their faces. We sang:
>
>> Behold the Saviour of mankind,
>> Nail'd to the shameful tree!
>> How vast the love that him inclined,
>> To bleed and die for thee.
>
> It was one of the most triumphant hours I have ever known.

Charles recorded again in his journal: "I preached with power and freedom in the Marshalsea. I prayed by Mrs. Cameron who owned herself convinced. She had been a Deist, because it is so incredible [that] the Almighty God should condescend to die for his creatures."

In 1739, John wrote in his *Journal* of visiting Newgate prison in Bristol and ministering to the inmates:

> April 26. At Newgate, I was led to pray that God would bear witness to His word. Immediately one, and another, and another sunk to the earth; they dropped on every side as thunderstruck. One of them cried out aloud. We besought God in her behalf and He turned her heaviness into joy. A second being in the same agony, we called upon God for her also; and He spoke peace unto her soul. In the evening, one was so wounded by the sword of the Spirit, that you would have imagined she could not live a moment. But immediately His abundant kindness was shown, and she loudly sang of His righteousness.
>
> April 27. All Newgate rang with the cries of those whom the word of God cut to the heart; two of whom were in a moment filled with joy, to the astonishment of those that beheld them.
>
> April 30. While I was preaching at Newgate, a woman broke out into strong cries and tears. Great drops of sweat ran

down her face, and all her bones shook; but both her body
and soul were healed in a moment.

Both brothers frequently visited Newgate prison in London. On
November 9, 1739, they went early in the morning "to do the last good
office to the condemned malefactors." After the Communion, the
Wesleys were not allowed to ride in the cart to the place of execution,
so they followed in a coach down Holborn in London. Outside St. Giles
in the Fields, the procession stopped in front of the new church to
honor the ancient custom of allowing the condemned men to drink a
last tankard of ale. By the time they reached Tyburn in Hyde Park, the
place of execution, the usual immense crowd, avid to see the men hang,
was already waiting eagerly. The Wesleys sang hymns with the men as
they were made ready for death. "It was the most glorious instance I
ever saw of faith triumphing over sin and death," recalled John Wesley.
He asked one man who was weeping yet looking upward with the rope
around his neck, "How do you feel your heart now?"

The man replied calmly, "I feel at peace which I could not have
believed possible. And I know it is the peace of God, which passes
understanding."

A few moments later, the hangman led the cart forward, and the
man hung until he died. Then both Wesleys preached the gospel to
the crowd, Charles giving an impassioned sermon on repentance, faith,
and the love of God. Recalled Charles: "When the cart drew off not
one struggled for life. We left them going to meet their Lord, ready
for the Bridegroom. . . . I spoke a few suitable words to the crowd, and
returned full of peace in our friends' happiness. That hour under the
gallows was the most blessed hour of my life." In his *Journal*, John Wesley
wrote that "tears ran down the cheeks" of one of the condemned who
was moved by his preaching, but the fact that his handwriting is shaky
and he was unable to write in his *Journal* the following day suggests that
John was deeply disturbed by the hanging.

In December 1784, John visited Newgate in London and preached
to forty-seven prisoners who were condemned to death:

> While they were coming in, there was something very
> awful in the clink of their chains. But no sound was heard,

either from them or the crowded audience, after the text was named: "There is joy in heaven over one sinner that repents, more than ninety and nine just persons, that need not repentance." The power of the Lord was eminently present, and most of the prisoners were in tears. A few days after, twenty of them died at once, five of whom died in peace. I could not but greatly approve of the spirit and behaviour of Mr. Villette, the ordinary; and rejoiced to hear that it was the same on all similar occasions.

Throughout their lives, both John and Charles Wesley continued their prison ministry, regularly visiting Newgate in Bristol, the Castle and Bocardo prisons in Oxford, and Newgate and Marshalsea prisons in London. In 1753, John described the latter prison as "a nursery of all manner of wickedness. . . . Oh shame to man that there should be such a place, such a picture of hell upon earth." In 1761, John wrote to the *London Chronicle* describing the appalling conditions in Newgate prison in Bristol where "so great was the filth and the stench, misery and wickedness, it shocked all who had a spark of humanity left."

Even in the last years of his life, frail and in ill-health, Charles continued to visit Newgate prison in London where he preached "the condemned sermon," considering it a final opportunity to save the soul of the prisoner about to be hanged. Henry Moore, who accompanied Charles on at least one of these visits, wrote: "I witnessed with feelings which I cannot describe the gracious tenderness of his heart. I saw the advantage of proclaiming the Gospel to those who knew they were soon to die, and felt that they had greatly sinned." Charles' last published collection of hymns, *Prayers for Condemned Malefactors*, was dedicated to prisoners. In one copy of this hymnbook, published in 1785, someone, maybe even Charles himself, had written: "these prayers were answered, Thursday, April 28, 1785, as nineteen malefactors, who all died penitent. Not unto me, O Lord, not unto me."

At the Methodist conference of 1778, in response to the question "Is it not advisable for us to visit all the jails we can?" John replied: "By all means. There cannot be a greater charity." He wrote numerous articles in which he publicized the inhumane conditions in which prisoners lived, and he preached "charity sermons" during which collections were taken for prisoners.

John Wesley had the chance to meet the prisoner reformer John Howard in Dublin on July 28, 1787, a few years before both died, and wrote of the encounter: "I had the pleasure of a conversation with Mr. Howard, I think one of the greatest men in Europe. Nothing but the mighty power of God can enable him to go through his difficult and dangerous employments. But what can hurt us if God is on our side?" Howard himself recalled his encounter with Wesley: "I was encouraged by him to go vigorously with my own design. I saw in him how much a single man might achieve by zeal and perseverance. And I thought, why not I do as much in my way as Mr. Wesley has done in his, if I am only as assiduous and persevering? And I determined I would pursue my work with more alacrity than ever."

At the beginning of 1789, Howard called at Wesley's home in London on his way to Europe, but John had left for Ireland. Alexander Knox recalled Howard saying: "Present my respects and love to Mr. Wesley. Tell him I hoped to have seen him once more. Perhaps we may meet again in this world; but if not, we shall meet, I trust, in a better." Howard and John Wesley never did meet again, for Howard contracted typhus in Kherson, now Ukraine, while visiting a prison. He died aged sixty-three in January 1790.

15

MAKE THEM FREE
THAT THEY MAY BE
FREE INDEED

Thou Saviour of all, make them free,
that they may be free indeed.

—JOHN WESLEY

n 1735, when John and Charles Wesley decided to sail for Georgia as missionaries, John had declared that he was going to the New World to preach to the "heathens." But he was referring to American Indians, not black slaves, for slavery was banned in the colony. The 1732 charter to Georgia declared that each resident would be free, and it prohibited the importation and use of slaves.

However, the Wesleys were soon given a glimpse of slavery when they visited Charleston, South Carolina, in August 1736. John visited a church and conversed with a number of slaves, expressing his disappointment at their lack of knowledge of the Christian faith. The following April, he met a black slave girl when he visited the town of Ponpon and whose attention to his instruction he described as "inexpressible." Later, John made progress with a black boy he met in Purrysburg, whom he found "both desirous and very capable of instruction." Such was his success that he proposed a program of itinerant instruction for the slaves. Wrote John: "First, to inquire after and find out some of the most serious of the planters. Then, having inquired of them which of their slaves were best inclined and understood English, to go to them from plantation to plantation, staying as long as appeared necessary at each." John mentions that some of the planters expressed an interest, but the scheme never got off the ground. Curiously, John never mentions the brutality of the slave trade, even though it is likely that, on occasion, he witnessed it.

In contrast, when Charles saw for himself the evils of slavery, he recorded it in his journal:

> It were endless to recount all the shocking instances of diabolical cruelty which these men (as they themselves) daily practise upon their fellow-creatures and that on the most trivial occasions.
>
> Mon. August 2nd, 1736. I had observed much, and heard more, of the cruelty of masters towards their negroes; but now I received an authentic account of some horrid instances thereof. The giving a child a slave of its own age to tyrannize over, to beat and abuse out of sport, was, I myself saw, a common practice. Nor is it strange, being thus trained up in cruelty, they should afterwards arrive at so great perfection in it; that Mr. Star, a gentleman I often met at Mr. Lasserre's, should, as he himself informed Lasserre, first nail up a negro by the ears, then order him to be whipped in the severest manner, and then to have scalding water thrown over him, so that the poor creature could not stir for months after. Another much applauded punishment is, drawing their slaves' teeth. One Colonel Lynch is universally known to have cut off a poor negro's legs; and to kill several of them every year for barbarities.
>
> I shall only mention one more related to me by a Swiss gentleman, Mr. Zouberbuhler, an eye-witness, of Mr. Hill, a dancing-master in Charleston. He whipped a she-slave so long that she fell down at his feet for dead. When, by the help of a physician, she was so far recovered as to show signs of life, he repeated the whipping with equal rigour and concluded with dropping hot sealing-wax upon her flesh. Her crime was over-filling a tea-cup.
>
> These horrid cruelties are the less to be wondered at, because the government itself countenances and allows them to kill their slaves, by the ridiculous penalty appointed for it,

of about eleven pounds sterling, half of which is usually saved by the criminal informing on himself. This I can look upon as no other than a public act [statute] to indemnify murder.

Although Charles was shocked by the conditions of the slaves and the savage punishments meted out to them, he did not consider slavery wrong or the slave trade a crime against humanity at that point. Neither, surprisingly, did George Whitefield, despite writing and publishing "A Letter to the Inhabitants of Maryland, Virginia, and North and South Carolina Concerning Their Negroes" in which he criticized slave owners' treatment of their slaves:

> Your dogs are caressed and fondled at your tables, but your slaves, who are frequently styled dogs or beasts, have not equal privilege. They are scarce permitted to pick up the crumbs that fall from their masters' tables. Indeed, some . . . have been, upon the most trifling provocation, cut with knives, and have had forks thrown into their flesh; not to mention what numbers have been given up to the inhuman usage of cruel taskmasters, who, by their unrelenting scourges, have ploughed upon their backs, and made long furrows, and at length brought them even to death itself. I hope there are few such monsters of barbarity suffered to subsist among you.

Yet Whitefield still refused the logic of condemning slavery and the slave trade, even though he went on to claim "but sure am I that it is sinful, when bought, to use them as base as, indeed worse than brutes. . . . Your slaves, I believe, work as hard if not harder than the horses whereon you ride."

The 1732 Georgia charter decreed that every person residing in or born in the province would be free, and Georgians were prohibited from the importation and use of "Black Slaves or Negroes." Unfortunately, petitions from landowners to allow slavery led to the practice becoming lawful in 1740. John Wesley wrote to the French abolitionist Anthony Benezet: "Mr. Oglethorpe you know went as far as to begin settling a colony without Negroes, but at length the voice of those villains prevailed who sell their country and their God for gold, who laugh at human nature and compassion, and who defy all religion, but that of getting money. It is certainly our duty to do all in our power to check this growing evil. . . . But I fear it will not be stopped till all the kingdoms of the earth become the kingdoms of our God."

Whitefield advocated slavery because he believed the land could only be worked properly by negroes. According to Whitefield, Abraham in the Old Testament had slaves, and slavery was permissible as long as the slaves were treated well. Colonel William Stephens, the Secretary of Georgia, pointed out that Governor Oglethorpe had specifically banned slavery, stating: "Slavery is against the Gospel, as well as the fundamental law of England. We refused, as Trustees, to make a law permitting such a horrid crime." Whitefield had limited knowledge of the appalling conditions in which slaves were forced to work and the barbarous way in which they were treated. His naivety was exploited by those who envied the prosperity of slave-owning Carolina.

By 1745, Whitefield, believing that Bethesda, his house for orphans, could never expand nor Georgia prosper without slaves, and convinced that he could convert them to Christianity, decided to support the mounting agitation for the repeal of the act which excluded negroes from the colony and prevented the inhabitants from owning slaves. Despite the opposition of the leader of the Salzburger Protestants, John Martin Bölzius, who was a friend of John Wesley, and the Moravians, who both deplored slavery on principle, Whitefield remained unmoved. He became a slave owner, eventually owning twenty-five slaves. "I trust many of them will be brought to Jesus" he said in his defense, naively assuming other slave owners to be as enlightened in their treatment of slaves as he was. Whitefield's attitude towards slavery was expressed in a letter to a Mr. B. written in Bristol on March 22, 1751:

> As for the lawfulness of keeping slaves, I have no doubt, since I hear of some that were bought with Abraham's money, and some that were born in his house. And I cannot help thinking, that some of those servants mentioned by the Apostles in their epistles, were or had been slaves. It is plain, that the Gibeonites were doomed to perpetual slavery, and though liberty is a sweet thing to such as are born free, yet to those who never knew the sweets of it, slavery perhaps may not be so irksome.

However this be, it is plain to a demonstration, that hot countries cannot be cultivated without negroes. What a flourishing country might Georgia have been, had the use of them been permitted years ago? How many white people have been destroyed for want of them, and how many thousands of pounds spent to no purpose at all? Had Mr. Henry been in America, I believe he would have seen the lawfulness and necessity of having negroes there. And though it is true, that they are brought in a wrong way from their own country, and it is a trade not to be approved of, yet as it will be carried on whether we will or not; I should think myself highly favoured if I could purchase a good number of them, in order to make their lives comfortable, and lay a foundation for breeding up their posterity in the nurture and admonition of the Lord.

Whitefield also described ministering to slaves in North Carolina on his second trip to America:

I went, as my usual custom . . . among the negroes belonging to the house. One man was sick in bed, and two of his children said their prayers after me very well. This more and more convinces me that negro children, if early brought up in the nurture and admonition of the Lord, would make as great proficiency as any among white people's children. I do not despair, if God spares my life, of seeing a school of young negroes singing the praises of Him Who made them, in a psalm of thanksgiving. Lord, Thou has put into my heart a good design to educate them; I doubt not but Thou wilt enable me to bring it to good effect.

Ironically, in his will, George Whitefield bequeathed his slaves, together with the rest of his property in America, to Lady Selina Huntingdon, one of the leading supporters of Methodism in Britain.

Even though John Wesley read Thomas Southerne's anti-slavery play *Oronooko* in 1726–7 and taught a negro boy during his return voyage from Georgia in 1737–8, he did not become actively involved in the anti-slavery movement until the 1770s. However, in 1758 while preaching in Liverpool, he met and dined with John Newton, a thirty-three-year-old ex-slave trader who had embraced Christianity during a storm at sea some years earlier. Newton, who later wrote the famous hymn "Amazing Grace," inspired by his change of heart about slavery, had continued as a captain of a slave ship while a Christian, though he hated the work. When Wesley met him he was a tide surveyor and a disciple of George Whitefield, and it was partly due to John's pamphlet *Thoughts upon Slavery* that Newton realized the true evil of the practice.

John Wesley's *An Earnest Appeal to Men of Reason and Religion* (1744) greatly impressed Nathaniel Gilbert who inherited a plantation in Antigua in the Caribbean. He sought out Wesley when he returned to England, and during this visit, John baptized two slaves belonging to Gilbert. When Gilbert returned to Antigua, he began preaching to his slaves. By the end of the eighteenth century, the island had become largely Methodist.

Two events prompted Wesley to give more serious consideration to publicly entering the debate on slavery. In February 1772, while traveling from Dorking to London, he read the French Quaker Anthony Benezet's *Some Historical Account of Guinea* and was appalled by Benezet's descriptions of slavery in the British Colonies in America and the Caribbean. Wesley said: "I read nothing like it in the heathen world, whether ancient or modern and it infinitely exceeds, in every instance of barbarity, whatever Christian slaves suffer in Mahometan countries." The same year, the abolitionist Granville Sharp brought a lawsuit before the Lord Chief Justice Mansfield (who was also known as William Murray and had been saved from bullies by Charles at Westminster School) of the Court of King's Bench, to stop the export to Barbados of American runaway slave James Somerset, who had been recaptured in London. Lord Mansfield's famous judgment was that a slave setting foot in England came under the general ruling that "whenever and wherever a slave sets foot on English soil he was from that moment free."

Wesley condemned both the slave trade and slavery, describing them as "that execrable sum of all villainies, commonly called the slave trade." To slave owners, John declared: "O, whatever it costs, put a stop to its cry before it be too late. . . . Your hands, your bed, your furniture, your house, your lands, are at present stained with blood." And to slave traders, he urged: "Today, resolve, God being your helper, to escape for your life. Regard not money! . . . Whatever you lose, lose not your soul: Nothing can countervail that loss. Immediately quit the horrid trade." When the supporters of the slave trade asserted that negro slaves were necessary in the West Indies because white men were unable to work in that hot climate, John replied, "It were better that all those islands were altogether sunk in the depth of the sea than that they should be cultivated at so high a price as the violation of justice, mercy, and truth." When told that the slave trade was essential to the commercial prosperity of England, John replied: "Better no trade than trade procured by villainy. . . . Better is honest poverty than all the riches brought by the tears, and sweat, and blood of our fellow creatures."

John Wesley wrote to the editor of the *Monthly Review*, arguing strongly against the treatment of slaves. In 1774, Wesley published his treatise *Thoughts upon Slavery* as a fifty-three-page pamphlet which sold for a shilling. In it he referred to slavery as:

> . . . an obligation of perpetual service which only the consent of the master can dissolve, and moreover which allows the master to alienate the slave, in the same manner as his cows and horses.
>
> It is common for several hundred of them to be put on board one vessel, where they are stowed together in as little room as is possible for them to be crowded. It is easy to suppose what conditions they must soon be in, between heat, thirst and stench of various kinds. So there is little wonder that so many should die in passage, but rather that any should survive.
>
> Notwithstanding ten thousand laws, right is right and wrong is wrong. There must still remain an essential difference between justice and injustice. . . . Give liberty to whom liberty is due, that is, to every child of man, to every partaker of human nature. Let none serve you but by his own act and deed, by his own voluntary action. Away with all whips, all chains, all compulsion! Be gentle toward all men and see that you invariably do with every one as you would he should do unto you.

Wesley, quoting the observations of Sir Hans Sloane in his treatise, graphically described the appalling punishments meted out to the slaves:

> . . . they frequently geld them or chop off half a foot; after
> they are whipped till they are raw all over, some put pepper
> and salt upon them; some drop melted wax upon their skin;
> others cut off their ears and constrain them to broil and eat
> them. For rebellion—that is, asserting their native liberty,
> which they have as much right to as to the air they breathe—
> they fasten them down to the ground with crooked sticks on
> every limb, and then applying first by degrees, to the feet and
> hands they burn them gradually upward to the head.

Wesley sent a copy of *Thoughts upon Slavery* to Benezet, who had it published in America. One author has claimed that in America, the treatise "probably exerted a greater influence upon the public conscience than any book ever written, not excepting *Uncle Tom's Cabin*, for the reception of which it prepared the way." Publication in Ireland and Europe followed, and thirteen editions of the treatise were published in the United States over the next thirty years. One of those who read the pamphlet was John Newton, whose eyes were finally opened to the iniquity of the slave trade. He became an active opponent of slavery and a major influence on William Wilberforce.

Wesley did not stop there, however. In his *Calm Address to Our American Colonies*, published in 1775, he wrote incisively about the evils of slavery and gave a clear illustration of who was and who was not enslaved, so none of the colonists should mistake his concern. Said Wesley: "You and I and the English in general, go where we will and enjoy the fruit of our labours: This is liberty. The Negro does not: This is slavery." And in a pointed remark to slave-owners in the American colonies he said, "this equally concerns every gentleman that has an estate in our American plantations; yes, all slave-holders, of whatever rank and degree, seeing men-buyers are exactly on a level with men-stealers." John maintained that no one had the right to discuss the principle of liberty when involved in the slave trade, and the conflict in America was all most certainly God's judgment on Britain's involvement in the evil trade.

His opposition to slavery was well known among Methodists in America, a fact reinforced by the minutes of conferences held in 1780, in which it was stated that the owning of slaves was a cause for expulsion

from the Methodist movement. In America it actually became a badge
of virtue among Methodists for a slave-owning convert to free their
slaves.

John repeated his opinions in *A Serious Address to the People of
England with Regard to the State of the Nations*, published in 1778, and in
an article entitled "A Summary View of the Slave Trade," published in
the *Arminian Magazine* in 1788. The year before when the Committee
for the Abolition of the Slave Trade was formed, Wesley sent a letter of
support to the committee, stating that its objective should not just be
the abolition of the slave trade but to strike at the very heart of "the
shocking abomination of slavery" itself. Later that year, he wrote to one
of its members, Thomas Funnell, offering whatever help he could give.
John warned that there would be "vehement opposition both by slave
merchants and slave holders; and they are mighty men." He informed
Funnell that he would reprint:

> A large edition of the tract I wrote some years since,
> Thoughts upon Slavery, and send it (which I have an oppor-
> tunity once a month) to all my friends in Great Britain and
> Ireland; adding a few words in favour of your design, which
> I believe will have some weight with them. I commend you
> to Him who is able to carry you through all opposition and
> support you in all discouragements and am Gentlemen, Your
> hearty well-wisher.

A month earlier in October 1787, John corresponded with Granville
Sharp, who had founded a society for the abolition of slavery, saying,
"ever since I heard of it . . . I felt a perfect detestation of the horrid
Slave Trade, but more particularly since I had the pleasure of reading
what you have published upon the subject." In March 1788 John, now
in his eighty-fifth year, bravely preached against slavery in Bristol, the
center of the slave trade in Britain, declaring "that the poor outcasts
might find a way of escape and their chains be broken in asunder." At
the end of his sermon he declared that the following day would be a
day of prayer and fasting in remembrance of slaves.

In February 1791, John Wesley set out in his two-horse chaise with
his assistant, James Rogers, for what proved to be his last mission, to

console a friend in Leatherhead. During the journey, Rogers read to him from a new book that Wesley had helped finance, entitled *The Interesting Narrative of the Life of Olaudah Equiano, or Gustavus Vassa*. It was the autobiography of Vassa, an African born slave, who in 1745 had been kidnapped, transported to Virginia, sold into slavery in Barbados, and then educated and sent by his master to England where he was baptized, joined the Royal Navy, and had a number of adventures in the West Indies. Wesley was so moved by Vassa's story, which turned out to be the last book he read, that he wrote what proved to be his final letter, to William Wilberforce in 1791, encouraging him to pursue his crusade to abolish slavery throughout the British Empire:

> MY DEAR SIR, Unless the Divine Power has raised you up to be Athanasius, contra mundum, I see not how you can go through your glorious enterprise, in opposing that execrable villainy, which is the scandal of religion in England and of human nature. Unless God has raised you up for this very thing, you will be worn out by the opposition of men and devils. But, if God is for you, who can be against you? Are all of them together stronger than God? O! be not weary in doing well! Go on in the name of God and in the power of his might, till even American slavery (the vilest that ever saw the sun) shall vanish away before it.
>
> Reading this morning a tract, wrote by a poor African, I was particularly struck by that circumstance—that a man who has a black skin, being wronged or outraged by a white man, can have no redress; it being a law, in all our colonies, that the oath of a black against white goes for nothing. What villainy is this.
>
> That He who has guided you from your youth up, may continue to strengthen you in this and all things, is the prayer, Dear Sir,
>
> Your affectionate servant.

There is no record that Charles was directly involved in the abolitionist movement like his brother John, but he did help two former African princes in Bristol during the 1770s who had been enslaved for six years and who demonstrated "both the outward visible sign and the inward spiritual grace in a wonderful manner and measure."

In 1785, Charles had the opportunity to meet William Wilberforce, an event the rising young politician and ardent abolitionist recorded in his journal:

> I went, I think in 1785 to see [Hannah Moore], and when I came into the room Charles Wesley arose from the table, around which a numerous party sat at tea, and coming forwards to me, gave me solemnly his blessing. I was scarcely ever more affected. Such was the effect of his manner and appearance that it altogether over set me, and I burst into tears, unable to restrain myself.

Wilberforce was so moved by his encounter with Charles that in 1792, he arranged for Charles' widow, Sally, to receive an annual pension of £60 a year until her death.

16

GIVE ALL YOU CAN

Gain all you can.
Save all you can. Give all you can.

—JOHN WESLEY

M anuel Gonzales, a Portuguese who visited England
during the eighteenth century, wrote:

Few nations are more burdened with them
[the poor], there not being many countries where
the poor are in a worse condition. Those who were
unemployed or in prison, widows, orphans and children born
out of wedlock, were often condemned to a miserable life
of destitution, hunger and ill-treatment. Even poor people
who were employed were often forced to work long hours for
little reward, made even smaller by unfair deductions from
their pay.

John Wesley had seen "with my own eyes," throughout Britain,
"thousands starving because out of work"—people who could afford
only "a little coarse food every other day." He spoke of a woman who
gathered "Stinking sprats from a dunghill" to feed her children and
another who collected bones left by dogs in the streets, "making broth
of them to prolong a wretched life." This was in stark contrast to the
rich who were, according to Wesley, "abounding with all the necessaries,
the conveniences, the superfluities of life." He commanded one wealthy

follower to "Go and see the poor and sick in their poor little hovels. Take up your cross, woman!" Later he urged this woman to "Creep in among these in spite of dirt and an hundred disgusting circumstances, and thus put off the gentlewoman." Wesley spoke angrily against the "wickedly, devilishly false" view of the upper classes that many were poor due to idleness. John wrote in 1757: "I love the poor. In many of them I find pure, genuine grace, unmixed with paint, folly and affectation. I bear the rich and love the poor; therefore I spend almost all my time with them."

On May 7, 1741, John wrote in his *Journal*:

> I reminded the United Societies that many of our breth-ren and sisters had not needful food: many were destitute of convenient clothing; many were out of business, and that I had done what in me lay to feed the hungry, clothe the naked, employ the poor, visit the sick; but was not alone sufficient for all these things, and therefore, desired all whose hearts were as my heart:
>
> 1. To bring what clothes each could spare to be distrib-uted among those that wanted them.
> 2. To give weekly a penny or what they could afford for the relief of the poor and sick.

John reported in his *Journal* of visiting the sick and poor in the districts on the south bank of the River Thames during the winter of 1753:

> On Friday and Saturday I visited as many more as I could. I found some in their cells under ground; others in their garrets, half-starved both with cold and hunger, added to weakness and pain. But I found not one of them unemployed, who was able to crawl about the room. . . . If you saw these things with your own eyes, could you lay out money in orna-ments or superfluities?

In 1777, John described visiting members of the Bethnal Green society in East London:

Many of them I found in such poverty as few can conceive without seeing it. Oh, why do not all the rich that fear God constantly visit the poor! Can they spend part of their spare time better? Certainly "every man shall receive his own reward according to his labour."

Such another scene I saw the next day in visiting another part of the society. I have not found any such distress, no, not in the prison of Newgate. One poor man was just creeping out of his sickbed to his ragged wife and three little children, who were more than half naked and the very picture of famine. When one brought in a loaf of bread, they all ran, seized upon it, and tore it in pieces in an instant. Who would not rejoice that there is another world?

Wesley and the Methodists' views of how wealth and privilege were wasted and abused in eighteenth-century Britain proved to be highly offensive to many members of the aristocracy, including the Duchess of Buckingham, who wrote a scathing letter to Lady Selina Huntingdon:

These Methodist doctrines are most repulsive and strongly tinctured with impertinence and disrespect towards their superiors, in perpetually endeavouring to level ranks, and to do away with all distinction. It is monstrous to be told that you have a heart as sinful as the common wretches that crawl the earth. This is highly offensive and insulting; and I cannot but wonder that your Ladyship should relish any sentiments so much at variance with high rank and good breeding.

The threat of war over the American colonies affected trade, which led to rising unemployment and poverty in Britain during the 1770s. John commented that he observed thousands of unemployed "standing in the streets, with pale looks, hollow eyes and meagre limbs," and formerly well-to-do families forced to scavenge in the fields "to pick up turnips which the cattle had left." Wesley wrote to Lord Dartmouth, Secretary of State for the Colonies, on June 14, 1775, about his fears for the nation: "As I travel four or five thousand miles a year, I have an opportunity of conversing freely with more persons of every denomination than anyone else in the three kingdoms. I cannot therefore but know the general disposition of the people, English, Scots and Irish; and I know an huge majority of them are exasperated all to madness."

While he was studying at Oxford University, an incident dramatically changed John Wesley's perspective on money. He had just finished paying for some paintings for his room when one of the chambermaids came to his door. It was a cold winter's day, and he noticed that she had nothing to keep her warm but a thin, linen gown. He reached into his pocket to give her some coins to buy a coat, but found he had too little left. Immediately, the thought struck him that God was not pleased with the way he had spent his money. He asked himself, "Will your Master say, 'Well done, good and faithful steward?' You have adorned your walls with the money which might have screened this poor creature from the cold! O justice! O mercy! Are not these pictures the blood of this poor maid?"

In February 1766, a man who had been defrauded of a large fortune and was now starving called on Wesley, pleading for his help, but John discovered that he had run short of money. He therefore asked him to call again. Just before he arrived, someone gave John twenty guineas so that he was able to buy clothes for the man and send him back to his home city of Dublin.

Once, when his chaise got stuck in a rutted road in Ireland, Wesley proceeded on foot, leaving his friends to get help to drag the carriage out. A poor man who had been thrown out of his home because he could not afford the rent of twenty shillings approached John in deep distress. When Wesley gave him a guinea (twenty-one shillings), the man knelt down in the road to pray for his benefactor.

For almost four years, John lived on a diet consisting mainly of potatoes, partly for health reasons but also to save money, saying, "What I save from my own meat will feed another that else would have none." When Parliament imposed a tax on gold and silver plate and Wesley received a demand for the plate that it was assumed, as an eminent clergyman, he possessed, he replied: "Sir: I have two silver teaspoons at London and two at Bristol. This is all the plate which I have at present, and I shall not buy more while so many around me want bread. I am sir, your most humble servant. John Wesley."

Some complained that John was naive when it came to money, but he vigorously defended his approach to giving: "I have heard today that I do not know the value of money. What! Don't I know that twelve pence make a shilling, and twenty-one shillings a guinea. Don't I know that if given to God, it's worth heaven through Christ. And don't I know that if hoarded and kept, it's worth damnation to the man who hoards it." At the age of seventy-seven, John Wesley wrote, "I cannot help leaving my books behind whenever God calls me hence; but in every other respect my own hands will be executors." One Methodist recorded his astonishment that Wesley could not walk the few feet from his study to the pulpit without distributing coins to the "poor old people of his society," giving £10 or £20 in one go to needy tradesmen. Ralph Waller has commented that "It is interesting that John Wesley, who grew up in an atmosphere of pervasive debt, spent so much of his time and energy in later life feeding, clothing and educating poor people, and providing shelter for them."[48]

This was not only what Wesley practiced throughout his life, but also what he preached. "The Use of Money" was one of John's favorite sermons, and he first preached it in 1744. His need to repeat the sermon was rooted in his belief that the proper use of money was the real test of a person's Christian life. He also felt that it was his duty to arouse the conscience of his Christian stewardship—its use of money and time, which were gifts of God, and its responsibility to other members of the community.

Wesley earned more that £30,000 during his lifetime from the sale of his books, sermons, and other publications, and he gave most of it away. He kept a careful account of all his expenditures and receipts up until a few months before he died. He paid himself £30 a year. When he received £200 from his four-volume *Concise History of England*, he gave it all away in a week. When he inherited £1,000 from a supporter, it was given immediately to the needy. One year he earned £1,400 and gave virtually all of it away. John wrote to his sister, Patty Hall, "money never stays with me; it would burn me if it did. I throw it out as soon as possible, lest it should find a way into my heart." By giving his money

---

[48] Waller, *John Wesley*, 9.

away Wesley declared, "I am effectually secured from laying up treasure upon earth." In "The Use of Money" John stated:

> But let not any man imagine that he has done anything, barely by going thus far, by "gaining and saving all he can", if he were to stop there. All this is for nothing, if a man go not forward, if he does not point all this at a farther end. Nor, indeed, can a man properly be said to save anything, if he only lays it up. You may as well throw your money into the sea, as bury it in the earth. And you may as well bury it in the earth, as in your chest, or in the Bank of England. Not to use it, is effectively to throw it away.

He said even more dramatically: "Having gained all you can, and saved all you can, give all you can; else your money will eat your flesh as fire and will sink you to the nethermost hell. . . . If a man observed the first two rules and not the third, he will be twofold more the child of hell than he was before."

On January 21, 1740, at Lawford's Gate near Bristol, John provided food to more than one hundred and fifty people who were on the verge of starvation due to severe frosts that prevented them from working. The following year he organized a collection of clothes that were distributed to the poor and needy. In the bitterly cold winter of 1763 when the River Thames froze over, he opened a soup kitchen at the Foundery and distributed financial relief. *Lloyd's Evening Post* reported that "Great numbers of poor people had pease pottage and barley broth given them at the Foundery, at the expense of Mr. Wesley; and a collection was made, in the same place of worship, for further supplying the necessities of the destitute, at which upwards of £100 was contributed."

Two years later, he organized collections to aid London's unemployed weavers, and before this he had offered employment to women who were out of work in the knitting industry. To provide more long-term relief, Wesley proposed that every member of the London Methodist Society provide one penny a week to help the poor and sick and donate any spare clothing. Over a period of twenty years, the London society collected and gave £14,000 to those in need.

Wesley established a charitable fund providing small, interest-free loans to the needy among his London members. The maximum was initially fixed at twenty shillings, and the principal had to be repaid within three months. Twenty years later, the scheme was still going strong with the capital exceeding £120 and the loan limit raised to £5.

Housing for widows and the sick was another problem Wesley confronted. He took over two houses adjacent to the Foundery which became known as the Poorhouse. It provided a home for sixteen people, including nine poor widows, one blind woman, and two children. John also employed two schoolmasters at the Foundery to provide an elementary education for children who roamed the streets like "wild ass's colts." Other projects included supporting humanitarian schemes outside of the Methodist organization. One such scheme was the Strangers Friend Society established by retired soldier John Gardner, which helped those in utter destitution.

Throughout his life, even in old age, he would go door to door collecting money to feed and clothe the poor. In the week beginning December 5, 1785, at the age of eighty-two, he spent every hour he could spare "in the unpleasing but necessary work of going through the town and begging for poor men. . . . if I do it not, nobody else will." The famous writer Dr. Samuel Johnson complained indignantly about Wesley's concern for the poor after having dinner with him in 1783: "The dog enchants you with his conversation and then breaks away to go and visit some old woman!"

In January 1787, John wrote in his *Journal* of again trying to raise money for the poor:

> Monday 8, and the four following days, I went a-begging for the poor. I hoped to be able to provide food and raiment for those of the society who were in pressing want, yet had no weekly allowance; these were about two hundred. But I was much disappointed. Six or seven, indeed, of our brethren, gave ten pounds apiece. If forty had done this, I could have carried my design into execution. However, much good was done with two hundred pounds, and many sorrowful hearts made glad.

It is an irony indeed that as Methodism's emphasis on thrift, hard work, and discipline lifted many members out of poverty, Wesley worried that greater financial prosperity would lead to a decline in spiritual fervor. He wrote in 1787: "The Methodists in every place grow diligent and frugal; consequently they increase in goods. Hence they proportionately increase in pride, in anger, in the desire of the flesh, the desire of the eyes, and the pride of life. So, although the form of religion remains, the spirit is swiftly vanishing." "But I can afford it" was a remark that John often heard when he challenged members of the societies who lavished their wealth on themselves. In disgust he would reply: "Oh, lay aside forever that idle, nonsensical word. No Christian can afford to waste any part of the substance which God has entrusted him with."

When some Methodists justified themselves by giving a tenth of their income, Wesley declared, "Render unto God, not a tenth, not a third, not half, but all that is God's, be it more or less." Commented John: "I have not known threescore rich persons, perhaps not half the number, who, as far as I can judge, were not less holy than they would have been, had they been poor. . . . How many rich persons are there among the Methodists," enquired Wesley, "who actually do deny themselves and take up their cross daily? Who of you that are now rich deny yourselves just as you did when you were poor?" And from his observations, he came to the conclusion that it was a challenge for an individual to amass great wealth while retaining their religious zeal. Even to Ebenezer Blackwell, one of Wesley's wealthiest and most loyal laymen, he wrote, "What an amazing thing it will be if you endure to the end."

John implored wealthy Methodists to make a provision in their wills to provide funds to worthy causes. John said, "Surely if I did little good with my money while I lived, I would at least do good with it when I could live no longer." He particularly appealed to people who had no heirs: "And if you have not children, upon what scriptural principle can you leave behind you more than will bury you?" To those who declared to him, "I must provide for my children," he would reply: "Certainly. But how? By making them rich? Then you will probably make them heathens, as some of you have done already. Leave them enough to live on, not in idleness and luxury, but by honest industry." When asked to explain how he would provide for his own children if he had any, he replied, "I ought then to give each what would keep him above want, and to bestow all the rest in such manner as I judged would be meet for the glory of God."

In sermons and pamphlets, John passionately denounced the distilling of alcohol and its detrimental impact on society, particularly on the poor. In 1772, in a pamphlet entitled *Thoughts upon the Present Scarcity of Provisions*, Wesley claimed that a half of all the grain produced in England was distilled into alcohol, or what he termed "liquid fire." He declared, "It would be better for England that half the grain crop should be thrown into the sea, rather than convert it into deadly poison." John described as "blood money" wealth derived from selling alcohol. In an article entitled "A Word to the Drunkard," Wesley appealed to the manhood of the drunkard: "Are you a man? God made you a man, but you made yourself a beast. Never call yourself a man. You are beneath the greater part of the beasts that perish."

John founded a number of schools and adult learning programs. He also produced inexpensive literature for the poor. His literary output was prodigious, producing, with few exceptions, a number of works each year. These included English, French, Latin, Hebrew, and Greek grammar books, all of which sold for a penny, and *A Complete English Dictionary* and a *Concise History of England* in four volumes. He also published a vast body of literature for his preachers and members of the societies. In 1763, John published the two-volume *A Survey of the Wisdom of God in the Creation: or A Compendium of Natural Philosophy* because, he said, "I wished to see this short, full, plain account of the visible creation directed to its right end: not barely to entertain an idle, barren curiosity; but to display the invisible things of God, his power, wisdom and goodness." One of his most ambitious educational projects was his fifty-volume *Christian Library* (1749–55) which included some of the best works in practical divinity that Wesley abridged and made available to the public, although he was careful to exclude any favorable references to predestination. He said of this project that it would extract "all that is most valuable in the English tongue . . . to provide a complete library for those who fear God." John was also the first great religious leader to realize the value of leaflets for religious and educational purposes. As early as 1745 he was "giving away some thousands of little tracts among the poor people," and in 1772 he organized the world's first tract society. Through this endeavor he was able to reach and inform members of the working class who were unable to read his books.

In 1745, at Kingswood, three miles from Bristol, John Wesley founded the first of four schools (two of which were charity schools). This school provided an education for forty children of miners in the area. In addition, he founded two other charity schools, one at the Foundery in London and the other in Bristol. In 1748 a large sum, £800, was donated by a Mrs. Gumley, one of the few members of the upper classes who supported Methodism. The money was for the establishment of a fee-paying boarding school at Kingswood, primarily for the sons of Methodist lay preachers. The school's regime owed much to John's upbringing and educational experiences. It placed strong emphasis on religious instruction, discipline, and correction. According to Charles, the school was for "a little flock, a chosen seed [who would] shun the paths of men . . . listen for the voice of truth," and be the next generation of "ambassadors for the King of Kings."

Kingswood accommodated fifty children between the ages of six and twelve (John believed anyone older to be already corrupted by the world). Students were expected to rise daily at 4.00 a.m. for private devotions, followed by public worship at 5.00 a.m. The boys endured a punishing curriculum John designed that consisted of reading, writing, arithmetic, English, French, Latin, Greek, Hebrew, History, Geography, Rhetoric, Logic, and Ethics, Geometry, Algebra, Science, and Metaphysics. No time was allotted for play, and there were no school holidays. Charles visited the school regularly and was involved in assisting with disciplinary issues. He also taught the boys his hymns, many of which were published in 1763 in a collection entitled *Hymns for Children*. Despite the draconian schedule, its founder, John Wesley, was still revered by its pupils as evidenced by a letter John received from the then headmaster, Frances Owen: "The young folk heard that I am addressing you, Dear Sir, and with one voice beg to present their duty. They are counting the time when some of them hope to see you in Bristol."

The Methodists did not invent the concept of Sunday schools, but the movement aided their development, and John was an enthusiastic supporter. A Methodist named Hannah Ball established a school for the religious training of children on Sunday in the town of Wycombe in 1769. This was twelve years before Richard Raikes, the founder of the Sunday school system, opened his first school. Ball described the school in a letter to John: "The children meet twice a week, every Sunday and Monday. They are a wild little company, but seem willing to be instructed. I labour among them, earnestly desiring to promote the interests of the Church of Christ." It was another Methodist, Sophia Cooke, who suggested the idea of Sunday schools to Robert Raikes. One day in Gloucester, Cooke and Raikes observed a large number of ragged children in the streets. Struck by their poverty-stricken condition, Raikes said to Cooke: "What shall we do for these poor, neglected children?" She replied, "Let us teach them to read and take them to church," which is what they did the following Sunday.

John urged his followers to start Sunday schools, writing in his *Journal* on April 18, 1787, "Notice having been given at Wigan of my preaching a sermon for the Sunday schools, the people flocked from all quarters in such a manner as never was seen before." He also wrote to Richard Rodda, who had founded a number of Sunday schools near Chester: "It seems these will be one of the great means of reviving religion throughout the nation. I wonder Satan has not yet sent out some able champions against them." In praise of Sunday schools he remarked: "This is one of the best institutions which has ever been seen in Europe for some centuries."

John may have been a harsh disciplinarian, but he had a genuine love for children and always had a smile and a kind word for a child. Often he would request his carriage a half hour before he needed it and took as many children as he could for a ride before beginning his regular work of the day. The children in turn loved him. At Oldham,

Wesley wrote, "The children clung around me. After singing, a whole troop closed me in and would not be content till I had shook each of them by the hand." At Bolton in 1785, when about five hundred children surrounded him after he had spoken to them, he remarked. "Such an army got about me when I came out of the chapel, that I could not disengage myself from them."

17

JOHN WESLEY
THE PHYSICIAN

Cleanliness is indeed next to Godliness.

—JOHN WESLEY

John Wesley had a lifelong interest in the prevention and cure of disease. He began reading medical books in his spare time soon after arriving at Oxford. John Gambold, a member of the Holy Club at Oxford University, remarked on Wesley's perceived prowess in the medical field: "His knowledge of the world and his insight into physic were often of use to us." John was greatly influenced by the Bath physician Dr. George Cheyne's book *An Essay on Health and Long Life* (1724). It was the first medical book written for popular consumption in England which advocated exercise, eating sparingly, and drinking copious amounts of water. John's interest in medical matters intensified as he prepared to go to Georgia as a missionary in 1735, hoping to be "some service to those who had no regular physician among them."

While in America, he participated in at least one autopsy, and studied the herbal remedies and healing practices of the indigenous Indians. He was well acquainted with the latest medical and scientific literature and was highly knowledgeable of natural science. In his five-volume work, *A Survey of the Wisdom of God in the Creation: Or a Compendium of Natural Philosophy*, John summarized Isaac Newton's theories.

Wesley was skeptical of the benefits of the medical practices of his day and observed, "I have had numberless proofs that regular physicians do exceedingly little good." He had good reason to be skeptical. In the *London Pharmacopoeia* of 1721, issued by the College of Physicians, drugs included ingredients such as "dogs' excrement, earthworms and moss from the human skull." When John discovered a massive misappropriation of funds at a hospital in Winchester, he commented scathingly, "Tis a thing worthy of complaint when public charities designed for the relief of the poor are embezzled and deprecated by the rich."

Wesley was determined to provide effective and affordable medical care to the poor who could not afford the exorbitant fees charged by medical practitioners:

> But I was still in pain for many of the poor that were sick: there was so great expense and so little profit. And first I resolved to try whether they might not receive more benefit in the hospitals. Upon the trial, we found there was indeed less expense—but no more good done than before. I then asked the advice of several physicians for them, but still it profited not. I saw the poor people pining away and several families ruined and that without remedy. . . . At length I thought of a kind of desperate expedient. "I will prepare and give them physic myself."

He engaged the services of a chemist and an experienced surgeon, and in December 1746, he began offering free medical treatment to the poor on a Friday at the Foundery in London. About thirty people came for treatment on the first Friday. Within three weeks, 300 people had been treated, growing to about 600 within 6 months. Wesley and the local Methodist society covered the total cost of more than £40 over that period of time. He claimed that 9 out of 10 people who had been treated were greatly improved within 6 weeks and many were cured of diseases that they had suffered from for more than 40 years. One of those cured was William Kirkham, a weaver who had suffered from a persistent cough for years. Wesley enquired:

"How long have you had it?" He replied "About threescore years; it began when I was eleven years old." I was nothing glad that this man should come first, fearing our not curing him might discourage others. However I looked up to God and said, "Take this three or four times a day. If it does you no good, it will do you no harm." He took it two or three days. His cough was cured, and he has not returned to this day.

So successful was the London clinic that Wesley soon opened dispensaries in Bristol and Newcastle.

In 1747, John Wesley published *Primitive Physick; or An Easy and Natural Method of Curing Most Diseases.* It was essentially a collection of folk remedies and a common sense approach to treating a wide range of ailments. The word "primitive" in its title referred not to primitive remedies but to Wesley's desire to return to what he believed to be an ancient standard in medical practice based on the principles of observation and experience. Revised and expanded a number of times, twenty-three editions were issued during Wesley's lifetime with the thirty-seventh and last edition published in 1859, as well as being translated into French and Welsh. The work was still in use in the nineteenth century and could be found in a majority of British households, particularly those of the poor. The book sold for a mere shilling, compared to William Buchan's *Domestic Medicine* (1769) which sold for six shillings.

Primitive Physick was divided into two sections. The first dealt with preventative medicine and listed rules for good health. It contained six themes: Cleanliness, Diet, Exercise, Sleep, Regular Habits, and the Avoidance of Violent Stress. Wesley was keen to remind the members of the Methodist societies of the importance of personal hygiene, diet, and their conduct. Wrote Wesley to Hugh Sanderson, a Methodist preacher in Northern Ireland:

> If you regard your health, touch no supper but a little milk or water gruel. This will by the blessing of God secure you from nervous disorders. . . . Avoid all familiarity with women. This is deadly poison both to them and you. You cannot be too wary in this respect. . . . Avoid all nastiness, dirt, slovenliness. . . . Do not stink above ground. . . . Whatever clothes you have, let them be whole. . . . Let none ever see a

> ragged Methodist. Clean yourself of lice. . . . Do not cut your
> hair, but clean it, and keep it clean. Cure yourself and family
> of the itch: a spoonful of brimstone will cure you. . . . Use no
> tobacco unless prescribed by a physician. It is an uncleanly and
> unwholesome self-indulgence. . . . Use no snuff. . . . Touch no
> dram. It is liquid fire . . . a sure though slow poison.

The second part of the publication contained more than 900 cures for 280 medical conditions. Remedies included cold-water bathing, poultices, hot and cold drinks, and purges and potions of cheap and easily acquired ingredients. For tuberculosis, Wesley recommended, "Every morning cut a little turf of fresh earth and, laying down, breathe in the hole for quarter of an hour." To treat a head cold he suggested paring "very thin the yellow rind of an orange, roll it up inside out and thrust a roll into each nostril. . . . For one seemingly killed by lightning . . . or suffocated, plunge him immediately into cold water or blow slowly with bellows down his throat. This way revives a person seemingly drowned. It is still better if a strong man blows into his mouth."

Some of the proposed cures were bizarre, to say the least, including the use of cow dung, ground-up spider web, and crushed warts found on the inside of horses' legs. When his brother Charles was dying, Wesley's remedies included binding a warm onion and thin slices of beef across the pit of the stomach, and a jelly of bread crusts and lemon juice mixed with sugar. Others could be potentially dangerous, including his recommendation of three pounds of quicksilver (mercury) for a twisted gut. Wesley even had a cure for old age: electricity, along with tar-water and "decoction of nettles." In the fifth edition, published in 1755, Wesley reduced or omitted altogether ingredients that he considered "extremely dangerous," including opium, Peruvian bark, steel, and quicksilver.

Wesley claimed that those who owned the book had "a physician always in the house and one that attends without fee or reward." Those remedies he could guarantee personally, he marked with the letter "T" (tried) or "I" (infallible). He also recognized the problem of diseases, such as scurvy, and was aware of James Lind's *Treatise of the Scurvy* published in 1753. By 1780, Wesley was advocating two oranges a day and one or two spoonfuls of lemon juice and sugar, morning and evening, as a cure for scurvy, and he did so decades before it was discovered that scurvy was caused by a lack of vitamin C.

In March 1789, in Gloucester, a poor widow's only daughter was suffering from severe pains in her side and back, her skin was yellow, her legs were swollen, and she had a persistent cough. Wesley was preaching that night at Gloucester and the widow was able to consult him about her daughter's case. John listened to her sad account and said that he would call the next morning. "I am to preach at Tewkesbury at twelve o'clock, and shall pass your cottage." When he came, he informed the girl, "I have thought over your state, and will give your mother a remedy which, with God's blessing, I trust will do you good; and if God spares my life, I will call upon you when I come this way again." The medicine that Wesley gave the girl resulted in her complete healing.

In March 1790, exactly a year after his first visit, Wesley returned to Gloucester and visited the widow: "I see that you are blessed by God with faculties to use the medicines mercifully given by God for our use, so that I will instruct you in some further remedies that I have discovered lately, and as my body will soon be laid with the clods of the valley, waiting for the resurrection, I shall like to give you these remedies. Use them for God, and may He bless you, and be with you." Wesley gave her a small manuscript, in his own handwriting, containing instructions for the treatment of a number of common diseases. Her daughter's son, who became an eminent physician in the north of England, afterwards acknowledged that Wesley's remedies, handed down to him by his grandmother, had been the most successful he had prescribed during fifty years of practicing as a doctor.

To one female member of his Connexion he advised: ". . . to have enough air at night: it would not hurt you to have the window a little open. When you have the tickling cough, chew a small bit of bark (as big as half a peppercorn), swallow your spittle four or five times, and then spit out the wood. . . . Try if red currants agree with you; if they do, eat as many as you can."

John Wesley's approach to health and medicine, however, was not without its critics. One described *Primitive Physick* as "a little book, on

sale at all Methodist meeting houses; an absurd, fantastic compila-
tion of uncritical folklore," while the eminent London physician and
founder of the Royal Humane Society, Dr. William Hawes, referred to
Wesley's work as that of a "dangerous quack." However, the criticism
served to draw attention to *Primitive Physick* and sales soared. In gratitude, Wesley wrote to Hawes: "Dear Sir, My bookseller informs me that
since you published your remarks on the Primitive Physick there has
been a greater demand for it than ever. If, therefore, you would please
publish a farther remarks, you would confer a farther favour upon Your
humble servant."

Wesley may have been condemned as a quack and an amateur, but
he vigorously defended his practice of medicine:

> For more than twenty years, I had numberless proofs that
> regular physicians do exceedingly little good. From a deep
> conviction of this I have believed it my duty within these four
> months last past to prescribe such medicines to 600–700 of
> the poor as I knew were proper for their several disorders.
> Within six weeks, nine in ten of them who had taken these
> medicines were remarkably altered for the better and many
> were cured of diseases under which they had laboured 10,
> 20, 40 years. Now, ought I have let one of these poor wretches
> perish because I was not a regular physician? To have said,
> "I know what will cure you, but I am not of the College; You
> must send for Doctor Mead?" Before Dr. Mead had come in
> his chariot the man might have been in his coffin. And when
> the doctor was come, where was his fee? What! he cannot live
> upon nothing! So, instead of an orderly cure, the patient dies;
> and God requires his blood at my hands.

Many agreed with Wesley's sentiments, including W. J. Turrell,
who commented that in "hygiene and preventive medicine Wesley is
an acknowledged pioneer, a voice crying in the wilderness . . . a voice
of great power and penetration because of the enormous personal
influence he came to have throughout the whole nation." Dr. Robert
Parry, a medical officer of health for the City of Bristol, wrote, when
referring to the famous nineteenth-century social reformer Edwin
Chadwick: "He did not start the fight, of course. One hundred years

before him John Wesley fought his great fight for hygiene; he was the greatest health educator of the eighteenth century in Britain." While the author H. Vanderpool maintains that "More than any other figure in Christendom, John Wesley actively involved himself with the theory and practice of medicine as well as the principles and practice of ideal physical and mental health."

John Wesley was one of the pioneers of the use of electricity as a medical treatment, describing it as the "soul of the universe." He began using electrotherapy in November 1756 to treat various conditions, including epilepsy, angina, and cramp. He made the treatment available to all so that "any that desire it might try the virtue of this surprising medicine" and went on to install electric shock machines at all of his clinics. According to Wesley, electricity cured him of a number of conditions, and he was certain a friend's "gout in the stomach" was in fact angina pectoris. "I therefore advised him to take no more medicines, but to be electrified through the breast. . . . the violent symptoms immediately ceased." In 1760, he published *The Desideratum: Or Electricity Made Plain and Useful by a Lover of Mankind and of Common Sense.* This publication was based on his use of electricity in the free medical clinics that he had established for the poor in London, Bristol, and Newcastle a decade earlier.

> I ordered several persons to be electrified, who were ill of various disorders; some of whom found an immediate, some a gradual cure. From this time I appointed, first some hours in every week, and afterward an hour in every day, wherein any that desired it might try the virtue of this surprising medicine. Two or three years after, our patients were so numerous that we were obliged to divide them; so part were electrified in Southwark, part at the Foundery, others near St. Paul's, and the rest near the Seven Dials. The same method we have taken ever since; and to this day, while hundreds, perhaps thousands, have received unspeakable good, I have not known one man, woman, or child, who has received hurt thereby.

In his *Primitive Physick*, he suggested that more than twenty medical conditions could be helped by electric shock treatment, although he believed it was most effective for nervous disorders. It is interesting to note that as early as 1733, Wesley claimed that "lying in bed [is the] chief real cause of all nervous diseases . . . why nervous diseases are so much more common among us than among our ancestors . . . by soaking so long between warm sheets, the flesh . . . is parboiled, and becomes soft and fleshly. The nerves . . . are quite unstrung."

Wesley purchased an electrical machine and tried it first on himself for lameness and neuralgia, noting that there was a gradual improvement. He recorded in his *Journal*: "By the same means I have known two persons cured of an inveterate pain in the stomach, and another of a pain in his side which he had ever since he was a child." When someone asked him at a Methodist conference "Why did you meddle with electricity?" he replied, "For the same reason as I published the *Primitive Physick*—to do as much good as I can." And in a letter to the *Gentleman's Magazine*, published in May 1747, Wesley reported the cure of rheumatic pain by electrification. "Who knows what farther experiment and discoveries such an incident may lead to?"

18

ON THE WINGS
OF HEAVEN

. . . multitudes of every kind and degree are daily
turned from the power of darkness to God . . .

—JOHN WESLEY

John Wesley enjoyed a natural affinity with the Irish people and was highly successful in his evangelistic campaigns in Ireland. Methodism was the only Protestant branch of Christianity to achieve any significant impact on Ireland during the eighteenth century. In Dublin, Wesley had his largest following outside of London. John visited Ireland forty-two times between 1747 and 1789 and spent the equivalent of five-and-a-half years of his life ministering to the Irish. Approximately 14,000 Irish became Methodists during his lifetime and many immigrated to North America, extending his influence to the American colonies and then the United States of America. Charles was able to conduct two evangelistic campaigns in Ireland, before marriage and ill health curtailed his ministry.

Thomas Williams, a Methodist lay preacher, founded a Methodist society in Dublin in the 1740s. By August 1747, when John Wesley embarked on his first visit to Ireland, the society had around two hundred members. Soon after John's departure, gang warfare broke out in Dublin, and the Methodist meeting house was burned to the ground. It was at this point that John asked Charles to follow in his footsteps and reinforce what had been established in the country, with Charles recording in his journal somewhat sardonically, "I received a second summons from my brother, hastening me to Ireland."

Charles arrived in Dublin with three companions on September 9, 1747. He discovered that the Methodists had leased a weaver's shed in Cork Street, but the lodgings they had arranged for them turned out to be a squalid slum: "A family of squalling children, a landlady just ready to lie in, a maid who has no time to do the least thing for us, are some of our inconveniences. Our two rooms for four persons . . . and I groan for elbow room; our diet answerable to our lodgings; no one to mend our clothes; no money to buy more."

Charles was confronted with a far more daunting task than John because the city was experiencing one of its periods of intense conflict between the city's rival gangs. He saw a woman beaten to death and competing mobs fight each other until the ground ran red with blood. He was also appalled when the courts acquitted a man who had killed another by jumping on his stomach. The nascent Methodist society was not spared in the violence, as Charles recorded: "A mixed rabble of Papists and Protestants broke open our room . . . and a warehouse, stealing or destroying the goods to a considerable value; beat and wounded several with clubs, etc; tore away the pulpit, benches, window-cases, etc and burnt them openly . . . swearing they would murder us all."

Undeterred, Charles rallied the growing society and preached with courage and determination: "I began my ministry with, 'Comfort ye, comfort ye my people', etc. None made disturbance till I ended. Then the rabble attended us with the usual compliments to our lodgings." And Charles reported on preaching in the open air on his first Sunday in Dublin: "After commending our cause to God, I walked to the green. I believed the Lord would make bare his arm in our defence. I called in his name, 'Come unto me, all ye that are weary,' etc. His power was upon the hearers, keeping down the opposition. . . . Returning, we were insulted by a gathering mob." He even preached under the wall of the army barracks so that ordinary soldiers could hear him despite the opposition of their officers. On October 7, he commented with amusement how a number of soldiers "skulked down, kneeling or sitting on the ground, behind the women" to avoid being seen.

Charles set up two meeting places in Dublin and preached regularly at the city's Newgate prison. Mob violence, however, was never far from the surface, with Charles recording that "In our return from intercession we were stoned for the length of a street or two. Here I received the first blow since I came to Dublin." On October 30, Charles mentions being hit by a stone while preaching, although he was not seriously hurt.

When Charles and his three helpers reached Athlone in the province of Leinster, they were met by a group of thugs intent on stopping their progress:

> I observed the man who had knocked down J. Healey striking him on the face with his club; [I] tried to stop him, which drew him upon me and probably saved our brother's life. . . . They had gathered against our coming great heaps of stones, one of which was sufficient to beat out our brains. . . . One struck Mr. Force on the head; at whom Mr. Handy made a full blow. He turned and escaped part, yet it knocked him down and for the present disabled him. As often as we returned we were driven off by showers of stones. Some were for returning home but I asked if we should leave our brother in the hands of his murderers.
>
> . . . The man who wounded J. Healey was the priest's servant, and rode his master's horse. He was just going to finish the work with his knife, swearing desperately that he would cut him up, when a poor woman from her hut came to his assistance, and swore as stoutly that he should not cut him up. The man half killed her with a blow from J. Healey's whip, yet she hindered him till more help came. . . .
>
> We found J. Healey in his blood at the hut, to which the woman and her husband had carried him. He recovered his senses at the hearing of my voice. We got him to Athlone. . . .
>
> We marched very slowly for the sake of our patient, till we came to the field of battle. It was stained with blood abundantly. We halted and sang of triumph and praise to God, who gives us the victory through our Lord Jesus Christ.

Later Charles reported, "I returned to Dublin half dead with the rain and snow."

Charles and his fellow Methodists had little success among Roman Catholics (particularly as they spoke English to a largely Gaelic-speaking populace), but the Protestant community, especially those who had recently arrived from England, Wales, and Scotland, responded enthusiastically. Charles said in his journal:

> [Never had I spoken] to more hungry souls. They devoured every word [and] some expressed their satisfaction in a way peculiar to them and whistled for joy. . . . The people of Tyril's [sic] Pass were wicked to a proverb; swearers, drunkards, Sabbath-breakers, thieves, etc, from time immemorial. But now the scene is entirely changed. Not an oath is heard, or a drunkard seen among them. They are turned from darkness to light.

News of Charles Wesley's Irish campaign reached England, and his friend Howell Harris expressed his admiration at what Charles was achieving and encouraged him: "Go on my dear honoured brother— and blaze abroad the flame of Jesus our God." George Whitefield urged Charles to "turn thousands and tens of thousands more into righteousness and shine as stars for ever and ever." However, the constant traveling and often violent opposition put a great strain on Charles' health. It was agreed that he should return home in March 1748.

In the autumn of 1748, Charles returned to Ireland for the second time and what proved to be the last time. At Kinsale he received a severe blow to the side of his head, but in Cork he was encouraged by his reception:

> Outward wickedness has disappeared, outward religion succeeded. . . . At five I took the field again: but such a sight I have rarely seen! Thousands and thousands had been waiting some hours, Protestants and Papists, high and low. . . . I cried after them for an hour, to the utmost extent of my voice, yet without hoarseness or weariness.
>
> Wherever we go, we are received as angels of God. . . . One poor wretch told me, before his wife, that he had lived in drunkenness, adultery, and all the works of the devil, for

twenty-one years; had beaten her every day of that time; and never had any remorse till he heard us: but now he goes constantly to church, he behaves lovingly towards his wife, abhors the thing that is evil, especially his old sins. This is one instance out of many.

After Charles left Ireland, the Grand Jury at the Cork Assizes branded him, in his absence, as "a person of ill fame, a vagabond, and a common disturber of His Majesty's peace," and they "prayed that he might be transported." Charles was to write about the Catholic clergy in Ireland: "All the Catholic priests take wretched pains to hinder the people from hearing us," and, according to Charles, they told the people that "all manner of wickedness is acted in our society, except the eating of little children." When Daniel Sullivan, a Methodist layman, appealed to the mayor of Cork for protection, the latter replied: "It is your own fault for entertaining these preachers. If you will turn them out of your house I will engage there shall be no more harm done, but if you will not turn them out, you must take what you will get."

The opposition in Ireland intensified during John's second visit in 1748. He wrote, "That any of the Methodist preachers were alive is a clear proof of an overruling Providence." In Dublin he encountered opponents "hallooing and calling names," while in Birr and preaching to a "dull, rude, senseless multitude," a riot erupted when a Carmelite friar cried out, "You lie! You lie!" In 1749, John returned to Ireland with Grace Murray for his third campaign that lasted for three months. "A few years ago, if we heard of one notorious sinner truly converted to God, it was a matter of solemn joy to all that loved or feared him: and now, that multitudes of every kind and degree are daily turned from the power of darkness to God, we pass it over as a common thing! O God, give us thankful hearts."

A fourth visit followed from April to June 1750. And again his preaching in Cork provoked riots and his effigy was burned. He also found it so difficult to find lodgings (with one inn keeper setting her dogs on him) that he once was forced to ride for ninety miles in a day.

In Limerick, Wesley preached to the Palatines, German Protestant refugees who had been allowed to settle there a generation before.

Methodism took root, and the movement grew to the point where three individuals—Philip Embury, Barbara Heck, and Robert Strawbridge—emigrated to New York and Maryland where they assisted in establishing Methodist societies.

The Irish often gave Wesley a hostile reception when he visited their country. At Cork in 1750, the mayor sent the town drummers and his officials to disturb the congregation, and they arrived where Wesley was preaching with a vast mob. The drummers were noisy enough, but Wesley continued his discourse. When he went out and asked one of the officials to keep the peace, the man answered, "Sir, I have no orders to do that." The rabble threw whatever came to hand, but nothing hit Wesley. He walked forward quietly, looked every man in the face, the rioters opening right and left as he passed along. When he reached his friend's house, a woman stood in the doorway to prevent him from entering. Just then, one of the mob aimed a blow at Wesley, which missed and knocked the woman down flat. All he had to do was to step into the house and no one followed him.

Ten days later another immense crowd assembled near the army barracks in Cork, where Wesley was preaching. When he had finished, seven or eight of the soldiers marched in front and a whole troop behind, so that he passed safely through the rabble with his military bodyguard.

In the same year, John wrote from Dublin: "I had the satisfaction of observing how greatly God had blessed my fellow labourers, and how many sinners were saved from the error of their ways. Many of these had been eminent for all manner of sins. Many had been Roman Catholics; and I suppose the number of these would have been far greater had not the good Protestants, as well as the popish priests, taken true pains to hinder them." And later he commented: "O what a harvest might be in Ireland did not the poor Protestants hate Christianity worse than either popery or heathenism!" Yet, he was not always so charitable about the Irish Catholics, writing in his *Journal* in June 1758: "how little the Irish Papists are changed in a hundred years. Most of them retain the same bitterness, indeed, and thirst for blood as ever, and would as freely cut the throat of all the Protestants as they did in the last century. . . . But as to the nature of religion, the life of God in the soul, they know no more (I will not say, than the priest, but) than the beasts of the field."

John wrote to an Irish Methodist preacher in 1769 warning of the vices that plagued Ireland:

> Use no snuff unless prescribed by a physician. I suppose no other nation in Europe is in such vile bondage to this silly, nasty, dirty custom as the Irish are; but let the Christians be in this bondage no longer. . . . Touch no dram. It is liquid fire. It is a sure, though slow poison. It saps the very springs of life. In Ireland, above all countries in the world, I would sacredly abstain from this, because the evil is so general. To this, and snuff, and smoky cabins, I impute the blindness which is so exceeding common throughout the nation.

In 1757, Whitefield visited Ireland for three weeks, supporting the work of the Wesleys. He commented, "Everywhere the glorious Emmanuel smiled upon my labours." Huge crowds greeted him in Dublin, but he also faced severe persecution, as was recorded by an observer:

> . . . on Sunday afternoon, after preaching in Oxmantown-green, a place frequented by the Ormon and Liberty boys, who often fight there, he narrowly escaped with his life.
>
> In the time of sermon and prayer a few stones were thrown at him, which did not hurt. But when he had done and thought to return home the way he came, access was denied, and he was obliged to go near a half mile through hundreds of papists. Finding him unattended, for a soldier and four preachers who came with him fled, they threw vollies of stones upon him from all quarters, and made him reel backwards and forwards, till he was almost breathless, and all over a gore of blood.
>
> At last, with great difficulty, he staggered to the door of a preacher's house which was kindly opened to him. For a while he continued speechless and panting for breath; but his weeping friends having given him some cordials and washed his wounds [they were afraid that their house would be attacked], a coach was procured, in which, amidst the

oaths, imprecations and threatenings of the rabble, he got safe to his lodgings.

Even in the 1770s, opposition to Wesley and the Methodists could still be intense and violent. Samuel Wood, who later became a preacher, recalled as a child John visiting his home city of Waterford:

> I shall never forget the feelings excited within me when I was hardly five years old, in April 1773, when I saw that venerable servant of God, the Rev. John Wesley, shamefully treated by a rude and desperate mob while he was preaching in the Bowling Green, Waterford. I felt all my blood rushing into my face. I stood at the table upon which Mr. Wesley was standing; and while I heard the shouting of the crowd, and saw the dead animals and cabbage stalks flying around his hoary head, I was filled with pity and horror. I wished that I were a man. I clinched my little fists. Some person came to remove the "child;" but "the child" resisted and would not be removed, until a gentleman, afterward well known as Sir John Alcock rushed forward, took Mr. Wesley in his arms off the table and conveyed him in safety to Mr. Scott's. He [Mr. Wesley] afterward inquired who "the child" was who so bravely stood by the table. I was brought to him. He put both his hands upon my head and blessed me, in the presence of my mother. Dear Mr. Wesley must have been seriously injured but for the manly intervention of Mr. Alcock. Such was my first sight of, and such my first introduction to, my venerable and much-beloved father and friend, the Rev. John Wesley.

Luke Tyerman, in his three-volume *The Life and Times of the Rev. John Wesley*, recalled an incident that occurred when Wesley was invited to dine with one of the officers at the army barracks in Sligo:

> A large party of friends were assembled to meet the venerable visitor at dinner; and, while the meal was in progress, he [Wesley] suddenly laid down his knife and fork, clasped his hands, and lifted up his eyes, as in the attitude of praise and prayer. In an instant, feasting was suspended, and all the guests were silent.
> Wesley then gave out, and sang with great animation, "And can we forget, in tasting our meat, the angelical food

which ere long we shall eat. When enrolled with the blest, in glory we rest, and for ever sit down at the heavenly feast?" The happy old man, so near to the gates of heaven, then quietly resumed his knife and fork; and all felt that this beautiful spontaneous episode, in the midst of an Irish dinner, had done them good.

Of his ministry in Dublin, Wesley wrote: "In some respects the work of God in Dublin was more remarkable than even in London. (1) It is far greater, in proportion to the time and to the number of people. (2) The work was more pure." By the year 1844, there were 50,000 Methodists in Ireland. In 1752, five years after Wesley had first visited Ireland, he held the first Irish Methodist annual conference.

John Wesley visited Ireland for the last time in 1789, eighteen months before he died, by which time he was held in great affection and esteem. At Clanard he held a service at 5.00 a.m. and three or four times as many people as the house where he was staying could contain turned up to hear him speak. And as he passed through the town of Ballyhay, he recorded that the "poor people flocked round me on every side, and would not be contented, till I came out of the chaise, and spent some time with them in prayer." At Pallas no building was large enough to hold the vast crowd that came to see him. According to a Mr. Crookshank, who spoke of those with whom Wesley stayed on his last trip to Dublin, "They seemed to think it a blessing to have him under their roof; and such a sacred influence attended his words that it was no ordinary privilege to have the opportunity of listening to his conversation." And a Mr. Stopford, who witnessed his departure from Ireland, recalled:

> Multitudes followed him down to the ship. Time had done its work: "the keepers of the house trembled and the strong man bowed himself." Wesley was then eighty-seven years old [he was in fact eighty-six]. Before he went on board the vessel he gave out a hymn and they sang. He then kneeled with the multitudes upon the ground and offered a fervent prayer for those who were present, for their families, and for God's blessing upon the Church, and especially upon Ireland. He then shook hands with them. Many wept and a number fell

upon his neck and kissed him. The scene was tenderly impressive. After Mr. Wesley went on board the ship he stood upon the deck with uplifted hands blessing them, while those on the shore waved their handkerchiefs till the winds of heaven wafted him out of their sight, and they beheld him no more.

19

INTO THE LIONS' DEN

Crucify him!

—THE MOB AT WALSALL, 1743

oth John and Charles Wesley were initially opposed to preaching in the open, believing that it would only lead to more conflict with the Church of England, particularly as it would involve preaching in someone else's parish. Shut out of most Anglican churches, George Whitefield claimed that he had no other choice but to preach in the open, declaring that there were too many members of the clergy who "believe only an outward Christ . . . [whereas we] believe that He must be inwardly formed in our hearts also."

Planning to return to Georgia in 1739, Whitefield hoped that John would take over from him and wrote to him to come and observe for himself what God was doing. "There is a glorious door opened among the colliers. You must come and water what God has enabled me to plant. . . . I am a novice. You are acquainted with the great things of God. Come, I beseech you, come quickly. I have promised not to leave this people till you or somebody come to supply my place." However, John felt unequal to the call and had written to James Hutton, "We are all young men—though I hope few of you so young in spiritual, experimental knowledge, as your poor brother, J. Wesley." He was also convinced that he would soon die due to the pressures of ministry.

Charles was also opposed to him going. In a quandary, John asked the Fetter Lane Society to decide. After a futile debate, he requested the casting of lots "and by this it was determined that I [John] should go."

John arrived in Bristol on Saturday, March 31, 1739. Whitefield was overjoyed to see him: "I was much refreshed with the sight of my honoured friend, Mr. John Wesley, whom God's providence has sent to Bristol. 'Lord, now let your servant depart in peace.'" John, however, was shocked the following day to witness Whitefield preaching on a bowling green, writing in his *Journal*: "In the evening I reached Bristol and Mr. Whitefield was there. I could scarce reconcile myself at first to this strange way of preaching in the field of which he set an example on Sunday, having been all my life (till very lately) so tenacious of every point relating to decency and order that I should have thought the saving of souls almost a sin if it had not been done in a church."

The next day, Whitefield left Bristol for Wales with John praying for "some portion of his spirit." But rather than follow his example into the fields, Wesley preached at one of the local societies to a packed and overflowing hall. On April 2, however, he went to one of Whitefield's "pulpits"—a mound in a brickyard—and decided to take a momentous step: "At four in the afternoon, I submitted to be more vile and proclaimed in the highways the glad tidings of salvation, speaking from a little eminence in a ground adjoining the city, to about three thousand people." Even more shocking for John was that he had not preached in his canonicals—gown, cassock, and bands—because they were still en route from London. He wrote to his friend Hutton: "Dear Jemmy, I want my gown and cassock every day. O how is God manifested in our brother Whitefield! I have seen none like him."

After preaching in the brickyard in the afternoon, that evening John spoke of the Acts of the Apostles at a packed meeting room in Baldwin Street, Bristol, where the doors and windows were opened wide, "by which means all that was spoken of the true Christian life described in the end of the 2nd chapter of the Acts was heard clearly by those in the next room, and on the leads, and in the court below, and in the opposite house, and the passage under it." Wrote John of this hectic period:

Every morning I read prayers and preached at Newgate [Bristol]. Every evening I expounded a portion of Scripture at one of or more societies. Every Monday, in the afternoon, I preached abroad, near Bristol; on Tuesday, at Bath Two-Mile Hill alternately; on Wednesday, at Baptist Mills; every other Thursday, near Pensford; every other Friday, in another part of Kingswood; on Saturday, in the afternoon, and Sunday morning, in the Bowling Green (which lies near the middle of the city); and on Sunday, at eleven near Hanham Mount, at two at Clifton, and at five on Rose Green; and hitherto, as my days, so my strength has been.

Between April and December 1739, John preached 500 sermons, with according to his calculations, 50,000 people hearing his preaching in the first month alone. When James Hervey, a former member of the Holy Club, raised his concerns about open-air preaching, John replied: "I have now no parish of my own, nor probably ever shall . . . [so] I look upon all the world as my parish. . . . This is the work I know God has called me to, and I am sure that His blessing attends it."

James Hutton described vividly the impact of open-air preaching by Whitefield and the Wesleys and those who heard them:

They were composed of every description of persons, who, without the slightest attempt at order, assemblies, crying "Hurrah!" with one breath, and with the next bellowing and bursting into tears on account of their sins; some poking each other's ribs, and others shouting "Hallelujah!". It was a jumble of extremes of good and evil. . . . Here thieves, prostitutes, fools, people of every class, several men of distinction, a few of the learned, merchants, and numbers of poor people who never had entered a place of worship, assembled in crowds and became godly.

Charles was still reluctant to preach in the open air (despite doing so at Tyburn in November 1738), particularly as his brother Samuel vehemently denounced field preaching. But Charles was stunned by the impact of Whitefield's preaching to more than 20,000 at Moorfields, an eighteen-acre area of parkland not far from Fetter Lane in London. Charles wrote on June 23, 1739: "My inward conflict continued. I perceived it was fear of man, and that by preaching in the field next Sunday, as George Whitefield urges me, I shall break down the bridge and become desperate." Charles did indeed become "desperate," for the following day he preached in the open air at Moorfields and found the experience overwhelming:

> I found near ten thousand helpless sinners waiting for the word at Moorfields. I invited them in my Master's words, as well as name, "Come unto me, all ye that travail, and are heavy laden, and I will give you rest." The Lord was with me, even me, his meanest messenger, according to his promise. . . . My load was gone, and all my doubts and scruples. God shone upon my path, and I knew THIS was his will concerning me.

When Mrs. Kirkham, mother of Oxford Methodist Robert, saw Charles preaching in the open, she confronted him:

> "What, Mr. Wesley, is it you I see? Is it possible that you who can preach at Christ Church, St Mary's &c., should come hither after a mob?" I cut her short with, "The work which my Master gives me, must I not do it" and went to my mob, or (to put it in the Pharisees' phrase) this people which is accursed. Thousands heard me gladly, while I told them the privilege of the Holy Ghost, and exhorted them to come for Him to Christ as poor sinners. I continued my discourse till night.

In 1738, Charles had begun preaching in churches without a prepared sermon, instead opening the Bible and taking his theme from whatever passage of Scripture was presented to him. He would always first seek to be allowed to preach in a local church. In 1739 he wrote when preaching in Gloucester: "Before I went into the streets and highways, I sent according to custom, to borrow the use of the church. The minister, being one of the better disposed, sent back a civil message that he would drink a glass of wine with me but would not lend me his pulpit for fifty guineas. Mr. Whitefield, however, did lend me his field, which did just as well." Charles was then able to exhort about 2,000 sinners to repent and believe the gospel. He also preached to a multitude again at Moorfields on the outskirts of London. In Runwick in August 1739, he recorded:

> The minister . . . lent me his pulpit. I stood at the window (which was taken down) and turned to the larger congregation of above two thousand in the church yard. They appeared greedy to hear, while I testified "God so loved the world, that He gave His only begotten Son." . . . In the afternoon . . . the church was full as it could crowd. Thousands stood in the church yard. It was the most beautiful sight I ever beheld. . . . In this amphitheatre they stood, deeply attentive, while I called upon them in Christ's words, "Come unto Me, all that are weary." The tears of many testified that they were ready to enter into rest. God enabled to lift up my voice like a trumpet, so that all distinctly heard me. I concluded with singing an invitation to sinners.

And Charles continued, declaring the price that was often paid by those who followed Christ:

> Christianity flourishes under the cross. None who follow after Christ want that badge of discipleship. Wives and children are beaten. . . . Today Mary Hannay was with me. While she continued a drunkard, a swearer, and company-keeper, it was very well; she and her father agreed entirely. But from the time of her turning to God, he has used her most inhumanely. Yesterday he beat her, and drove her out of doors, following her with imprecations and threatenings to murder her, if ever she returned.

✠ ✠ ✠

According to Tyson, "Behind the almost frenetic energy of their itinerant ministry lay the Wesley's substructure of societies, classes and bands. It was this infrastructure that gave eighteenth-century Methodism its staying power."[49]

By the early 1740s, two additional Methodist chapels were established in London: one in a former Huguenot chapel in "Seven Dials" in

---

[49] Tyson, *Assist Me to Proclaim*, 78.

West Street, the other in a former Unitarian chapel called "Snowfields" in Bermondsey, Southwark.

The number of Methodist societies was also expanding throughout the country. Smaller groups called bands, consisting of five or six persons of the same age and sex, had been established within the societies for more mature believers, with women leading the female bands. Each band met privately to "confess their faults one to another and pray for one another that they may be healed." Methodist societies were required to abide by John's "Rules for the United Societies" and met several times per week, but not during scheduled Anglican church services. Methodists were expected to attend worship and the sacrament at their local parish church, as well as their society and band meetings. However, there was no support for those who were not deemed committed Christians and were not in a band.

In February 1742 when John asked for financial assistance from the societies to cover the debt incurred from building the Foundery and New Room meeting places, a sea captain called Foy suggested a solution: "Let every member of the society give a penny a week till the debt is paid." When Foy was informed that many were too poor to pay even a penny, he replied: "Then put eleven of the poorest with me; and if they can give anything, well; I will call on them weekly; and if they can give nothing, I will give for them as well as for myself. And each of you call on eleven of your neighbours weekly; receive what they give, and make up what is wanting." "In a while," wrote John, "some of these informed me that they found such and such a one did not live as he ought. It struck me immediately; this is the thing, the very thing, we have wanted so long."

Accordingly, he divided his societies into small groups, which were called classes (from the Latin classis or "division"). They met weekly for prayer, Bible study, and pastoral care. The classes were generally larger than the bands, were not divided by age, sex, or marital status, and were open to all in the society, not just those who had voluntarily banded together. At the head of each group John appointed a class leader, who became the supervisor of the class. All Methodists were required to join a class, and each member was examined on a periodic basis and given a ticket by either John or Charles to certify they were right with God and their fellow class members.

In 1744, the societies were joined together into a network, or "Connexion" as John called it, so they could share their resources. In 1746, the societies of John's Connexion were linked together into regional preaching circuits, of which there were seven at first: London, Bristol, Cornwall, Evesham, York, Newcastle, and Wales. John then assigned two or three of his lay preachers to each circuit or "rounds" for a month at a time. These preachers traveled around the circuits, preaching, exhorting, and examining the members of the societies.

✠ ✠ ✠

Lady Selina Huntingdon urged John to minister to the illiterate and godless coal miners of Newcastle-upon-Tyne in the northeast of England, claiming: "They have churches, but they never go to them! And ministers, but they seldom or never hear them! Perhaps they may hear you. And what if you save (under God) one soul?" Heeding her call, in May 1742 John traveled north and preached first in Birstal, the hometown of one of his foremost lay preachers, John Nelson, who had first heard John preach at Moorfields.

After preaching in Birstal, John headed for Newcastle-upon-Tyne, accompanied by John Taylor, one of Lady Huntingdon's protégés, and was shocked by "so much drunkenness, cursing, and swearing (even from the mouths of little children) do I never remember to have seen and heard before in so small a compass of time. Surely this place is ripe for him who 'came not to call the righteous, but sinners to repentance.'"

On the morning of Sunday, May 30, 1742, John and Taylor walked down to the center of Sandgate, the poorest area of the town, and began to sing the Hundredth Psalm, with John recording, "Three or four people came out to see what was the matter." More came until the street and every side ally were packed with an estimated 1,500 people eager to hear John preach. When he preached again in the afternoon, 20,000 people gathered, the largest crowd he had ever addressed up to that time.

Observing the people, when I had done, to stand gaping and staring upon me, with the most profound astonishment, I told them, "If you desire to know who I am, my name is John Wesley. At five in the evening, with God's help, I design to preach here again."

At five, the hill on which I designed to preach was covered, from the top to the bottom. I never saw so large a number of people together, either at Moorfields, or at Kennington Common. I knew it was impossible for the one half to hear, although my voice was then strong and clear; and I stood so as to have them all in my view, as they were ranged on the side of the hill. . . .

After preaching, the poor people were ready to tread me under foot, out of pure love and kindness. It was some time before I could possibly get out of the press. I then went back another way than I came; but several were got to our inn before me; by whom I was vehemently importuned to stay with them, at least for a few days, or, however, one day more.

Such was the overwhelming response that John purchased land to build a meetinghouse cum orphanage similar to the New Room and Foundery. He called it the Orphan House. Newcastle would become the third center of John and Charles' ministry, forming what became known as the "Methodist Triangle" with London and Bristol. The Orphan House became John's northern headquarters and consisted of a preaching house, a school, and Sunday school, residential accommodation, and later a medical dispensary.

After preaching in Newcastle in May, John decided to return to London via his childhood home of Epworth, but the curate, John Romley, an implacable opponent of the Wesleys, refused to allow him to preach at his church. However, after the service, John Taylor announced to the parishioners outside as they were leaving that "Mr. Wesley, not being permitted to preach in the church, designs to preach here at six o'clock." That evening, John was confronted with "such a congregation as I believe Epworth never saw before," recording: "I preached at Epworth about eight, on Ezekiel's vision of the resurrection of the dry bones. And great indeed was the shaking among them: lamentation and great mourning were heard, God bowing their hearts so that on every side as with one accord, they lifted up their voice and wept aloud. Surely He who sent his Spirit to breathe upon them will hear their cry and will help them."

According to Luke Tyerman:

> [John] Wesley's preaching on his father's grave was attended with amazing power. On one occasion, the people on every side wept aloud; and on another, several dropped down as dead; Wesley's voice was drowned by the cries of penitents; and many there and then, in the old churchyard, found peace with God, and broke out into loud thanksgiving. A gentleman, who had not been at public worship of any kind for upwards of thirty years, stood motionless as a statue. "Sir," asked Wesley, "are you a sinner?" "Sinner enough!" said he, and still stood staring upwards, till his wife and servant, who were both in tears, put him into his chaise and took him home.

John ended up staying for a week, preaching each evening in the Epworth churchyard and one the following Sunday at the parish church in Wroot, having been invited by the rector John Whitlamb, his sister Molly's widower. John preached at Wroot in the morning and afternoon, "but the church could not contain the people, many of whom came from far." That evening, he preached for the last time standing on his father's gravestone in Epworth's church cemetery.

John visited Newcastle again in November, after Charles had been there. John founded a Methodist society which he described as "a wild, staring, loving society." He returned in 1743 and preached in the nearby mining villages of Chowden, which he described as "the very Kingswood of the north," and Plessey, whose inhabitants he recorded as "in the first rank for savage ignorance and wickedness of every kind."

Throughout the 1740s, John and Charles Wesley preached fearlessly in the open all over Britain, often facing brutal persecution whipped up by envious and disgruntled clergyman, local officials, and magistrates who were convinced that the Wesleys were fomenting Jacobite revolution, even though they strenuously confirmed their allegiance to the Crown. Commented John, "It was my rule confirmed by long experience, always to look a mob in the face." At Halifax market cross in

Yorkshire, he did just that, but was pelted with stones by the crowd, one of which cut him badly on the face. In Roughlee in Lancashire, John was beaten to the ground while the local constable "sat well pleased close to the place, not attempting in the least to hinder them."

In London the mobs were stirred up by outraged publicans and pimps who found customers deserting them for prayer meetings, and by thieves, pickpockets, and louts who had passed the word that the law would not protect Methodists. Once a mob tried to pull the roof off the Foundery. On another day when John was preaching outside in Charles Square north of the city, a rabble drove an ox at the attentive crowd, but the animal ran left and right and "at length broke through the midst of them clear away, leaving us calmly rejoicing and praising God."

At Deptford in London, while John was preaching, "many poor wretches were got together, utterly devoid both of common sense and common decency, who cried out aloud, as if just come from 'among the tombs.'" In London, "many men of the baser sort" mixed themselves with the women in the congregation and behaved indecently. A constable commanded them to keep the peace, in answer to which they knocked him down. In Long Lane while John was preaching, the mob pelted him with stones, with one huge one barely missing his head. In Marylebone, he faced a hail of stones, while in Whitechapel, a stone struck him between the eyes, but wiping away the blood, he continued preaching as if nothing had happened.

At Wrestlingworth, John preached by moonlight, and at Guisborough, he preached under a sun so hot that he recorded that there "was so vehement a stench of stinking fish, as was ready to suffocate me." In the county of Wiltshire, John was preaching from a table on a village green "when a rabble came furiously upon us, bringing a bull which they had been baiting." The bull ran wildly on either side. Wesley stopped preaching and led the people in hymns and prayer for nearly an hour.

> The poor wretches at length seized upon the bull, now
> weak and tired, after having been so long torn and beaten,
> both by dogs and men; and by main strength, partly dragged
> and partly thrust him in among the people.

When they had forced their way to the little table on which I stood, they strove several times to throw it down, by thrusting the helpless beast against it. I once or twice put aside his head with my hand, that the blood might not drop upon my clothes; intending to go on as soon as the hurry should be over. But, the table falling down, some of our friends caught me and carried me right away on their shoulders; while the rabble wreaked their vengeance on the table. We went a little way off, where I finished my discourse without any noise or interruption.

John recorded what happened when he preached in Bolton:

At one I went to the Cross at Bolton. There was a vast number of people, but many of them utterly wild. As soon as I began speaking, they began thrusting to and fro, endeavouring to throw me down from the steps on which I stood. They did so once or twice, but I went up again and continued my discourse. They then began to throw stones; at the same time some got upon the Cross behind me to push me down; on which I could not but observe how God overrules even the minutest circumstances. One man was bawling just at my ear, when a stone struck him on the cheek and he was still. A second was forcing his way down to me, till another stone hit him on the forehead. It bounded back, the blood ran down, and he came no farther. The third being got close to me, stretched out his hand and in the instant a sharp stone came upon the joints of his fingers. He shook his hand and was very quiet till I concluded my discourse and went away.

John arrived in Wednesbury in Staffordshire on October 20, 1743, mounted a horse block in the town center, and started preaching "to a far larger congregation than was expected on 'Jesus Christ, the same yesterday and today and forever.' I believe everyone present felt the power of God and no creature offered to molest us, either going or coming; but the Lord fought for us and we held our peace." However, it proved to be the lull before the storm. That afternoon, as John was writing in the house of Francis Ward, the leader of Wednesbury's Methodist society, they and the other Methodists in the house heard a horn summoning a mob that soon surrounded the house. John calmly announced that they would pray, and they knelt as he and others prayed extempore. The howls and threats outside died down until within half-an-hour, when someone looked out the door, "not a man was left." John suggested he had better leave as the mob was after him, but they begged him to stay. At about 5.00 p.m. their opponents returned in greater numbers, swelled by those from the nearby mining town of Darlaston. "Bring out the minister!" they cried. "We'll have the minister!" Wesley told a fearful colleague to go to the front door and bring in the ringleader "by the hand." Those in the room were astonished by what happened next. The ringleader entered, his face contorted with rage. John smiled and spoke to him quietly. "After a few sentences interchanged between us, the lion was become a lamb." Wesley told him to fetch one or two others and he brought a man and a woman, both in a rage, "but in two minutes they were as calm as he."

John then went to the door, stood on a chair, and the crowd became quiet. He asked what they wanted. When they replied that they wanted him brought to justice, he agreed, "with all my heart." He spoke a few words about the love of God and the mob cheered. The woman ringleader cried out, "The gentleman is an honest gentleman and we will spill our blood in his defence!"

The crowd wanted to leave at once, so Wesley set off at their head. Most of the Methodists had fled out the back door of the house while the mob was screaming at the front, but three men and Methodist Joan Parks kept close as an escort, while William Sitch held John's arm throughout. As darkness fell, a heavy downpour began and they were soaked before they reached Bentley Hall between Wednesbury and Darlaston, where a Mr. Lane, a justice of the peace, was already in bed. His son asked for their complaint and somebody replied: "Why an't please you, they sing psalms all day; nay and make folks rise at five in the morning. And what would your worship advise us to do?" "To go home and be quiet," replied Lane, who by this time had risen from his bed.

They then dragged Wesley to the magistrate who lived outside of Walsall, but when they reached his house at 7.00 p.m. he too was in bed. The now friendly mob decided to take Wesley back to Wednesbury with fifty acting as an escort, while the rest returned to their homes. Barely had they left Walsall when a great multitude advanced to meet them and a fight broke out. The Darlaston mob made what defense they could, but they were weary as well as outnumbered, so that in a short time many had been knocked down while the rest ran away. The Darlaston collier woman who had sworn to defend Wesley, charged the Walsall mob "and knocked down three or four men, one after another. But many assaulting her at once, she was soon overpowered, and had probably been killed in a few minutes (three men keeping her down and beating her with all their might), had not a man called to one of them, 'Hold, Tom, hold!'" Tom stopped beating the woman for he recognized the voice of Walsall's champion prizefighter "Honest Munchin," whose real name was George Clifton.

The screaming mob dragged Wesley, Joan Parks, and Sitch towards Walsall down the steep and wet cobbled streets. One slip and Wesley would have gone down and they would have trampled him to death, but he managed to keep upright. Some tried to hit him, but somehow missed. One man who "came rushing through the press, and raising his arm to strike, on a sudden let it drop, and only stroked his head, saying, 'What soft hair he has!'"

As they hustled him along, Wesley saw a large house with an open door. He stopped and tried to enter, but a man dragged him back by his long hair and would have pulled him down had not Sitch bitten his arm. The mob propelled them down the street until Wesley saw another open door at a chandler's (candlemakers) shop. The chandler, who was standing at the door, refused to let him in, saying they would pull his house down if he did, but unknown to John, the man was the newly-appointed mayor of Walsall, William Hazelwood. The mob, assuming that Wesley's stop was deliberate, calmed a little.

"Will you hear me?" shouted John.

"No, no! Knock his brains out! Kill him!" replied the crowd.

"What evil have I done? Which of you have I wronged?" responded Wesley in his defense. He then spoke of the love of God for the next quarter of an hour until his voice failed.

The braying mob, led by Honest Munchin, roared again, "Bring him away! Strip him!"

"You needn't do that. I will give you my clothes," replied Wesley.

"Crucify him!" shrieked the crowd.

Undeterred, John, his voice recovered, began to pray aloud.

Suddenly, Munchin turned to him and said, "Sir, I will spend my life for you: follow me, and not one soul shall touch a hair of your head."

The mob parted, and Wesley's escort took him down the slippery street towards the flooded brook at the bottom of the town. But before they could cross the footbridge at the mill dam, the crowd began to bay for his blood again. "Throw him in!" cried some. A man hit Wesley hard in the mouth, but Munchin got him and Sitch across the bridge and into the meadows where they were soon lost to their pursuers in the darkness. Speaking of this incident in his *Journal*, John wrote:

> By how gentle degrees does God prepare us for his will! Two years ago a piece of brick grazed my shoulders. It was a year after that the stone struck me between the eyes. Last month I received one blow, and this evening two, one before we came into town and one after we were gone out, but both were as nothing. For though one man struck me on the breast with all his might, and the other on the mouth with such force that the blood gushed out immediately, I felt no pain from either of the blows than if they had touched me with a straw.
>
> It ought not to be forgotten that when the rest of the society made all haste to escape for their lives, four only would not stir, William Sitch, Edward Slater, John Griffiths and Joan Parks. These kept with me resolving to live or die together, and none of them received one blow, but William Sitch who held me by the arm, from one end of the town to the other. He was then dragged away and knocked down, but he soon rose and got to me again. I afterwards asked him what he expected when the mob came upon us. He said, "To die for Him who had died for us." And he felt no hurry or fear, but calmly waited till God should require his soul of him.
>
> I asked J. Parks if she was not afraid when they tore her from me. She said, "No, no more than I am now. I could trust God for you as well as for myself. From the beginning I had a full persuasion that God would deliver you. I knew not how,

but I left that to Him and was as sure as if it were already done." I asked if the report was true that she had fought for me. She said, "No, I knew God would fight for his children." And shall these souls perish at the last?

When I came back to Francis Ward's, I found many of our brethren waiting upon God. Many also whom I never had seen before, came to rejoice with us. And the next morning, as I rode through the town in my way to Nottingham, every one I met expressed such a cordial affection that I could scarce believe what I saw and heard.

Charles was waiting in Nottingham for John. "My brother came delivered out of the mouth of the lion. He looked like a soldier of Christ. His clothes were torn to tatters." As a postscript, Charles was to record later that Munchin petitioned to join the local Methodist society. "I took several new members into the Society; and among them, the young man whose arm was broke [during the riot], and [upon trial] Munchin, the late captain of the mob. He has been constantly under the Word since he rescued my brother. I asked him what he thought of him [John]. "Think of him!" said he [Munchin]. "That is a man of God; and God was on his side, when so many of us could not kill one man."

Opposition and riots continued throughout the 1740s, one of the worst being in Colne in Lancashire in the summer of 1748, where the curate, the Reverend George White, preached against John and stirred up a rioting mob. John and his colleagues were punched, stoned, clubbed, dragged by their hair, hurled into the river, and taken forcibly by the drunken mob to see the curate who demanded that they leave town. John replied that he "would sooner cut off his hand than make such a promise," and one of his companions, William Grimshaw, declared, "he was ready to go to prison or death for Christ's sake."

Charles Wesley, while renowned as a prolific hymn writer, was also a courageous and tenacious evangelist. He preached powerfully in fields, town markets and squares, village greens, and church graveyards. At Kingswood and St. Ives, he preached to miners at the mine entrances, and at Plymouth and Portsmouth, he preached at the docks, standing on bales of cotton or crates of merchandise waiting to be loaded on to ships. Charles said of those he ministered to in Newcastle: "I told them sincerely that I would rather be the Keelman's chaplain than the King's. There is no expressing their love for me; they would even pluck out their eyes [Matthew 5:29] and give them to me." One observed:

> When Mr. Charles Wesley came back from Newcastle, the Lord was with him in such a manner, that the pillars of hell seemed to tremble: many that were famous for supporting the devil's kingdom, fell to the ground while he was preaching, as if they had been thunder-struck. One day he had preached four times; and one that had been amongst the people all day said at night, twenty-two had received forgiveness of their sins that day.

Charles always urged his fellow Methodists to "turn the other cheek" and to "resist not evil." He often suffered brutal persecution, but there were times when those who were listening came to his defense. In his journal, Charles describes how the wives of the Newcastle Keelmen (boatmen who guided coal barges up and down the River Tyne) attacked a local detractor who sought to make a disturbance while Wesley was preaching:

> I live by the gospel and renewed my strength to preach it this morning. . . . Breakfasted at a constant hearer of the Word and several of the poor Keelman (Keel-women I should say) flocked to us. They related some instances of their zeal which pleased them more than me. At that [instance] a gentleman happening to say, while I was preaching, that I should be sent to Bedlam [a mental hospital], a stout woman collared and kicked him down the hill. More of her fellows joined in the pursuit so that he was forced to fly for his life. Another poor scoffer they put into the pond. I do indeed believe that were they to offer me violence, the people would stone them; but by and by, I trust they will learn to suffer wrong and to turn the other cheek.

In Leeds, Charles barely avoided serious injury when the floor of the upper room where he was speaking collapsed under the weight of the congregation. He and hundreds of others fell as "heaps upon heaps" to the floor. Charles, who only sustained a bruised hand and a scraped head, remarked, "Never did I more clearly see that not a hair of our head can fall to the ground without our heavenly father."

In Grimsby, Charles recorded that "several poor wild creatures, almost naked, ran about the room, striking down all they met" until he was able to win over their leader and then they began fighting among themselves. At Hexham in Northumberland, the only place that Charles was allowed to preach was the local cock-fighting pit. While he preached, the cocks fought each other and the crowd roared. Charles recounted, "I expected Satan would come and fight me on his own ground."

In Thorpe in Yorkshire, Charles wrote rejoicingly in his journal: "Blessed be God, I got no hurt, but only eggs and dirt. My clothes indeed abhorred me, and my arm pained me a little by little by a blow I received in Sheffield." While at Worcester, he was subjected to "lewd, hellish language" and had so much "dust and dirt" hurled at him that he was "covered from head to foot and almost blinded."

In Cardiff in Wales, while Charles was preaching, some of the women who were listening were kicked and had their clothes set on fire by rockets. The table on which Charles was standing was hacked to pieces and his Bible wrenched from his hands, with one of the persecutors declaring that he would persecute the Methodists to his dying day.

In September 1740, Charles, despite being in poor health, courageously stepped in to stop a riot that had erupted among the miners of Kingswood over the rising cost of corn. He persuaded some to stop rioting and then defended them when they were attacked by the remaining rioters: "I rode up to one ruffian who was striking one of our colliers [who had agreed to stop rioting] and prayed him rather strike me. He would not, he said, for all the world, and was quite overcome. I turned upon one who struck my horse, and he also sunk like a lamb. Wherever I turned, Satan lost ground."

In 1742 at Oxford, Charles preached what would probably become his most famous sermon, "Awake Thou That Sleepest," based on Ephesians 5:14. The sermon proved to be a massive success and became the most frequently published and purchased Methodist pamphlet.

In Devizes in Wiltshire, Charles and his companion the Reverend John Meriton faced a rioting mob that was spraying the house where they were staying with water from the town's fire engine. The jets of water broke the windows and flooded the ground floor rooms, forcing Charles and his followers to move upstairs:

> The Mayor's maid came . . . and begged me to disguise myself in women's clothes, and try to make my escape. . . . The rioters without continued playing their engine . . . but their number and fierceness increased, and the gentlemen plied them with pitchers of ale, as much as they could drink. . . . Our enemies, at their return, made their main assault at the back door, swearing horribly they would have me, if it cost them their lives. . . . Now we stood in jeopardy every moment. Such threatenings, curses and blasphemies I have never heard. They seemed kept out by a continued miracle. . . .
>
> They were close to us, on every side, and over our heads, untiling the roof. I was diverted by a little girl, who called to me . . . "Mr. Wesley! Mr. Wesley! creep under the bed; they will kill you; they are pulling down the house." Our sister Taylor's faith was just failing, when a ruffian cried out, "Here they are, behind the curtain!" At this time we fully expected their appearance, and returned to the furthermost corner of the room. . . .
>
> In about an hour after the last general assault the answer of faith came, and God made bare his arm. Soon after three, Mr. Clark knocked at the door, and brought with him the persecuting constable. He said, "Sir, if you will promise never to preach here again, the gentlemen and I will engage to bring you safely out of town." My answer was, "I promise no such thing."

Charles did eventually agree to leave the town, commenting: "We rode a slow pace up the street, the whole multitude pouring along on both sides, and attending us with loud acclamations. Such fierceness and diabolical malice I have not seen in human faces. They ran up to our horses, as if they would swallow us; but they did not know which was Wesley."

Charles preceded John, traveling to the west of England in February 1743, preaching in a number of towns, including Bath, which he viewed as a modern-day Sodom. In May, he headed north to Staffordshire, then Yorkshire, and then to the West Midlands, where in Walsall he was confronted by a baying mob as he walked through the streets "to the noisy greetings of our enemies." They railed, blasphemed, and mocked as he made his way to the steps in front of the market house. After he had finished preaching and was leaving, he was set upon by a group of thugs who pulled him down from the steps and beat him to the ground twice as he tried to get up:

> The street was full of Ephesian beasts (the principal man setting them on) who roared and shouted and threw stones incessantly. Many struck, without hurting me. I besought them in calm love to be reconciled to God in Christ. While I was departing, a stream of ruffians was suffered to bear me from the steps. I rose, and having given the blessing, was beat down again. So the third time, when we had returned thanks to the God of our salvation. I then, from the step[s], bade them depart in peace, and walked quietly back through the thickest rioters. They reviled us, but had no commission to touch an hair of our heads.

Charles was not confronted by serious opposition in Birmingham and Nottingham, but when he visited Sheffield, he found the Methodists "as sheep in the midst of wolves." The local clergy roused a mob to pull down the recently built Methodist meetinghouse. The house where he was staying also came under attack. In fact, "the stones flew so thick" that Charles decided to step outside and face the mob. A stone struck him in the face, and an army officer accused him of treason:

> Hell from beneath was moved to oppose us. As soon as I was in the desk [pulpit] with David Taylor, the flood began to lift up their voice. An officer (Ensign Garden) contradicted and blasphemed. I took no notice of him and sang on. The stones flew thick, hitting the desk and people. To save them and the house, I gave notice [that] I should preach out[side] and look the enemy in the face.

The Captain ran at me with great fury . . . [and] drew his sword and presented it to my breast. My breast was immediately steeled. I threw it open and fixing my eye on his, smiled in his face and calmly said, "I fear God and honour the King." His countenance fell in a moment, he fetched a deep sigh, put up his sword and quietly left the place. One member of the local Methodist society had heard Garden say, "You shall see, if I do but hold my sword to his breast he will faint away."

The rioters followed and exceeded in their outrage all I have seen before. Those of Moorfields, Cardiff and Walsal [sic] were lambs [compared] to these. . . . Satan now put it into their heads to pull down the Society-house and they set to their work, while we were praying and praising God. It was a glorious time with us. Every word of exhortation sunk deep, every prayer was sealed and many found the Spirit of glory resting on them.

They laboured all night for their master and by morning had pulled down one end of the house. I could compare them to nothing but the men of Sodom, or those coming out of the tombs exceeding fierce.

The following day, Charles preached twice more in Sheffield, and in the evening, he walked to the center of the town to preach again: "We heard our enemies shouting from afar. I stood up in the midst of them and read the first words that offered. 'If God before us, who can be against us? He that spared not His own Son,' and etc. God made bare his arm in the sight of the Heathen and so restrained the fierceness of men, so that not one lifted up [his] hand or voice against us."

When preaching in the town of Widdup in Yorkshire, Charles again faced a disruptive mob:

Yesterday between twelve and one o'clock, while I was speaking to some quiet people without any noise or tumult, a drunken rabble came with clubs and staves, in a tumultuous and riotous manner, the captain of whom, Richard B. by name, said he was a deputy-constable and that he was come to bring me to you. I went with him; but I had scarcely gone ten yards when a man of his company struck me with his fist in the face with all his might; quickly after, another threw his stick; but another of your champions, cursing and swearing in the most shocking manner and flourishing his club over his head, cried out, "Bring him away!"

But it was not just John and Charles who faced violent persecution. In September 1740, William Seward, one of Charles' early converts and an ardent Whitefield supporter, was struck in the eye and killed while preaching in South Wales, becoming the first Methodist martyr. A year later, at Bala in Wales, Howell Harris barely escaped with his life after being attacked by a mob. As one observed:

> The women were as fiendish as the men, for they besmeared him with mire, while their companions belaboured him with their fists and clubs, inflicting such wounds that his path could be marked in the street by the crimson stains of his blood. The enemy continued to persecute him . . . striking him with sticks and with staves, until overcome with exhaustion he fell to the ground . . . [and they] abused him, though prostrate.

In London, while Harris was preaching at Whitefield's meetinghouse, the Tabernacle, opponents broke in and started beating the congregation with wooden staves. Harris, however, was unmoved, reporting: "Had bullets been shot at me, I felt I would not move. Mob raged. Voice lifted up, and though by the power going with the words my head almost went to pieces, such was my zeal that I cried, 'I'll preach Christ till to pieces I fall!'"

When Howell Harris and John Cennick were preaching in the town of Swindon, they were attacked by a raging mob:

> The mob fired guns over our heads holding the muzzles so near to our faces that we were made as black as tinkers with the powder. We were not affrighted, but opened our breasts, telling them we were ready to lay down our lives. . . . then they played an engine on us which they filled out of the stinking ditches. While they played on Brother Harris I preached; and when they turned the engine on me, he preached. . . . The next day they gathered about the home of Mr. Lawrence who had received us, and broke all of his windows with stones, cut and wounded four of his family, and knocked down one

of his daughters. . . . After we left the town, they dressed up
two images, called one Cennick and the other Harris, and
then burnt them.

On another occasion when Cennick spoke of the blood of Christ,
a butcher shouted, "If he wants blood I'll give him plenty." He then
ran back to his shop to get a bucket full of blood, but was stopped by
a bystander from throwing it over Cennick. In the ensuing struggle it
was tipped all over the butcher.

George Whitefield was also attacked when preaching in the town
of Hampton, writing:

> No sooner had I entered the town than I heard the blow-
> ing of horns and the ringing of bells for the gathering of the
> mob. . . . I preached on a large glass platform. "And seeing the
> grace of God, he exhorted them with full purpose of heart to
> cleave to the Lord." I finished my sermon and pronounced the
> blessing just as the ringleader of the mob broke in upon us. . . .
> I went into the house [of Thomas Adams] and preached upon
> the stair case to a large number of serious souls; but these real
> troublers of Israel soon came in to mock and mob us. But . . .
> power being given us from above, I leapt down stairs, and all
> fled away before me. However, they continued making a noise
> about the house till midnight, abusing the poor people as they
> went home, and broke one young lady's arm in two places.
> Brother Adams they threw a second time into the pool;
> he received a deep wound in the leg. John C[room]'s life,
> that second Bunyan, was much threatened. Young W-H- they
> wheeled in a barrow to the pool side, lamed his brother and
> grievously hurt several others.
> Hearing that two or three clergyman were in the town,
> one of whom was a Justice of the Peace, I went to them. But
> instead of redressing, they laid the cause of all the grievance
> at my door. But by the help of God I shall persist in preaching
> myself and in encouraging those who I believe are truly moved
> by the Holy Ghost.

In Exeter, where the Methodists had a growing following, a witness
who was not a Methodist reported a savage attack on a meetinghouse:

The rioters entered the Methodist meeting-house, interrupted the minister with obscene language, and fell upon him
in a most furious manner with blows and kicks. They treated
every man they could lay their hands upon with such abuse
and indignity as is not to be expressed.

But what is more than all was their abominable treatment
of the poor women. Some were stripped quite naked. Others,
notwithstanding their most piercing cries for mercy were forcibly held by some of the wicked ruffians, while others turned
their petticoats over their heads and forced them to remain in
that condition . . . the poor creatures being afterward dragged
through the [sewer]. . . . The riot continued for several hours.
The mob had their full swing. It is true no one was actually
murdered, but the whole Society were put into great danger
and fear for their lives.

A mob captured Thomas Lee at Pately, hurled him into a sewer,
then dragged him to a bridge and threw him into a river. Peter Jaco at
Warrington was struck so violently on his chest with a brick that blood
poured out of his mouth, nose, and ears. At Ackham the mob seized
John Nelson, and one observed that he was "knocked down eight times.
As he lay on the ground, not able to get up, they dragged him by the
hair of his head upon the stones for twenty yards, kicking him on the
sides and thighs as they went along. Then six of them stood on his body
and thighs in order to 'tread the Holy Ghost out of him.'"

Methodist supporters were not just threatened with physical harm.
A gardener who had served his master for fifty years was discharged
for "hearing the Methodists." While at Charlton, a group of farmers
made an agreement to refuse work to any who went to hear Methodist
preachers. At Hornberry, a landlord evicted all Methodists from his
properties, while Joseph Periam was placed in an insane asylum by his
father for "being Methodistically mad." Even at the Wesleys' alma mater,
Oxford University, Methodist undergraduates were ridiculed for their
faith and were required to sign a document renouncing "the practices
and purposes of the people called Methodists." As late as 1768, six
students were expelled from Oxford for holding "Methodistical tenets."

Methodist lay preacher James Wheatley was dragged by his hair through the streets of Norwich. Moses Dale was carried around Northwich on a butcher's block, dumped in the marketplace, and his persecutors blew through cow horns into his ears until he was almost deafened. Others were press ganged in to the army, and four Methodist lay preachers were killed at the battle of Fontenoy against the French on May 11, 1745. John Evans, whose legs were blown off by chain shot, was laid across a cannon to die, where he preached for as long as he could speak. John Wesley commented proudly of these preachers, "For what pay could we procure such men to do this service—to be always ready to go to prison or to death?"

20

POWER FROM ABOVE

. . . the more they raged, the more power I found from above.

—CHARLES WESLEY

When John and Charles Wesley visited Cornwall in the southwest of England in 1743, England was at war with France, Spain, and Prussia in the War of the Austrian Succession. There were rumors of a French invasion and a Jacobite uprising in Scotland in support of the Young Pretender, Prince Charles Edward Stuart—Bonnie Prince Charlie. Some magistrates and clergy claimed that the Methodists were Jacobites and French agents. Using this they exploited the fears of the local people. One of John's traveling companions, John Downes, was positively identified as the Young Pretender, while it was claimed later that the preacher calling himself John Wesley was an imposter as "Mr Wesley is dead," when in fact it was his brother Samuel who had died in 1739.

Charles was the first to visit Cornwall in July 1743. He was preaching at the house of fish curer, John Nance, in St. Ives in Cornwall when a violent mob forced its way into the meeting and began demolishing the interior of the building:

> I had just named my text at St. Ives . . . when an army of
> rebels broke in upon us. They began in a most outrageous
> manner, threatening to murder the people, if they did not

[leave] that moment. They broke the sconces, dashed the windows in pieces, tore away the shutters, benches, poor-box and all but the stone walls. Several times they lifted up their hands and clubs to strike me, but a stronger arm restrained them. . . . they beat and dragged the women about, particularly one of great age and trampled on them without mercy. The longer they stayed and the more they raged, the more power I found from above. I bade the people stand still and see the salvation of God; resolving to continue with them and see the end. . . . The ruffians fell to quarrelling among themselves, broke the town clerk's (their captain's) head, and drove one another out of the room. . . . Having kept the field, we gave thanks for the victory; and in prayer the Spirit of glory rested upon us.

Undeterred, the next day Charles preached in St. Ives again with "No weapon formed against thee shall prosper" as his text. Another riot ensued, with the crowd led by the son of the town's mayor. "The gentleman had resolved to destroy all within doors. He struck out the candles with his cane and began courageously beating the women. I laid my hand upon him, and said, 'Sir, you appear like a gentleman: I desire you would show it by restraining these of the baser sort. Let them strike the men, or me, if they please, but not hurt the poor helpless women and children.'" Almost immediately the man came to his senses, and he and the attackers left the room. Charles preached again that afternoon. "I proved the devil a liar by preaching in the room at five. The words I first met were Isa. 54: 'For thou shalt break forth on the right hand and on the left. Fear not; for thou shalt not be ashamed: neither be thou confounded; for thou shalt not be put to shame. Behold, I have created the smith, and the waster to destroy. No weapon that is formed against thee shall prosper.'"

The following day he preached at Gwennap Pit, a natural amphitheater formed by old mine workings that had collapsed near Redruth "to near two thousand hungry souls."

On Sunday, July 24, he preached in the village of Wednock. The local ministers urged a mob to attack him and his followers because they claimed they were "Popish emissaries."

At Wednock many listened to my description of our
Lord's sufferings from Isaiah 53. After the evening service I
would have finished my discourse; but the minister's mob fell
upon us, threatening and striking all that came near. They
swore horribly they would be avenged upon us, for our making
such a disturbance on the Sabbath-day. . . . They assaulted us
with bricks and stones and endeavoured to pull me down. I
bade them strike me, and spare the people. . . . We were now
encompassed with a host of men, bent on mischief, with no
visible way of escape; but the Lord has many ways. He touched
the heart of one of our persecutors, who came up to me, took
my hand, and besought me to depart in peace, assuring me he
would preserve me from all violence. Another gentleman did
the same. I told them I had an unseen Protector. . . . I walked
on slowly with all the rabble behind. One of the brethren
attended me. . . . About six we rested at brother Nance's. The
enemy still pursued. I went out and looked them in the face,
and they pulled off their hats and slunk away.

Charles concluded his first visit to Cornwall on August 7, 1743,
with another meeting at Gwennap Pit, where it was estimated that ten
thousand people came to listen.

Later that month, John Wesley arrived in Cornwall after preaching
to a great crowd in Exeter on the site of Rougemount Castle. This was
the first of thirty-three visits to the county. Wesley traveled around
Cornwall with his companions John Downes and John Nelson, making
little impression at first, with Wesley complaining in September, "I still
could not find a way into the hearts of the hearers, although they were
earnest to hear what they understood not." He then decided to hire a
small fishing boat to visit the nearby Isles of Scilly: "I had had for some
time a great desire to go and publish the love of God our Saviour, if
it were but for one day, in the Isles of Scilly. . . . So . . . John Nelson,
Mr. Shepherd and I, with three men and a pilot, sailed from St. Ives."

Wesley preached to the soldiers, sailors, and laborers working to
fortify the islands against the expected French invasion. Said Wesley,
"After the sermon I gave them some little books and hymns, which
they were so eager to receive that they were ready to tear both them
and me to pieces."

Returning to St. Ives on the mainland, they were forced to sleep on a stone floor night after night. Nelson recorded: "He [John] had my greatcoat for his pillow and I had Burkitt's Notes on the New Testament for mine. . . . One morning, about 3 o'clock, Mr. Wesley turned over, and, finding me awake, clapped me on the side saying, 'Brother Nelson, let us be of good cheer: I have one whole side left!'" (The skin on his other side had been rubbed raw by the stone).

Traveling from village to village, Wesley and Nelson (John Downes was ill with a fever) were often hungry. Nelson recalled: "As we returned, Mr. Wesley stopped his horse to pick the blackberries, saying, 'Brother Nelson, we ought to be thankful that there are plenty of blackberries; for this is the best country I ever saw for getting a stomach, but the worst that I ever saw for getting food. Do the people think we can live for preaching?'"

Later, while riding alone, John stopped at a cottage where a woman, Alice Daniel, was removing honeycomb from a hive. He asked for water, and Alice invited him in and gave him barley bread and honey. John saw it as a chance to preach the gospel, and both Alice and her husband, John Daniel, a godless miner and smallholder, became committed Christians. They even extended their cottage to provide accommodation for Wesley and other itinerant preachers.

As in Staffordshire, John Wesley saw conversions and met violence. The mob at St. Ives broke into Nance's house where John was staying. John stopped preaching and went out to face the mob. Someone delivered a blow to his head before he was able to lead the ring leader by the hand to a pulpit where his courage and powerful words were able to quell the worst of the rioters. The next day, John preached to around 10,000 near Gwennap Pit. When darkness fell he was still preaching to the multitude, "and there was on all sides the deepest attention; none speaking, stirring or scarce looking aside. Surely here, though in a temple not made with hands, was God worshipped 'in the beauty of holiness.'" Early the next morning, John was awoken by the sound of singing. A group of tin miners, afraid they might miss his departure, were "singing and praising God" outside the house as a farewell. He wrote in his *Journal* that he then "preached once more on 'Believe on the Lord Jesus Christ and you shall be saved.' They all devoured the Word."

John returned to Cornwall in the spring of 1744 and preached at the amphitheater of Gwennap Pit, which he described as:

> ... by far the finest I know in the Kingdom. It is a round, green hollow, gently shelving down, about fifty feet deep; but I suppose it is two hundred across one way, and near three hundred the other. . . . [I] stood on the wall in the calm still evening, with the setting sun behind me, and almost an innumerable multitude before, behind and on either hand. Many likewise sat on the little hills, at some distance from the bulk of the congregation. But they could all hear distinctly.

On John's third tour of Cornwall in June 1745, he was issued with a warrant to forcibly enlist him into the army by a local magistrate and clergyman, Dr. Borlase, even though as an ordained member of the clergy he was exempt. John Nelson had already been enlisted in the Midlands. Charles had led public prayers for Nelson and raised money to hire a substitute soldier to take his place. Wrote Nelson: "Several would have given bail for me, but I was told one hundred pound was refused. I am too notorious a criminal to be allowed such favours. Christianity is a crime which the world can never forgive."

The intervention of Lady Selina Huntingdon and Charles Wesley eventually secured his release, but curiously, John did nothing to help Nelson. Tom Maxfield, John's assistant, was seized while preaching at Crowan, a few miles away, and Wesley arrived too late to rescue him. A few days later it was John's turn. He had just concluded an evening open-air meeting at St. Just's when a member of the local gentry declared, "Sir, I have a warrant from Dr Borlase and you must go with me." They agreed to go the next morning, but when they arrived, Borlase was not at home and John was released. That afternoon, Wesley was preaching from the doorway of a cottage in his cassock, gown, and bands to a large crowd when the bailiff of the local squire, Beauchamp, rode his horse violently through the crowd and confronted John. Recorded Wesley:

> Most of the people stood still as they were before and began singing an hymn. Upon this Mr. B. lost his patience and

cried out with all his might, "Seize him, seize him, I say, seize the preacher for His Majesty's service." But no one stirring, he rode up and struck several of his attendants. . . . Perceiving still that they would not move, he leaped off his horse, swore he would do it himself, and caught hold of my cassock crying, "I take you to serve His Majesty." A servant taking his horse, he took me by the arm, and we walked arm in arm for about three quarters of a mile. He entertained me all the time, with the "wickedness of the fellows belonging to the society."

When he was taking breath, I said, "Sir, be what they will, I apprehend it will not justify you in seizing me in this manner, and violently carrying me away, as you said, to serve His Majesty." He replied, "I seize you? And violently carry you away? No, Sir, no. Nothing like it. I asked you to go with me to my house, and you said you was willing; and if so, you are welcome and if not, you are welcome to go where you please."

Beauchamp, who was no friend of Borlase and may have been a secret Jacobite, knew that Wesley as a clergyman could not be enlisted and instead put John on a horse, mounted his own, and rode back with him to the cottage. However, worse persecution was to come.

In Falmouth, a big crowd surrounded the house of a woman that Wesley was praying for and chanted, "Bring out the Canorum"—the local term for Methodist.

No answer being given, they quickly forced open the outer door and filled the passage. Only a wainscot-partition was between us, which was not likely to stand long. I imme-diately took down a large looking glass which hung against it, supposing the whole side would fall in at once. When they began their work with abundance of bitter imprecations, poor Kitty was utterly astonished and cried out, "O Sir, what must we do!" I said, "We must pray." Indeed at that time, to all appearance, our lives were not worth an hour's purchase. She asked, "But Sir, is it not better for you to hide yourself? To get in the chest?" I answered, "No. It is best for me to stand where I am."

Among those without were the crews of some privateers which were lately come into the harbour. Some of these, being angry at the slowness of the rest, thrust them away and coming up all together, set their shoulders to the inner door, and cried out, "Avast, lads, avast!" Away went all the hinges at once and the door fell back into the room.

I stepped forward at once into the midst of them and said, "Here I am. Which of you has anything to say to me? To which of you have I done any wrong? To you? Or you? Or you?" I continued speaking till I came, bareheaded as I was (for I purposely left my hat that they might all see my face), into the middle of the street and then raising my voice, said, "Neighbours, countrymen! Do you desire to hear me speak?" They cried vehemently, "Yes, yes. He shall speak. He shall. Nobody shall hinder him." But having nothing to stand on and no advantage of ground, I could be heard by a few only. However, I spoke without intermission and, as far as the sound reached, the people were still.

A number of sympathizers advised John to leave from the rear of the house that backed onto the sea and go by boat to his next destination while they sent his horse on. John recorded:

A few of the fiercest ran along the shore, to receive me at my landing. I walked up the steep narrow passage from the sea, at the top of which the foremost man stood. I looked him in the face and said, "I wish you a good night." He spoke not, nor moved hand or foot till I was on horseback. Then he said, "I wish you was in hell," and turned back to his companions.

About half-hour after five I began at Gwennap. I was afraid my voice would not suffice for such an immense multitude. But my fear was groundless, as the evening was quite calm and the people all attention. It was more difficult to be heard in meeting the society, amidst the cries of those on the one hand were pierced through as with a sword, and those, on the other, who were filled with joy unspeakable.

Despite the mob violence, as early as 1744 John Wesley could report from Cornwall that "It is remarkable that those of St. Just were the chief of the whole country for hurling, fighting, drinking and all manner of wickedness; but many of the lions are become lambs, are continually praising God and calling their old companions in sin to come and magnify the Lord together."

In July 1744, Charles Wesley made his second visit to Cornwall, this time accompanied by fellow Methodist John Meriton. Violent opposition was encountered again, including at St. Ives, with Charles recording how the mob "broke the windows of all who were suspected of Christianity," and "one of our sisters complained to the Mayor of some who had thrown into her house stones of many pounds' weight which fell on the pillow within a few inches of her sucking child."

Yet when he preached at Gwennap Pit that same month, he declared: "Here a little one has become a thousand. What an amazing work has God done in one year! The whole country is alarmed, and gone forth after the sound of the Gospel. In vain the pulpit's ring of Popery, madness, enthusiasm. Our Preachers are daily pressed to new places, and enabled to preach five or six times a day. . . . Societies are springing up everywhere."

When Charles returned to Cornwall for his third and final trip in July 1746, it was evident that the worst of the mob violence had subsided, even though one of his companions was accused of being the Young Pretender in disguise. At St. Ives, Charles wrote: "No one offered to make the least disturbance. Indeed, the whole place is outwardly changed in this respect. I walk the streets with astonishment, scarce believing it St. Ives. It is the same throughout the country. All opposition falls before us, or rather is fallen. . . . This also the Lord wrought."

At Gwennap he preached to an estimated 10,000 people and said later, "Seventy years' suffering were overpaid by one such opportunity."

John visited Cornwall again in September 1746, five months after the Jacobite rebellion ended with the defeat of Bonnie Prince Charlie and his forces at the Battle of Culloden. At the village of Brea, John found that "vehement opposers . . . opposed no more." He went on to preach at Sithney. "Before I had done the night came on; but the moon shone bright upon us. So I met them all together, and exhorted them not to leave their first love."

At St. Agnes, John Wesley was pursued, after preaching, by a young woman who was weeping bitterly and crying out, "I must have Christ;

I will have Christ. Give me Christ or else I will die!" Wesley and two or three others knelt down to claim the promise on her behalf. Soon, as he commented later, she was filled with peace unspeakable and they left her rejoicing in the Savior.

By 1747, it appeared that the battle had been truly won. When John returned to Cornwall, he was amazed at the difference: "We came to St. Ives before morning prayers and walked to church without so much as one huzza. How strangely has one year changed the scene in Cornwall! This is now a peaceable, indeed, an honourable station. They give us good words almost in every place. What have we done that the world should be so civil to us?" Richard Watson, in his biography *John Wesley*, published in 1831, remarked that when John passed through the towns and villages of Cornwall in later years, the windows of houses were filled with people anxious to see him and pronounce their blessing on him, even though he never mentioned this in his *Journal* or letters.

In July 1773, John preached at Gwennap Pit to an estimated 32,000 people, his largest audience ever, remarking, "Perhaps the first time that a man of seventy had been heard by thirty thousand persons at once!" In August 1789, John Wesley visited Cornwall for the last time. On the way, he attended a service at Exeter Cathedral and was impressed by the reverent congregation and uplifting music. The Bishop of Exeter, John Ross, invited him to dinner at the palace where Bishop Lavington had written his diatribes against Methodism. As they parted, Ross said to Wesley, "I hope I may sit at your feet in the kingdom of heaven."

In Falmouth, where in 1745 John had suffered among the most violent opposition that he was ever to encounter, it was also dramatically different, as he recalled:

> The last time I was here about forty years ago I was taken
> prisoner by an immense mob, gaping and roaring like lions:
> but how is the tide turned. High and low lined the streets,
> from one end of the two to the other, out of stark love and
> kindness, gaping and staring as if the King were going by. In
> the evening I preached on the smooth top of the hill, at a small
> distance from the sea, to the largest congregation I have ever
> seen in Cornwall, except in or near Redruth. . . . God moved

wonderfully on the hearts of the people, who all seemed to know the day of their visitation.

And he preached again at Gwennap Pit, remarking: "I suppose for the last time for my voice cannot now command the still increasing multitude. It was supposed they were now more than five-and-twenty thousand. I think it scarce possible that all should hear."

As a testimony of John and Charles' success, by the mid nineteenth century, 9 percent of church-goers in Britain were Methodists, but in Cornwall Methodists made up 65 percent of the population.

21

THE OLD SHIP

*I believe I shall not separate from the Church of
England till my soul separates from my body.*

−JOHN WESLEY

C harles Wesley had an undying love for the Church
of England. He ardently embraced the Church from
his youngest years, and here the influence of the two
Samuels—his father and elder brother—were para-
mount. Both were staunch Church of England men, and
their loyalty was compounded in young Charles with the kind of fervor
that brings absolute devotion. Charles' parents joined the Anglican
Church and embraced it with zeal. John Rattenbury has concluded
that Charles' "love for the Church was his deepest human loyalty,"
while one has commented that Charles' determined attempts to keep
Methodism within the Church of England was his life's work. According
to Tyson: "Charles Wesley's love for the Church of England, 'the Old
Ship,' was profound. It was one of the fundamental constants of his
life."[50] Recalled Adam Clarke, one of the early Methodist preachers:
"Mr. J. Wesley mildly recommended the people to go to the Church
and Sacrament. Mr. C. Wesley threatened them with damnation if they
did not." And it appears that Charles equated an attack on the Church
as an assault on himself.

---

[50] Ibid., 229.

Above all, Charles saw the Methodist movement as a renewal group within the Church, to revive, evangelize, and "leaven the whole lump." For him, involvement in Methodism required loyalty to the Anglican Church. In 1739, he wrote in his journal about two Methodists who wanted to separate from the Church: "We all consented that their names should be erased out of the Society-book because they disowned themselves [as] members of the Church of England."

John Wesley always had the ideal of an apostolic, primitive church that he sought to reintroduce to the contemporary Church of England as its foundation. Despite wavering at times under pressure from some of his lay preachers who wanted an independent Methodist movement, he remained a loyal member of the Church of England of which he was an ordained minister. John asserted: "We will not, dare not, separate from the Church. . . . And as we are not Dissenters from the Church now, so we will do nothing willingly, which tends to a separation from it. Therefore, let every assistant so order his circuit, that no preacher may be hindered from attending the church more than two Sundays in a month. Never make light of going to church, either by word or deed."

On the other hand, neither John nor Charles were oblivious to the corruption and compromise in the Church of England. In 1740, Charles mourned the decrepit state of the Church: "[God] opened my mouth again at the society, and I spoke in much grief and love of our desolate mother, the Church of England. My heart yearns towards her when I think upon her ruin and it pities me to see her in the dust." In April 1742, in a sermon he preached at Oxford University, he denounced the failure of the Church of England to proclaim the gospel, condemning sinners "to live and die without the image of God . . . on the brink of the pit, in the jaws of everlasting destruction." And in a sermon entitled "On a Single Eye" preached in 1789, John railed against worldly clergy in the Church of England, describing them as "vile, infamous wretches" and that "Hell is paved with souls of Christian priests."

By 1750, the lay preachers of the Methodist societies were the mainstay, of whom eighty-five had been recognized by John and sixty-eight were still active. Charles was perplexed why the Church of England refused to acknowledge such individuals who suffered for their faith, commenting that nothing moved them: "Neither persuasions nor threatenings, flattery nor violence, dungeons or sufferings of various kinds." However, unlike John, Charles realized that the Church would never embrace Methodism nor would members of the clergy join the movement as long as they depended on lay preachers who the Anglican Church accused of displaying "a wild and pernicious enthusiasm."

Charles perceived himself as the only one who could contain the growth in numbers and what he viewed as the misguided fervor of the lay preachers. He accepted John's invitation to become a special adviser to the preachers. Charles traveled throughout England hearing and investigating the lay preachers, and his first test case in attempting to control them was a cobbler called James Wheatley who was accused of immoral sexual behavior. Charles temporarily revoked Wheatley's right to preach and persuaded John to expel him from the movement when it became clear the allegations were true, commenting on Wheatley: "I threw away advice . . . [on him] for I could make no impression on him, or in any degree bow his stiff neck."

Charles discovered others who, in his opinion, were completely unfit to preach, including a preacher named Michael Fletcher. Charles said of Fletcher:

> Such a preacher I have heard and hope I never shall again. It was beyond description. I cannot say he preached false doctrine, or true, or any doctrine at all, but pure unmixed nonsense. Not one sentence did he utter that could do the least good to any one soul. Now and then a text of Scripture or a verse quotation was dragged in by the head and shoulders. I could scarce refrain from stopping him. . . . Of this I am infallibly sure, that if he ever had a gift for preaching, he has now totally lost it.

Charles had a clear understanding in his own mind that the role of lay preachers was to preach the Word, not perform the sacrament. And he was adamant that they should continue with their trades and professions, including a former tailor called Robert Gillespie, whom Charles was determined should return to his trade because of his "utter unworthiness to preach the Gospel." Writing to John Bennet (husband of Grace Murray), Charles said: "A friend of ours [John Wesley] (without God's counsel) made a preacher of a tailor. I, with God's help shall make a tailor of him again."

By the mid 1750s, Charles had become embroiled in conflicts with Methodist lay preachers demanding the authority to perform the sacrament, without being ordained by the Anglican Church. Many of these preachers were seeking a formal separation from the Church of England, and some sought licenses as Dissenting clergymen under the 1689 Act of Toleration that granted them legal protection from not abiding by the rules and regulations of the Church. In 1745, in his *Farther Appeal to Men of Reason and Religion,* John had clearly forbidden Methodist lay preachers from taking out Dissenters licenses, even though it was unlikely that an increasingly hostile Anglican Church would be willing to ordain Methodist ministers.

Impatient with the status quo, in 1754 two lay preachers—Charles Perronet, son of Vincent Perronet, Vicar of Shoreham, and Thomas Walsh—defied John and administered the sacrament in London and Reading. Much to Charles' chagrin, John did nothing, with him reporting in his journal: "I was with my brother, who said nothing of Perronet except, 'We have in effect ordained already.' He urged me to sign the preachers' certificates; was inclined to lay on hands; and to let the preachers administer [the sacrament]." Charles was convinced that John was under the influence of the lay preachers who were leading him into a separation from the Anglican Church. He wrote an "epistle" to John defending "the church whose cause I serve, whose faith I approve, whose altars reverence, and whose name I love."

John's apparent weakness and reluctance in dealing with the failings of the lay preachers angered Charles and made him doubt his brother's resolve to resist the calls for separation from the Church of England. John, on the other hand, was angered by Charles' refusal to shoulder what he considered his share of the burden of itinerant ministry. Charles expressed his concerns to Walter Sellon, an Anglican minister in November 1754: "They are continually urging him to separation, that is, to pull down all he has built, to put a sword in our enemies' hands, to destroy the work, scatter the flock, disgrace himself, and go out—like the snuff of a candle."

Sellon must have written to John about his concerns, for in December 1754 Charles corresponded again with Sellon, urging him to write to John a second time: "Dear Brother and Friend—write again and spare not, my brother took no notice to me of your letter. . . . Since the Melchisedechians [Charles' name for the lay preachers who wanted a priesthood without lineage or genealogy] have taken him in, I have been excluded [from] his cabinet council. They know me too well to trust him with me. . . . He is come so far as to believe a separation quite lawful, only not expedient. They are indefatigable in urging him to go so far, that he may not be able to retreat."

The Methodist annual conference in Leeds in May 1755 promised to be a battle between opponents and proponents of separation. Charles confided to Lady Huntingdon that he was dreading it: "Tomorrow I proceed to the Conference with a heavy heart. Yet I must trust in the Lord, that He will look to His own cause." The issue was indeed debated. John wrote in his *Journal*:

> Our Conference began at Leeds. The point in which we desired all the preachers to speak their minds at large was, whether we ought to separate from the Church. Whatever was advanced on one side or the other was seriously and calmly considered. And on the third day we were all fully agreed in that general conclusion, that (whether it was lawful or not) it was no way expedient.

John was convinced that Charles was overreacting about the possibility of schism and separation from the Anglican Church, writing to him in June 1755:

> Wherever I have been in England the societies are far more firmly and rationally attached to the Church than ever before. I have no fear about this matter. I only fear the preachers' or the people's leaving, not the Church, but the love of God, and inward or outward holiness. To this end I press them forward continually. I dare not, in conscience, spend my time and strength on externals. If (as Lady [Huntingdon] says) all

> outward establishments are Babel, so is this establishment [the
> Church of England]. Let it stand for me. I neither set it up
> nor pull it down. But let you and I build up the city of God.

John believed that Charles was blind and bigoted when it came
to the Church of England: "Your gross bigotry lies here, in putting
a man on a level with an adulterer because he differs from you as to
church government. . . . What a miserable confounding the degrees of
good and evil is this?" John Pawson, a lay preacher and an opponent of
Charles, shared John's view: "It is well known that Mr. Charles Wesley
was much prejudiced in favour of the clergy through the whole course
of his life, and that it was nothing but hard necessity that obliged him,
in any degree, to continue with the lay preachers." But Charles hit back,
writing to John: "Is it not your duty to stop Joseph Cownley and (such
like) from railing and laughing at the church? The short remains of my
life are devoted to this very thing, to follow your sons . . . with buckets
of water, and quench the flame of strife and division which they have,
or may kindle."

In 1756, John's resolve was again tested when Charles Perronet's
brother, Edward, published *The Mitre*, a polemic against the corruption
in the Church of England in which he described the Church as "the
ape of Rome" and the leadership "a blended spawn of church and state
which had been created from 'the pride of priests.'" Under pressure
from Charles, John ordered Perronet to stop selling his book. Copies
were confiscated, but the damage had been done. Charles said of
Perronet, "he has set himself against us . . . counteracting us with
our preachers, spiriting them up, poisoning, proselyting them to his
own wretched notions." Not stopping there, Charles, together with
Anglican clergymen William Grimshaw, Henry Venn, and Samuel
Walker, requested that John use the conference in 1756 to restrict the
activities of the lay preachers. Writing to Walker, Charles asserted: "My
brother ought, in my judgement, to declare in the possible strongest and
most explicit manner, his resolution to live and die in the communion
of the Church of England . . . [and] take all proper pains to instruct
and ground his preachers and his flock in the same." But Walker did
not hold out much hope of that happening because John had already

invested so much time and effort in employing lay preachers. Wrote Walker: "He has had too great a hand in setting them up, to think of pulling them down. It has been a great fault all along to have made low people of your council; and if there be not power left in your brother's hands to do as he sees fit, they will soon show him they will be their own masters."

To Charles' surprise and satisfaction, there were few calls for separation at the 1756 Conference, but John still refused to accept Charles' proposal to encourage the lay preachers to seek ordination. Disappointed, Charles confided to Walker that he only remained in the movement to stop the march towards separation: "I know my brother will not hear of laying aside his lay preachers. . . . I [fear] the tide will be too strong for him, and bear him away into the gulf of separation. . . . The restless pains of bad men to thrust me from the Methodists seems a plain argument for my continuing with them."

In 1758, John published his *Reasons against a Separation from the Church of England*, in which he argued that separation was undesirable, though not wrong, because it caused division. Charles responded by declaring:

> I am quite clear that it is neither expedient nor lawful for me to separate. I never had the least inclination or temptation to do so. My affection for the Church is as strong as ever; and I clearly see my calling which is to live and die in communion. This therefore I am determined to do, the Lord being my helper. . . . Would to God all the Methodist Preachers were, in this respect, like-minded.

The tension between Charles and the Methodist lay preachers rose considerably in 1760 when a number of the preachers in the Norwich circuit began to administer the Lord's Supper without either John's or Charles' knowledge or permission. This was a clear breach of Church of England law and represented a further step towards separation. When John was reluctant to either demand the preachers seek ordination or be expelled, Charles criticized his weakness in not confronting the preachers:

Dear Brother, I have thought and prayed about going to Norwich and am ready to go; but not on a fool's errand. Your [lack] of resolution yesterday saved you the reading of a long letter. Did you give Murlin [one of the preachers] and his fellows the least check? Did you blame them in the slightest word? What must be the consequence? The rest, secure in your weakness, will do what they list; will, sooner than you are aware, follow the example of those three, and draw as many disciples after them as they can, into a formal separation.

And in another letter to John, Charles wrote dramatically regarding the Norwich preachers: "Dear Brother, We have come to the Rubicon. Shall we pass, or shall we not? . . . The rest will soon follow their example, I believe because . . . they think they may do it with impunity. . . . More and more will give the sacrament, and set up for themselves, even before we die. . . . You have connived at it too long."

Charles made it clear to all that if the Methodists separated from the Church of England, he would leave the movement himself. To Nicholas Gilbert he wrote: "My soul abhors the thought of separating from the Church of England. You and all the preachers know, if my brother should leave it, I should leave him, or rather he [would leave] me. While they have any grace remaining they can never desire to part us, whom God has joined."

Charles declared stridently to John, "I am fully persuaded almost all of our preachers are corrupted already; more and more will give the sacrament and set up for themselves even before we die, and all except the few that get Orders [in the Church of England] will turn Dissenters before or after our death." Charles had harsh words for John, whom he blamed for not taking more decisive action: "You must wink very hard not to see all this. You have connived at it too long. But I now call upon you in the name of God to consider with me what is to be done? First to prevent a separation 2. To save a few uncorrupted preachers 3. To make the best of those that are corrupted."

At the 1760 Conference, John promised Charles that he would "gag the blatant beast once and for all," threatening to leave the movement if the lay preachers forced a separation with the Church Of England.

This was a major victory for Charles, and John wrote to his brother begging him to let the issue rest: "I have done at the last Conference all I can or dare do. Allow me liberty of conscience, as I allow you." In 1763, John established what was described as a "Model Deed" which stated that preaching houses were never to be called churches and that the only preachers allowed to preach at them had to be authorized by him and Charles.

In 1768, Charles attended the Methodist Conference for the first time in many years, with John reiterating his stance on remaining in the Church of England at the Conference, knowing this would please Charles:

> We will not, dare not, separate from the Church. . . . We are not seceders . . . and will do nothing willingly which tends to a separation from it. . . . Some may say "Our own service is public worship." Yes, in a sense; but not such as supersedes the church service. We never designed it should. We have a hundred times expressed the contrary. . . . I advise therefore all the Methodists in England and Ireland . . . constantly to attend the service of the Church, at least every Lord's day.

But this did not stop some Methodists from obtaining licenses or allay Charles' fears of separation, with Charles writing to Sally that year:

> My dear Sally, You are not acute enough to understand our policy. We have allowed our lay preachers to take out licences as Dissenting Protestants. To the Government they therefore say, "we are Dissenting Ministers"; to the Methodists they say "we are not Dissenters, but members of the Church of England." To Press Warrant of persecuting Justice, they say again: "we are Dissenters," to me at our next Conference, they will unsay it again. This is their sincerity, and my brother applauds their skillfulness— and his own.

Another crisis erupted in 1779 when John informed Alexander McNab, a lay preacher and superintendent of the Bristol circuit, that his services as a preacher were no longer required in Bath since an Anglican Church minister had been appointed in the city who was a supporter of Methodism. McNab refused to accept John's authority, began urging for separation from the Church of England, and was expelled from the Methodist movement. Consumed with bitterness, McNab began praying for John's death. Charles graphically wrote to his brother to stand his ground:

> You, single, are no match for near two hundred smooth-tongued. . . . Rouse yourself, before they flay you alive for your skin. Begin proving your sons one by one. Pray for wisdom, resolution and love.
>
> I would give up my wife and children, to cleave to you, if you stand firm and faithful to yourself, and the cause of God, and the Church of England.

John, however, backed down and reappointed McNab under pressure from John Pawson and other lay preachers. Charles was appalled, believing that there was a conspiracy among some of the preachers to overthrow John and separate from the Anglican Church. He declared that he would not attend the conference in 1780 just to witness everything he had worked so hard for be destroyed.

However, Charles did attend the Methodist conference in 1780, but only to please his brother. It was resolved to remain in the Church of England, yet he still feared that separation from the Church was inevitable, informing John: "Your design, I believe, was to keep all quiet. . . . By a very few words I could have provoked your preachers to lay aside the mask; but that was the very thing you guarded against; and I suppose, the reason for which you desired my presence was that I might be some sort of check on . . . [those wanting separation from the Church]."

A dilemma that John had to confront was who would succeed him when he died as he ruled the Methodist movement alone and owned all its property. As early as 1773, John had approached the popular Vicar of Madeley, John Fletcher, to take over the leadership of the Methodist movement, but Fletcher declined, citing he was unworthy of the position and lacked the physical stamina. In any case, by 1776 he was seriously ill and died in 1785 at the age of fifty-five. With no obvious successors—Charles had declined, citing poor health and family commitments—in February 1784, John issued his "Deed of Declaration" which transferred the governance of the Methodist movement to the "legal hundred" lay preachers following his death. Commenting on his decision, John said: "I simply set down those that, according to the best judgement, were most proper. But I am not infallible." Not all preachers excluded from the legal hundred accepted John's decision, although only five resigned, including John Hampson, his future biographer.

Another issue that John had to address was the Methodist movement in the American colonies. By 1774, there were seven itinerant preachers in America under the supervision of Thomas Rankin. Methodist membership had grown to more than 2,000. However, the outbreak of the American War of Independence in 1776 led to an exodus of Methodist preachers to Canada, the West Indies, and back to England, leaving only Francis Asbury, whom John had sent out in 1771. Asbury, who became known as the "Wesley of American Methodism," traveled 5,000 to 6,000 miles a year on horseback and preached 20,000 sermons over the next 45 years, a record to match Wesley himself. Asbury was so effective that by 1783, when a peace treaty was signed between Britain and the newly established United States of America, there were nearly 15,000 Methodists in the American states with members in 46 circuits led by 83 itinerant lay preachers. But Asbury was still the only ordained Methodist minister in America, and the Church of England rejected John's request in 1780 for additional ordinations.

As far back as 1746, John had read former lord chancellor, Lord Peter King's *Constitution of the Primitive Church* in which he stated that "In spite of the vehement prejudice of my education, I was ready to believe that . . . bishops and presbyters are essentially of one order." Bishop Stillingfleet's *The Irenicum* (1659) convinced John that the New Testament office of presbyter was the same as that of bishop. John had assurance that he possessed as much authority as a bishop to conduct ordinations into the ministry.

In June 1780, John foreshadowed his future actions by writing to Charles, saying: "Read Bishop Stillingfleet's Irenicum, or any impartial history of the ancient church, and you will think as I do. I verily believe I have as good a right to ordain as to administer the Lord's supper."

Thus on September 1, 1784, John "appointed" (although in private John called them ordinations) Dr. Thomas Coke as Superintendent for America, supported by lay preachers Richard Whatcoat and Thomas Vassey as elders. John even prepared a special American hymnbook that was about a fifth of the size of the one he had ironically published with Charles' assistance. John did not inform Charles of his intentions, knowing that he would disapprove.

When Charles discovered in November 1784 what his brother had done, he announced that he was "thunderstruck. I cannot believe it." Soon after, John published a vindication of his actions, claiming that American independence now meant the United States was "at full liberty simply to follow the Scriptures and the Primitive Church. . . . I violate no order and invade no man's right by appointing and sending labourers into the harvest." He assured Methodists that he remained "as firmly attached to the Church of England as ever." But Charles was not convinced by John's *Apology*, writing to a friend:

> The apology has so stunned and con[fuse]d me that I have not yet recovered the use of my brain. . . . He said he would never separate from the Church of England without my consent. Set this then to this age: his memory fails him. . . . I have the satisfaction of having stood in the gap so long, and staved off the evil for near half a century. And I trust I shall be able, like you, to leave behind me the name of an honest man. Which with all his sophistry he [John] cannot do.

On April 28, 1785, Charles wrote a letter to a Dr. Chandler, expressing his sentiments about John:

> After having continued friends for above seventy years, and fellow labourers for above fifty, can anything but death part us? I can scarcely yet believe it, that, in his eighty-second year, my Brother, my old, intimate friend and companion, should have assumed the Episcopal Character, ordained Elders, Consecrated a Bishop, and sent him to ordain our lay Preachers in America! I was then in Bristol, at his Elbow; yet he never gave me the least hint of his Intention. How was he surprised into so rash an action? He certainly persuaded himself that it was right.

Lord Mansfield told me last year, that "ordination was separation." This my Brother does not and will not see; or that he has renounced the Principles and Practice of his whole life; that he has acted contrary to all his Declarations, Protestations and Writings, robbed his friends of their boast, realized the Nag's head ordination, and left an indelible blot on his name, as long as it shall be remembered.

In a letter he wrote to John he declared: "Surely I am in a dream! Is it possible that J. W. should be turned Presbyterian? J. W. the schismatic grandson to J. W. the regicide! How would this disturb (if they were capable of being disturbed) my Father and Brother [Samuel] in paradise!" As Green has commented: "Charles saw more clearly than his brother the implications of what he had done and made no secret of his horror."[51]

In a long, rambling reply, John defended his actions:

Dear Brother, I will tell you my thoughts with all simplicity and wait for better information. If you agree with me, well; if not, we can, as Mr. Whitefield used to say, agree to disagree. . . . I firmly believe I am a scriptural episkopos [bishop or overseer], as much as any man in England, or in Europe; for the uninterrupted succession I know to be a fable, which no man ever did or can prove.

Charles felt betrayed by John's "madness." In August 14, 1785, he wrote to his brother urging him to read his *Reasons against a Separation from the Church of England* and concluded: "I am on the brink of the grave. Do not push me in, or embitter my last moments. Let us not leave an indelible blotch on our memory, but let us leave behind us the name and character of honest men." To Sally, he was more explicit. She suggested that the ordinations had turned the Methodists into a sect of Dissenters, which Charles agreed with:

You think right. "What has been done already, has fixt the Preachers Dissenters." Who would not live foursquare years for so glorious an end—to turn 7,000 Church of England

---

[51] Green, *John Wesley*, 149.

people Dissenters! My B[rother] cannot undo what has been done. His Bishop [Coke] may now ordain all the Preachers without his leave; or the 3 Scottish Preachers may do it (and will) without either of them.

John, however, was convinced that Charles was overreacting to the ordinations, claiming: "All those reasons against a separation from the Church, in this sense, I subscribe to still. What then are you frightened at? I no more separate from it now than I did the year 1758. I submit still (though sometimes with a doubting conscience) to 'mitred infidels'. . . . I walk still by the same rule I have done for between forty and fifty years. I do nothing rashly."

Coke did as John instructed and ordained Asbury as assistant superintendent, but he began attacking the ministers of the Church of England in America as "parasites and bottle companions of the rich and great." Coke and Asbury then began to ordain more ministers, called themselves bishops, and referred to the Wesleyan Church as the Methodist Episcopal Church of America.

Charles implored John to put a stop to the ordinations: "I believe . . . ordination is separation. . . . Stop here; ordain no more." Charles was sure that John had "set open the flood-gates." But John continued to ordain ministers for churches in America, and this was expanded to cover Scotland, Canada, and the West Indies. Although Charles was saddened by his brother's pragmatic approach, he focused his remaining time and energy on keeping Methodism as a renewal movement within the Church of England.

Charles attended the 1786 Conference, and the heated debate that was expected about separation never occurred, with, much to his relief, general agreement "to remain in the 'Old Ship'," despite the opposition of some dissenting preachers. Charles' only comment was to cry out "No!" during a debate on holding Methodist meetings during the hours of Anglican worship.

Charles did not attend the 1787 Conference, but a week before he preached in London against the "self created bishops and self made priests" who he was convinced would ruin the Methodist movement. He strongly advised society members to refuse to have communion with them. John Pawson expressed his and others' opposition to "such a hot, fiery spirit" and believed that Charles' views would never "bear the light at all."

By that year, the church in America was asserting its independence from the Wesleys and the Methodist movement in Britain. When John ordered the American Methodists to hold a conference to appoint Richard Whatcoat a general superintendent, they refused point blank, with Asbury commenting contemptuously, "For our old Daddy to appoint Conference when and where he pleased, to appoint a joint superintendent with me, were strokes of power we did not understand." Much to John's dismay, Asbury declared imperiously: "Mr. Wesley and I are like Caesar and Pompey: he will bear no equal, and I will bear no superior." When Asbury permitted Wesley's name to be voted out of the minutes of the American Conference, it was the last straw. John reacted by denouncing Asbury, "This completed the matter and showed that he had no connection with me."

Worse was to follow. After Coke's ordination of Francis Asbury, both assumed the title of bishop. In 1788, John wrote a scathing and sarcastic letter to Asbury: "My dear Franky. I study to be little; you study to be great. I creep; you strut along. . . . Do not seek to be something. Let me be nothing and 'Christ be all in all.' . . . How can you, how dare you, suffer yourselves to be called BISHOP. I shudder, I start at the very thought! Men may call me a knave or a fool; a rascal, a scoundrel, and I am content. But they shall never, by my consent, call me Bishop!"

John Wesley continued to maintain that the steps he took from 1784 onward did not constitute a separation from the Church of England, claiming in 1786, "Indeed, I love the Church as sincerely as ever I did; and I tell my societies everywhere, 'the Methodists will not leave the Church, at least while I live'." In 1787 he declared, "That when the Methodists leave the Church, God will leave them." As late as 1790, he remarked to Bishop Tomline of Lincoln that "the Methodists in general are members of the Church of England, they hold all her doctrines, attend her services and partake of her Sacraments."

John ordained at least twenty-seven Methodist preachers as presbyter and Thomas Coke as superintendent, but Charles continued to plead with his brother not to ordain ministers for service in England. In one of his last letters written on April 9, 1787, Charles urged John to "Stand to your own proposal. I leave America and Scotland to your latest thoughts and recognitions. . . . Keep your authority while you live. . . . You cannot settle the succession; you cannot divine how God will settle it." Charles believed, presciently as it turned out, that as soon as John died the Wesleyan Methodists would separate from the Anglican Church and establish their own order of ministry. But, as Tyson has said, "in the end, Charles got what he wanted most: he lived—and died—in the Church of England."[52]

---

[52] Tyson, *Assist Me to Proclaim*, 322.

22

THINGS ETERNAL

The best of all is God is with us.

—JOHN WESLEY

As early as 1773, Charles was writing ruefully of his declining health: "I do not want a heart to visit my dear friends at Newcastle, but a body." A myriad of ailments—pleurisy, neuralgia, lumbago, hemorrhoids, rheumatism, gout, and others—had taken their toll. A decade later, Charles referred to himself and his friend John Fletcher as being just "human ruins tottering in the grave," and a few years later he wrote of himself, "I creep along the streets, tottering over the edge of the grave."

Though Charles was devoting some of his energies to the promotion of his sons, Charles junior and Samuel's musical careers, he was still prison visiting, helping the poor, and preaching regularly, writing to Sally: "My work, I very well know, keeps me alive more than it wears me out. That and my life will probably end together." One of Charles' chief antagonists, John Pawson, described him in his old age as "like Samson shorn of his strength." Charles' ability to preach extemporaneously probably began to fail as he got older. John Wesley biographer John Telford described Charles opening his Bible and preparing to preach on "the first words presented," only drawing a blank and lifting his eyes to heaven as though waiting for divine assistance. Yet John wrote to Charles on June 27, 1781, saying, "From several I have lately heard that

God has blessed your preaching. See your calling!" Methodist preacher Henry Moore commented that, even in his later years, Charles had "the remarkable talent for uttering the most striking truth with simplicity, force and brevity." He even recalled that Charles had the energy to hurl a hymnal from the pulpit of City Road Chapel in the direction of one of his opponents, Thomas Coke, who was seated directly in front of him, just missing his head.

Whenever he was offered clerical positions that would have brought him a regular, comfortable income, Charles refused them, saying he would not forego his work among the Methodists in London. On one occasion when offered a significant legacy, he commented, "I know what I am now, but I do not know what I should be if I were thus made rich." On another occasion when he was recounting his father's imprisonment in a debtor's prison, his sister Martha criticized him for revealing such shameful details about the family. "If you are ashamed of poverty," replied Charles, "you are ashamed of your Master."

In the autumn of 1787, a frail and aged Charles made his final visit to Bristol, living alone in a rented room, for he had not the funds to pay for his family to join him. Charles said: "Silver and gold have I none. But I want none, neither do I run in debt for want of it." He wrote to his wife Sally: "My eyes fail me for writing and reading. Perhaps they may not be darkened, till they are closed," and he informed her that he didn't have the strength to finish packing to return home: "On Saturday night I thought myself near my [death] through an intense pain in my side. I had small hope of officiating yesterday, yet the Lord gave me back and increased my strength. Probably, I shall depart without taking leave [of Bristol]." The following day he again wrote to Sally gloomily: "Last night my troublesome old companion, lumbago, paid me a visit before the time. Tis well if he does not lay an embargo upon me; or possibly hasten my return home to be nursed." Charles returned to London exhausted, confessing to one of the London preachers: "I am known as a dead man out of my mind and am content."

By February 1788, Charles' health had further declined. He was rarely able to leave his bed. John urged his brother to hire a carriage and go out for a daily walk "for at least an hour a day. I would not blame you if it were two or three. Never mind the expense; I can make that up. You shall not die to save charges." He also offered various remedies, including binding a warm onion or thin slices of beef across the pit of the stomach and making a jelly from bread crusts and lemon juice mixed with sugar. John also advised Charles "to be electrified; not shocked but only filled with electric fire." He recommended that Sally seek the services of a Dr. Whitehead who was very highly regarded, but the doctor could do little to help because he found Charles' body was "reduced to the last extreme state of weakness."

Whitehead wrote of his admiration of Charles' strength and composure when confronted by death, his "unaffected humility and holy resignation to the will of God," and his "unshaken confidence in Christ, which kept his mind in perfect peace." He also wrote an account of Charles' last days:

> Mr. Charles Wesley had a weak body, and a poor state of health, during the greatest part of his life. I believe he laid the foundation of both, at Oxford, by too close application to study, and abstinence from food. He rode much on horseback, which probably contributed to lengthen out his life to a good old age. I visited him several times in his last sickness, and his body was indeed reduced to the most extreme weakness. He possessed that state of mind which he had been always pleased to see in others—unaffected humility and holy resignation to the will of God. He had no transports of joy, but solid hope and unshaken confidence in Christ, which kept his mind in perfect peace.

As Charles' health declined, his daughter Sally wrote to her uncle John that "He took solemn leave of all his friends. I once asked if he had any presages that he should die. He said, 'No'; but his weakness was such, that he thought it impossible he 'should live through March.' He kindly bade me remember him, and seemed to have no doubt but I should meet him in heaven."

Two weeks before his death, Charles prayed tearfully for those he considered his enemies, including Mary Freeman Shepherd, whom he blamed for influencing his son Samuel to become a Roman Catholic.

Cried Charles, "I beseech you, O Lord, by your agony and blood sweat that she may never feel the pangs of eternal death."

By March 1788, Charles' physical condition deteriorated still further. He had stopped eating. He became at times semi-conscious and was heard muttering "Let me die. Let me die." On March 28, his wife Sally asked him if he had any final message to give her and the children. His reply, "Only thanks, love, blessing."

Charles' daughter Sally recalled that her father seemed "totally detached from earth" and that he "spoke very little nor wished to hear anything read but the Scriptures. . . . All his prayer was, 'Patience and an easy death.' He . . . said to us all, 'I have a good hope [heaven].' When we asked him if he wanted anything, he frequently answered, 'Nothing but Christ.' Some person observed that the valley of death was hard to be passed. 'Not with Christ', he replied." And Sally recalled her father's last moments:

> Last morning, which was the 29th March, being unable to speak, my mother entreated him to press her hand, if he knew her; which he feebly did. His last words which I could hear were, "Lord, my heart—my God!" He then drew his breath short, and the last so gently, that we knew not exactly the moment in which his happy spirit fled. His dear hand was in mine for five minutes before, and at the awful period of his dissolution.

Charles had insisted that he should not be buried in a crypt at City Road Chapel prepared for him by his brother, but in a consecrated cemetery, saying emphatically, "I have lived and I die in the communion of the Church of England, and I will be buried in the yard of my parish church." John expressed his disappointment that Charles was not to be buried at City Road: "Tis pity but the remains of my brother had been deposited with me. Certainly that ground [behind City Road Chapel] is holy as any in England, and it contains a large quantity of 'bonny dust.'"

The letter informing John of his brother's death was misdirected and arrived too late for him to attend the funeral, but he was devastated by Charles' death. Preaching a fortnight later in Bolton, he broke down in the pulpit and wept along with the congregation when he read out the lines from one of Charles' hymns, "Wrestling Jacob": "My company before is gone, And I am left along with thee." He then said, "I have a brother who is as my own soul." He then recovered, preached, and prayed.

It says much for John's love for his brother that he decided to write Charles' biography. Age and a lack of time precluded him from finishing the work, but references in his *Journal* suggest that he did make a start on the project.

The Methodist conference of 1788 barely acknowledged Charles' passing in a list of preachers who had died that year, which included seven others, perhaps still resentful of his decision to stop his itinerant ministry and his determination to keep the Methodist movement within the Church of England. It reported: "Mr. Charles Wesley, who after spending fourscore years with much sorrow and pain, quietly retired to Abraham's bosom. He had no disease; but after a gradual decay of some months, 'The weary wheels of life stood still at last.'"

By the 1780s, John Wesley had become a respected and venerated figure who could not accept all the invitations he received to preach. Writing in 1785 he said: "The scandal of the Cross is ceased and all the kingdom, rich and poor, Papists and Protestants, behave with courtesy—indeed and seeming goodwill! It seems as if I had well-nigh finished my course, and our Lord was giving me an honourable discharge."

When the much persecuted Methodist lay preacher John Nelson died in 1774, his coffin was carried through the streets of Leeds attended by thousands who were weeping with grief. Perhaps as a sign of a little mellowing in his old age, John commented in 1789, "In my youth I was not only a member of the Church of England but a bigot to it, believing none but the members of it to be in a state of salvation."

Despite his age, John still continued with his punishing preaching itinerary. His health remained remarkably good for someone of his age, as he noted in his *Journal* in 1784: "I am as strong at eighty-one, as I was at twenty-one, but abundantly more healthy, being a stranger to the head-ache, tooth-ache and other bodily disorders which attended me in my youth. We can only say, 'The Lord reigneth!' While we live, let us live to him!" However, even he may have had a sense of his mortality. That same year a friend urged him to visit America again, to which he replied sadly, "No, I shall pay no more visits to the new worlds till I go to the world of the spirits."

A year later, on June 28, he recorded in his *Journal*:

> By the good providence of God, I finished the eighty-second year of my age. Is anything too hard for God? It is now eleven years since I have felt any such thing as weariness; many times I speak till my voice fails, and I can speak no longer. Frequently I walk till my strength fails, and I can walk no farther; yet even then I feel no sensation of weariness but am perfectly easy from head to foot. I dare not impute this to natural causes: it is the will of God.

Recalled John Hampson, Wesley's first biographer, of his latter years:

> . . . his appearance, till within a few years of his death, vigorous and muscular. His face, for an old man, was one of the finest we have seen. A clear smooth forehead, an aquiline nose, an eye the brightest and most piercing that can be conceived, and a freshness impressive of the most perfect health, conspired to render him a venerable and interesting figure.
> . . . cheerfulness mingled with gravity, a sprightliness which was the natural result of an unusual flow of spirits and was yet accompanied with every mark of the most serene tranquility. . . . In dress, he was a pattern of neatness and simplicity. . . . His manner, in private life, was the reverse of cynical or forbidding. It was sprightly and pleasant to the last degree; and presented a beautiful contrast to the austere deportment of many of his preachers and people, who seemed to have ranked laughter among the mortal sins. It is impossible to be long in his company without partaking his hilarity.

The Irish theological writer Alexander Knox, who accompanied Wesley in Ireland, recalled: "So fine an old man I never saw! The happiness of his mind beamed forth in his countenance: Every look shewed [sic] how fully he enjoyed, 'The gay remembrance of a life well spent.'"

John ascribed his good health to rising at 4.00 a.m. (helped by an alarm that "went off with a thundering noise"), followed by prayer and preaching at 5.00 a.m. He claimed that "though I am always in haste I am never in a hurry because I never undertake any more work than I can go through with perfect calmness of spirit."

On Midsummer's Day 1786, John Wesley rose in the early hours of the morning to pray and write a sermon. At 5:30 a.m., he set off in a chaise for Newton-on-Trent. On arrival, at 8.00 a.m., he took tea and then preached on Psalm 10:12. From Newton he travelled on to Newark for lunch at noon. After lunch, he preached on Ecclesiastes 9:10. At 2.35 p.m., he set out for Tuxford, where he spent half-an-hour with the people there, before journeying on to Retford to preach and say prayers at 6:15 p.m. This was followed by supper with his hosts and evening prayers in the family home, which he conducted, before retiring to bed at 9:30 p.m. Four days later, on his eighty-third birthday, he remarked in his *Journal*, "I am never tired (such is the goodness of God!) either with writing, preaching or travelling." When returning from a trip to the Netherlands in 1786, John so impressed a fellow traveler by reading a small-print edition of a book that she later recorded, "If the Methodists' principles keep their sight as clear as that to the age of 83, then I wish I had been educated in their sect."

John's mental faculties and enthusiasm did not diminish in his final years. He continued to exhibit a great interest and delight in all elements of his ministry, including a visit to a Sunday school in Bolton for 800 poor children, where 80 masters taught them reading and writing for free. Around 100 of the children sang for Wesley, and he claimed that not even the famed choir of King's College Chapel could equal the beauty of their singing.

John reached his eighty-fifth birthday in June 1788 in good health, except for "some difficulty in reading small print by candlelight." On January 1, 1789, he wrote, "If this is to be the last year of my life, according to some of those prophecies, I hope it will be the best." By the autumn of that year he noted some deterioration in his health: his sight had further "decayed," his strength was ebbing, and his memory for faces, names, and places had declined. "My sight is so decayed that

I cannot well read by candlelight; but I can write as well as ever. My strength is much lessened so that I cannot easily preach above twice a day. But, I bless God, my memory is not much decayed, and my understanding is as clear as it has been these fifty years."

By New Year's Day, 1790, however, there had been a dramatic change in his physical condition, as Wesley himself recorded:

> I am an old man, decayed from head to foot. My eyes are dim; my right hand shakes much; my mouth is hot and dry every morning; I have a lingering fever almost every day; my motion is weak and slow. However, blessed be God, I do not slack my labour: I can preach and write still. . . . I feel no pain from head to foot; only it seems nature is exhausted; and, humanly speaking, will sink more and more, till "the weary springs of life stand still at last."

John revealed later that year to a friend, "My body seems nearly to have done its work, and to be almost worn out." But Henry Moore was surprised by John's admission of physical deterioration: "Being in the house with him when he wrote thus, I was greatly surprised. I knew it must be as he said; but I could not imagine his weakness was so great. He still rose at his usual hour, four o'clock, and went through the many duties of the day, not indeed with the same vigour, but without complaint and with a degree of resolution that was astonishing."

On Good Friday 1790, John Wesley dedicated his last chapel at Oldham in Lancashire. "The new house would in no wise contain the congregation but I preached to as many as it could contain." In the congregation was a young boy, John Standering, who recalled the scene in his old age: "Mr. Wesley was of small stature, aged and wrinkled and feebled in body, and yet his voice was strong. He wore a three-cornered cocked hat, gown and bands. There was an immense concourse of people. After the sermon, Mr. Wesley requested all the children to sit around the altar and he passed around, laid his hands upon their heads, and offered a prayer for each child."

On July 16, 1790, John recorded his last entry in his expenses book. He wrote with a trembling hand: "For upwards of eighty-six years [he probably meant sixty-eight years] I have kept my accounts exactly. I will

not attempt it any longer, being satisfied with the continual conviction that I save all I can, and give all I can, that is, all I have."

John preached in the open air for the last time on October 6, 1790, beneath an ash tree in the churchyard of Rye, Kent, then at a meetinghouse in Colchester the following week. In the congregation that day was fifteen-year-old Henry Crabb Robinson, who became a famous diarist and literary figure. Crabb later recalled that momentous day:

> [He] stood in the wide pulpit and on each side of him stood a minister, and the two held him up, having their hands under his armpits. His feeble voice was barely audible; but his reverend countenance, especially his long white locks, formed a picture never to be forgotten. There was a vast crowd of lovers and admirers. It was for the most part a pantomime, but the pantomime went to the heart.

At John's last Methodist Conference in 1790, John Pawson observed that Wesley was now "nearly worn out and his faculties evidently were very much impaired, especially his memory." The preacher John Sutcliffe described the gathering of the leaders of the Methodist movement:

> A long table being placed across the chapel, which had no pews, Mr. Wesley sat in a chair at the head of the table, and about twenty venerable men on the benches, ten on each side, distinguished by bushy or cauliflower wigs, aged men that had borne the heat and burden of the day. Mr. Mather, as a sort of archdeacon . . . conducted the whole business of the Conference. Mr. Valton was the secretary, with his small quarto ledger.

Charles Atmore described meeting John in Newcastle in 1790: "We heard him preach in the evening, from 'He is before all things, and by Him all things consist.' He appears very feeble; and no wonder, he being nearly eighty-seven years of age. His sight has failed so much, that he cannot see to give out the hymn; yet his voice is strong and his spirits remarkably lively. Surely this good man is the prodigy of the present age."

On February 17, 1791, after preaching at Lambeth, John was taken ill. Although he struggled to keep several of his appointments, two days later, after rising early as usual, he was forced to return to bed for several hours. He seemed to recover some of his strength, and on Monday he traveled to Twickenham. The following day, he preached at the City Road Chapel. At 7.00 a.m., on Wednesday, February 23, Wesley set out in his two-horse chaise with James Rogers, his assistant, to visit a merchant friend named Belson in Leatherhead who had just lost his wife. While traveling, Rogers read to him the newly published autobiography of the former slave Gustavus Vassa. Wesley preached his last sermon at the home of his friend in Leatherhead. His text was "Seek ye the Lord, while He may be found, call ye upon Him while He is near."

Arriving home at City Road, Wesley had difficulty getting out of his carriage and climbing the stairs to his room. The following day, Rogers read more of Vassa's autobiography. John was so moved that he dictated a letter to William Wilberforce on February 24, signing it with a shaking hand, barely being able to hold the pen. Even his signature on the manuscript *Journal of Conference* the year before had been illegible. He wrote his last letter to America on February 1, 1791, saying: "Those that desire to write . . . to me have no time to lose, for time has shaken me by the hand, and death is not far behind. . . . Lose no opportunity of declaring to all men that the Methodists are one people in all the world, and that it is their full determination so to continue, Though mountains rise, and oceans roll, To sever us in vain."

On the afternoon of Tuesday, March 1, 1791, Wesley decided to get up. While faithful helpers Elizabeth Ritchie and Rogers were preparing his clothes, "he broke out in a manner which considering his extreme weakness astonished us all, in these blessed words: 'I'll praise my Maker while I've breath.'" John then sang two verses of Isaac Watt's metrical psalm before having to lie down again, exhausted. When he had recovered a little, he asked for pen and ink, but was unable to write anything.

"Let me write for you sir," asked Elizabeth Ritchie. "Tell me what you would say."

"Nothing—but that God is with us," replied Wesley.